Calvinism and Religious Toleration in the Dutch Golden Age

Dutch society has enjoyed a reputation, or notoriety, for permissiveness from the sixteenth century to present times. The Dutch Republic in the Golden Age was the only society that tolerated religious dissenters of all persuasions in early modern Europe, despite being committed to a strictly Calvinist public Church. Professors R. Po-Chia Hsia and Henk van Nierop have brought together a group of leading historians from the USA, the UK, and the Netherlands to probe the history and myth of this Dutch tradition of religious tolerance. This collection of outstanding essays reconsiders and revises contemporary views of Dutch tolerance. Taken as a whole, the volume's innovative scholarship offers unexpected insights into this important topic in religious and cultural history.

R. PO-CHIA HSIA is Edwin Earle Sparks Professor of European and Asian History at Pennsylvania State University. He is the author or editor of eight books on early modern Europe, including *In and Out of the Ghetto: Jewish–Gentile Relations in Late Medieval and Early Modern Germany* (Cambridge, 1995) and *The World of Catholic Renewal, 1540– 1770* (Cambridge, 1998).

HENK VAN NIEROP is Professor of Early Modern History at the University of Amsterdam and Director of the Amsterdam Centre for the Study of the Golden Age. He is the author or editor of a number of books on European and Dutch history, including *The Nobility of Holland: From Knights to Regents, 1500–1650* (Cambridge, 1993).

Calvinism and Religious Toleration in the Dutch Golden Age

Edited by

R. Po-Chia Hsia

Pennsylvania State University

and

Henk van Nierop

Universiteit van Amsterdam

PUBLISHED BY THE PRESS SYNDICATE OF THE UNIVERSITY OF CAMBRIDGE
The Pitt Building, Trumpington Street, Cambridge, United Kingdom

CAMBRIDGE UNIVERSITY PRESS
The Edinburgh Building, Cambridge CB2 2RU, UK
40 West 20th Street, New York, NY 10011-4211, USA
477 Williamstown Road, Port Melbourne, VIC 3207, Australia
Ruiz de Alarcón 13, 28014 Madrid, Spain
Dock House, The Waterfront, Cape Town 8001, South Africa

http://www.cambridge.org

First published 2002

Printed in the United Kingdom at the University Press, Cambridge

Typeface Plantin 10/12 pt.   *System* LaTeX 2$_\varepsilon$ [TB]

A catalogue record for this book is available from the British Library

Library of Congress Cataloguing in Publication data
Calvinism and religious toleration in the Dutch Golden Age / edited by
R. Po-Chia Hsia and Henk van Nierop.
      p.   cm.
Includes bibliographical references and index.
ISBN 0 521 80682 8
1. Calvinism – Netherlands – History.   2. Netherlands – Church history.
I. Hsia, R. Po-Chia, 1953–   II. Nierop, Henk F. K. van.
BX9424.5.N4 C35   2002
261.7′2′09492 – dc21   2001043850

ISBN 0 521 80682 8 hardback

Contents

Notes on contributors

WILLEM FRIJHOFF is Professor of Early Modern History at the Free University in Amsterdam. He is the author of many books, including *La société néerlandaise et ses gradués, 1575–1814: une recherche sérielle sur le statut des intellectuels* (Amsterdam, 1981), *Wegen van Evert Willemsz.: Een Hollands weeskind op zoek naar zichzelf 1607–1647* (Nijmegen, 1995), and *1650: Bevochten eendracht* (The Hague, 1999).

JONATHAN ISRAEL is Fellow of the Institute for Advanced Studies in Princeton. His many publications include *Dutch Primacy in World Trade, 1585–1740* (Oxford, 1989), *The Dutch Republic: Its Rise, Greatness, and Fall (1477–1806)* (Oxford, 1998), and *Radical Enlightenment: Philosophy and the Making of Modernity 1650–1750* (Oxford, 2001). He won the Wolfson Literary Prize for History in 1986. He is a Fellow of the British Academy and a member of the Royal Dutch Academy of Sciences.

BENJAMIN J. KAPLAN is Professor of Dutch History at University College London. He is the author of *Calvinists and Libertines: Confession and Community in Utrecht, 1578–1620* (Oxford, 1995) for which he won the Philip Schaff Prize and the Roland Bainton Prize in History and Theology.

CHRISTINE KOOI is Associate Professor of History at Louisiana State University and the author of *Liberty and Religion: Church and State in Leiden's Reformation, 1572–1620* (Leiden, 2000).

HENK VAN NIEROP is Professor of Early Modern History at the University of Amsterdam and Director of the Amsterdam Centre for the Study of the Golden Age. His publications include *The Nobility of Holland: From Knights to Regents, 1500–1650* (Cambridge, 1993) and *Het verraad van het Noorderkwartier: oorlog, terreur en recht in de Nederlandse Opstand* (Amsterdam, 1999).

RONNIE PO-CHIA HSIA is Edwin Earle Sparks Professor of European and Asian History at Pennsylvania State University. He is the author or editor of eight books on early modern Europe, including *In and Out of the Ghetto: Jewish-Gentile Relations in Late Medieval and Early Modern Germany* (Cambridge, 1995) and *The World of Catholic Renewal, 1540–1770* (Cambridge, 1998).

JUDITH POLLMANN is Lecturer in Modern History at the University of Oxford and Tutor at Somerville College, Oxford. She is the author of *Religious Choice in the Dutch Republic: The Reformation of Arnoldus Buchelius (1565–1641)* (Manchester, 1999) for which she won the Keetje Hodshon Prize for History of the Hollandsche Maatschappij der Wetenschappen.

MAARTEN PRAK is Professor of Economic and Social History at the University of Utrecht. His publications include *Gezeten burgers: de elite in een Hollandse stad, Leiden 1700–1780* (Dieren, 1985) and *Republikeinse veelheid, democratisch enkelvoud: sociale verandering in het Revolutietijdvak, 's-Hertogenbosch 1770–1820* (Nijmegen, 1999).

PETER VAN ROODEN is Reader in the Research Centre for Religion and Society at the University of Amsterdam. His publications include *Theology, Biblical Scholarship and Rabbinical Studies in the Seventeenth Century: Constantijn L'Empereur (1591–1648), Professor of Hebrew and Theology at Leiden* (Leiden, 1989) and *Religieuze regimes: over godsdienst en maatschappij in Nederland, 1570–1990* (Amsterdam, 1996).

JOKE SPAANS is Lecturer of the History of Christianity at the University of Amsterdam and the author of *Haarlem na de Reformatie: stedelijke cultuur en kerkelijk leven, 1577–1620* (The Hague, 1989) and *Armenzorg in Friesland 1500–1800: publieke zorg en particuliere liefdadigheid in zes Friese steden: Leeuwarden, Bolsward, Franeker, Sneek, Dokkum en Harlingen* (Hilversum, 1997).

SAMME ZIJLSTRA† was Research Fellow at the Fryske Akademy in Leeuwarden. He is the author *of Het geleerde Friesland – een mythe?: universiteit en maatschappij in Friesland en Stad en Lande ca. 1380–1650* (Leeuwarden, 1996) and *Om de ware gemeente en de oude gronden: geschiedenis van de dopersen in de Nederlanden 1531–1675* (Hilversum, 2000).

1   Introduction

Ronnie Po-Chia Hsia

Defending himself against criticisms that he was making war on his fellow co-religionists, Colonel Jean-Baptiste Stouppe, the Reformed Swiss commander of Louis XIV's troops in Utrecht during the occupation of 1672–3, retorted that the Dutch were not at all Reformed. 'It is well known . . . that in addition to the Reformed', Stouppe wrote in his tract *On the Religion of the Hollanders* (1673), 'there are Roman Catholics, Lutherans, Brownists, Independents, Arminians, Anabaptists, Socinians, Arians, Enthusiasts, Quakers, Borelists, Muscovites, Libertines, and many more . . . I am not even speaking of the Jews, Turks, and Persians . . . I must also report on an enlightened and learned man, who has a great following . . . His name is Spinoza. He was born a Jew and had not swore off allegiance to the Jewish religion, nor has he accepted Christianity. He is a wicked and very bad Jew, and not a better Christian either.'[1]

His criticisms aside, the Netherlands were indeed a Calvinist country, albeit tolerant of numerous religious communities, a fact celebrated in our visions of a Dutch Golden Age but much decried by contemporaries, even by those who enjoyed toleration. Consider the case of the Anabaptists, the most persecuted religious community during the early decades of the Reformation. In his 1633 preface to the *Martelaers Spiegel* Hans de Ries (1553–1638) lamented the languor of his fellow Mennonites. Contrasting the fervour of their forebears who were hunted down for their faith, De Ries chastised the Mennonites of his day for being 'cold and careless in religious matters'. He saw a community preoccupied with temporal affairs: 'the oxen must first be checked and the field inspected before one can come to the heavenly celebration. Wickedness is changed into pomp and splendor; goods are multiplied, but the soul is impoverished; clothes have become expensive, but interior beauty is gone; love has grown cold and diminished, and quarrels have increased.'[2] Such was the price for

---

[1] Cited in Willem Frijhoff, 'Hollands Gouden Eeuw', in *De gouden delta der Lage Landen. Twintig eeuwen beschaving tussen Seine en Rijn* (Antwerp, 1996), p. 192.

[2] *Martelaers Spiegel der Werelose Christenen . . .* , published in Haarlem, 1631–2; cited in Brad S. Gregory, *Salvation at Stake. Christian Martyrdom in Early Modern Europe* (Cambridge, MA, 1999), p. 244.

religious toleration, as the last Mennonite martyr died in 1574 in the northern Low Countries. In fact, the Mennonites found themselves in a new state and society, where religious toleration enabled a gradual process of economic and cultural assimilation.[3]

This new state, the United Provinces of the Netherlands, emerged out of the revolt against Spain in an alliance that guaranteed freedom of conscience; in the Union of Utrecht (1579), the rebel provinces agreed in article 13 that 'nobody shall be persecuted or examined for religious reasons'.[4] Not everyone concurred. From the beginning of the discussion on religious plurality in the Netherlands, the Calvinist Church vehemently opposed any official status for Catholicism, a position shared by other Protestant leaders during the long war with Spain, when Catholics remained a potential source of rebellion inside the new Dutch Republic. Anti-Catholic legislations remained in force throughout the seventeenth and eighteenth centuries, but their enforcement, as the contributions by Henk van Nierop and Christine Kooi show in this volume, was sporadic and uneven. The central paradox of the Dutch Republic is this: the existence of a confessionally pluralistic society with an official intolerant Calvinist Church that discriminated against Catholics, but whose pragmatic religious toleration elicited admiration and bewilderment in *ancien régime* Europe and whose longevity surpassed the perhaps more tolerant religious regime of the sixteenth-century Polish–Lithuanian Commonwealth.

The Netherlands in the Golden Age were a remarkable society. Not only did the different Christian confessions carve out social and political spaces in the Republic, Sephardic and Ashkenazic Jews also transformed Amsterdam into the centre of Jewish life in northern Europe during the seventeenth century. Individuals found porous boundaries. Consider the following examples: a Portuguese Jewish philosopher turned agnostic (Benedict Spinoza, 1632–77); a Mennonite poet converted to Catholicism (Joost van den Vondel, 1587–1679); and a poetess abandoning the Reformed Church for Rome, sending her sons to be educated in Leuven (Anna Roemersdochter Visscher, 1583–1651). That religious pluralism flourished in a polity with an official Calvinist Church made this story of toleration even more remarkable. How does one explain the

---

[3] See Alastair Hamilton, Sjouke Voolstra, and Piet Visser (eds.), *From Martyr to Muppy. A Historical Introduction to Cultural Assimilation Processes of a Religious Minority in the Netherlands: the Mennonites* (Amsterdam, 1994).

[4] M.E.H.N. Mout, 'A Comparative View of Dutch Toleration in the Sixteenth and Early Seventeenth Centuries', in C. Berkvens-Stevelinck, J. Israel, and G.H.M. Posthumus Meyjes (eds.), *The Emergence of Tolerance in the Dutch Republic* (Leiden/New York/Cologne, 1997), p. 41.

juxtaposition of Calvinist hegemony and religious toleration? The history of the Sephardim in Amsterdam provides an instructive example. Coming initially in the 1590s as Portuguese merchants and Christian converts, the so-called 'New Christians', Sephardic Jews in fact, were welcomed by the Regents of Holland but were strongly opposed by the Reformed clergy. When the *conversos* reverted to the open practice of Judaism, reaction from the Reformed Church was fierce. The *predikant* Abraham Coster attacked the Sephardim as an 'unclean people' who sought to build a public synagogue 'in which they can perform their evil and foolish ceremonies and spew forth their gross blasphemies against Christ and his holy Gospels, as well as their curses against the Christians and Christian authorities'.[5] Moreover, almost from the beginning of their settlement in Amsterdam, Protestant groups sought out the Jews for debates and conversion. In 1608 Hugh Broughton, the English pastor of the separatist community in Middelburg, wrote a polemic in Hebrew against Judaism. There were many attempts to convert the Jews in the seventeenth century, especially between 1640 and 1660.[6] Provocations and opposition aside, the Jewish community flourished because of the protection of the regents, who ignored most of the complaints of the Reformed clergy. What mattered to the regents was social peace; the pragmatism guiding magisterial policy stipulated that the Jewish community maintained internal discipline and kept watch over its own boundaries. By providing for their own poor and by strictly prohibiting the circumcision of Christian converts, the Amsterdam Jewish community maintained a stable relationship with the regents of the city that became the model for Jewish toleration in the rest of the Republic.

Social discipline and religious toleration, it would seem, went hand in hand in the Dutch Republic, unlike the case in the Holy Roman Empire, as Peter van Rooden argues in his contribution on attitudes towards Jews.[7] A linchpin in this arrangement was poor relief. By requiring the different religious communities to take care of their own poor, the regents effectively carved up Dutch society into clearly recognisable 'pillars' (*zuilen*), to use a term from later Dutch sociology, with sharply marked boundaries between the larger civil sphere and the separate religious spheres, as Joke Spaans argues in her essay. This genius in mapping social topography ensured that religious and civil identities were anchored in separate spaces,

---

[5] Cited in Miriam Bodian, *Hebrews of the Portuguese Nation. Conversos and Community in Early Modern Amsterdam* (Bloomington, IN, 1997), p. 59.

[6] R.G. Fuks-Mansfeld, *De Sefardim in Amsterdam tot 1795. Aspecten van een joodse minderheid in een Hollandse stad* (Hilversum, 1989), pp. 89–98.

[7] On social discipline and confessional conformity in Central Europe, see R. Po-Chia Hsia, *Social Discipline in the Reformation. Central Europe 1550–1750* (London, 1989).

which allowed for a nuanced articulation of the individual, the communal, and the civil in different representations. Expressions of loyalty to the House of Orange, for example, enabled all religious communities, including the Jews and Catholics, to celebrate a common patriotism, in spite of the unequal legal and civil status enjoyed by the different religious groups. Religious plurality was thus predicated upon a rigorous and vigilant patrolling of boundaries, undertaken by individuals, communities, and above all by the civil authorities. Order and discipline, therefore, laid the foundations for religious pluralism. The search for order propelled inner journeys of religious crossings, as was the case with Arnoldus Buchelius (1565–1641), who evolved from Catholic to Libertine and finally to Counter-Remonstrant, as Judith Pollmann shows in her contribution. The private and the public coexisted in the easygoing sociability of Buchelius with those not of the Calvinist Church and in his doctrinal intolerance of other religious communities. The construction of the vast grey zone of freedom between the private and the public, where different religious and immigrant groups must interact in daily life, was the work of civil authorities, who rigorously censored confessional polemic and defamations that could lead to disturbance of social peace.[8] It was the case in 1613 with Cornelis Buyck, brewer and deacon of the Calvinist Church in Woerden, who insulted his Counter-Remonstrant pastor as 'a false minister and a liar', and who was fined the enormous sum of fl. 350 (a worker's annual wages);[9] it applied to Hans Joostenszoon and his wife, Mennonites who converted to Judaism, and who in turn converted an elder of the Reformed Church in Grosthuizen, who were all three arrested, sentenced to die, and pardoned to exile in 1614;[10] and it was particularly true for those who confounded all religious boundaries by calling into question the fundamental doctrines of Christianity, as the followers of Spinoza and Descartes in Holland experienced at first hand the limits of toleration, as Jonathan Israel reminds us in his chapter.

Toleration, nevertheless, has served the Netherlands well. Visitors to the Republic in the seventeenth century associated religious pluralism with economic prosperity; and the image of an open society in an age of religious conformity has shaped Dutch self-image down to our day, as Ben Kaplan argues in his essay.

---

[8] Willem Frijhoff gives an incisive analysis to this process in his 'Dimensions de la coexistence confessionnelle', in C. Berkvens-Stevelinck, J. Israel, and G.H.M. Posthumus Meyjes (eds.), *The Emergence of Tolerance in the Dutch Republic* (Leiden/New York/ Cologne, 1997), pp. 213–37.

[9] Frijhoff, 'Dimensions de la coexistence', p. 236.

[10] Bodian, *Hebrews of the Portuguese Nation*, p. 60.

Our collection of essays focuses on the making of this toleration in the Dutch Golden Age, on the structure, contingency, agency, mechanism, and limitations of religious pluralism and toleration. Drawing together vastly divergent research interests and perspectives, our volume offers four conclusions and themes in the history of religious toleration: they concern periodisation, local diversity, the techniques of toleration, and comparative history.

Phases in the making of religious toleration

First, the making of religious toleration in the Dutch Republic seems to have evolved over three distinct phases. The first period, c. 1572 to 1620, was characterised by the attainment of Calvinist hegemony within the rebellious provinces. While claiming only about 20 per cent of the population of the north as full members, the Reformed Church achieved the status of official church (*publieke kerk*), while the doctrinal and ecclesiological conflicts between Remonstrants and Counter-Remonstrants ended up in the triumph of the more restrictive wing of Calvinism with the 1618 Synod of Dordrecht. During this first period, the most restrictive anti-Catholic legislations were enacted, although the Twelve Years' Truce in the war with Spain gave Catholics a reprieve in the actual enforcement of the edicts. The formation of the Mennonite community and the arrival of Sephardic Jews also made this initial period one of tremendous social change in the Netherlands, as the new society absorbed not only different Christian and Jewish communities, but immigrants from Iberia, France, the southern Low Countries, England, and Germany.

A second period, c. 1620 to 1700, coincided with the Golden Age of the Dutch Republic. A pragmatic and successful model of a pluriconfessional society evolved in the Netherlands, where a strong civil authority, especially in Holland, kept the peace between a hegemonic Reformed Church and the other religious communities. The separation between private and public spheres, the continued repression of Catholics during the span of the war and the beginning of Catholic missions launched from the south, the open toleration of the Jewish community, and the economic and cultural assimilation of the Mennonites characterised the success of religious toleration. Yet the limits of toleration were also clearly manifest in the repression against anti-Trinitarians, deists, agnostics, and atheists.

The third period spanned the eighteenth century until the end of the old Republic. The making of a system of religious pluralism was complete, resulting in a 'pillarized' society of separate communities under the watchful supervision of a strong civil authority. Improvements in the rights of Catholics represented the most significant development in a society where they still constituted nearly one-half of the population.

Local diversity

The chapters collected in our volume demonstrate the existence of great differences in religious toleration among towns, regions, and provinces in the Dutch Republic. Historians have long been aware of the predominance of Holland and Amsterdam in the economy, culture, and politics of the Netherlands. This was not the same for the history of religious toleration. The story of the Sephardim in the early modern Republic, for example, largely unfolded in Amsterdam; and the Amsterdam regents have been hailed in particular as exemplary of the liberal and tolerant attitude of the Dutch Republic.[11] Yet it was the Amsterdam regents who cracked down on the followers of Spinoza and Descartes in the last decades of the seventeenth century. Like all civil magistrates, the regents in Amsterdam were above all concerned with discipline and stability. If social peace was achieved with toleration in the towns of Holland, a different consideration guided the civil authorities in the eastern provinces of Utrecht and Overijssel. Maarten Prak argues that in towns dominated by guilds, such as Arnhem, Deventer, Nijmegen, Utrecht, and Zwolle, the Reformed Church exercised far greater political pressure and achieved a more repressive hegemony *vis-à-vis* minority religious communities. Catholics, for example, were excluded from guild membership and citizenship until the eighteenth century. By moving away from Holland, we immediately acquire a very different picture of society and religion in the Dutch Republic. We must constantly remember the sovereignty of the individual provinces and the importance of local custom in the new United Provinces.

Techniques of toleration

The most visible technique in favour of religious toleration was writing. During the early modern period, the Netherlands produced the most significant works in religious toleration and liberty; the names of Hugo de Groot, Coornhert, Wtenbogaert, and others come readily to mind. Toleration and plurality provided the theme for the formation of a textual and intellectual community that crossed religious boundaries. In addition to Remonstrant writers, members of other religious communities also defended liberty of worship; the importance of this textual tradition for

---

[11] Johan E. Elias, *Geschiedenis van het Amsterdamsche regentenpatriciaat* (The Hague, 1923).

one religious community is shown by Samme Zijlstra in his analysis of Mennonite ideals of toleration.

Litigation represented another technique in the struggle for toleration. Protracted lawsuits against anti-Catholic placards in Texel and Hoorn, for example, reflected the strong legal culture in the Netherlands and the availability of institutional recourse for minority groups to contest the application of repressive legislation. In fact, Catholics employed many techniques to counter religious persecutions, resorting to bribery, appealing to noble patrons, and counting on the laxity of local magistrates. The key to this contest was the struggle for equal civil rights by minority religious groups, which were eventually achieved by the end of the eighteenth century. A decentralised country with archaic constitutions and fragmented political authorities was not likely or inclined to impose religious conformity.

The Netherlands in comparative perspective

Finally, we would like to propose, more as a theme than as a conclusion, the importance of comparing religious plurality and toleration in the Dutch Republic with other societies in the early modern period. While the intellectual traditions have been studied in the larger European context,[12] a comparative social and political history of religious pluralism and toleration in early modern Europe has yet to be written. Despite scepticism of the depth of toleration in the Netherlands,[13] the Dutch Republic compared favourably to her neighbours. English Catholics, French Protestants, and suspect Judaisers in Spain and Portugal all endured far harsher treatments than their Dutch counterparts. Even in the Holy Roman Empire, where religious peace between the Christian confessions was established in 1555 and 1648, and where Jewish communities found protection among princes and magistrates, pathways through religious boundaries bristled with far more dangerous obstacles than in the Netherlands. To investigate the social and political context for religious pluralism is not to deny the achievements of the new Republic. By delineating the structures of toleration and by probing its limits, we can come to appreciate even more the achievements of a pragmatic and unsystematic arrangement that gave lustre to the Dutch Golden Age.

---

[12] See C. Berkvens-Stevelinck, J. Israel, and G.H.M. Posthumus Meyjes (eds.), *The Emergence of Tolerance in the Dutch Republic* (Leiden/New York/Cologne, 1997).

[13] See Marijke Gijswijt-Hofstra (ed.), *Een schijn van verdraagzaamheid. Afwijking en tolerantie in Nederland van de zestiende eeuw tot heden* (Hilversum, 1989).

2 'Dutch' religious tolerance: celebration and revision

Benjamin J. Kaplan

When foreigners visit the Netherlands today, certain items seem invari-
ably to stand on their touristic agenda: the Rijksmuseum, Anne Frank's
house, a boat ride through the canals. One of the more remarkable items
is a walk through Amsterdam's red light district, where, on a typical summer evening, in addition to the clientele, thousands of foreigners throng –
men, women, couples, even families. Such districts are not usually on the
itinerary of respectable tourists, but in Amsterdam a promenade there
serves a purpose: foreigners are invited to wonder at the tolerance – or, if
you prefer, permissiveness – that prevails in the Netherlands. In the same
district but during the daytime, the Amstelkring Museum extends essentially the same invitation. The museum preserves Our Lord in the Attic,
one of the roughly twenty Catholic *schuilkerken*, or clandestine churches,
that operated in Amsterdam in the latter half of the seventeenth century.
Nestled within the top floors of a large but unremarkable house named
The Hart, Our Lord does not betray its existence to the casual passer-by –
it has no tower, no stained-glass windows, no crosses on the outside –
and, but for the museum banner that hangs today on the building's front
façade, one could easily pass by it unawares. In its day, though, its existence was an open secret, like that of the other *schuilkerken*. Its discreet
architecture fooled no one, but did help to reconcile the formal illegal-
ity of Catholic worship with its actual prevalence. Today, the museum's
guidebook (English version) presents the church as 'a token of the liberalism of the mercantile Dutch in an age of intolerance'.[1]

Around the world, Dutch society is famous for its tolerance, which
extends to drug use, alternate lifestyles, and other matters about which
most industrial lands feel a deep ambivalence. But whence comes that
tolerance, that 'liberalism'? The guidebook hints at two answers. One is
that tolerance promotes commerce and thus is profitable; the other is
that the Dutch are simply a 'liberal', that is, tolerant, people. Tolerance
is represented as smart economics, but also as a national trait – a virtue

---

[1] *Amstelkring Museum: Our Lord in the Attic* (n.p., 1970), first page.

8

by most people's account, a vice by others', but either way as something rooted in the history, customs, and very character of the Dutch people. The Dutch, in other words, do not just practise tolerance: by their own account and others', they *are* tolerant; it is considered one of their defining characteristics.[2]

This is nothing new: 'Dutch' tolerance was already proverbial in the Golden Age, though the tolerance then under discussion extended only to religions. Indeed, as early as the sixteenth century, in the crucible of their Revolt against Spain, the Dutch – with Hollanders in the vanguard – began to define themselves as an especially, even uniquely tolerant people. That identity was cemented in the Golden Age, when Calvinists, Catholics, Mennonites, and a host of other religious groups lived peacefully alongside one another.[3] In our own century, the same notion of Dutchness has expanded beyond the religious, just as the concept of tolerance itself, rooted in the religious dilemmas of early modern Europe, has come to be applied to all forms of 'otherness'.

Logically, the argument that the Dutch practise tolerance because they are tolerant is nothing but a tautology, unless one believes in national character as an autonomous, causal force in history, which few scholars do today.[4] As a cultural construct, though, the argument continues to function as a powerful expression of national identity. In that capacity it provides a standard of behaviour against which the Dutch judge their society and government – severely sometimes, for example as concerns policy towards the ethnic minorities come in recent decades to live in the Netherlands. It also provides a framework for the interpretation of Dutch history. But here the problems begin, for the essentialising of 'Dutch'

[2] Hans Bots, 'Tolerantie of gecultiveerde tweedracht. Het beeld van de Nederlandse tolerantie bij buitenlanders in de zeventiende en achttiende eeuw', *Bijdragen en Mededelingen betreffende de Geschiedenis der Nederlanden* 107 (1992), 657; W.W. Mijnhardt, 'De geschiedschrijving over de ideeëngeschiedenis van de 17e- en 18-eeuwse Republiek', in W.W. Mijnhardt (ed.), *Kantelend geschiedbeeld. Nederlandse historiografie sinds 1945* (Utrecht/ Antwerp, 1983), p. 165; B. van Heerikhuizen, 'What is Typically Dutch? Sociologists in the 1930s and 1940s on the Dutch National Character', *Netherlands Journal of Sociology* 18 (1982), 103–26; R. van Ginkel, 'Typisch Nederlands . . . Ruth Benedict over het "nationaal karakter" van de Nederlanders', *Amsterdams Sociologisch Tijdschrift* 18 (1991), 43, 52; Ernest Zahn, *Regenten, rebellen en reformatoren. Een visie op Nederland en de Nederlanders* (Amsterdam, 1989), pp. 37–42; Herman Pleij, *Hollands welbehagen* (Amsterdam, 1998), pp. 37–42.

[3] On the complex relations between social practice and cultural identity, and problems of terminology, see Willem Frijhoff, 'Identiteit en identiteitsbesef. De historicus en de spanning tussen verbeelding, benoeming en herkenning', *Bijdragen en Mededelingen betreffende de Geschiedenis der Nederlanden* 107 (1992), 614–34.

[4] See, for the Netherlands, Rob van Ginkel's careful examination of twentieth-century ideas and discussions concerning Dutch national 'identity' and 'character': Rob van Ginkel, *Op zoek naar eigenheid. Denkbeelden en discussies over cultuur en identiteit in Nederland* (The Hague, 1999).

tolerance has for centuries involved mythologising, encouraged anachronism, and served partisan causes. In this way it has long obscured our
understanding of religious life in the Dutch Republic. Today it does the
same, but in a twofold manner: not just by propagating but also by provoking reactions, some of them exaggerated, against such mythologising,
anachronism, and partisanship.

The mythologising began early. In the sixteenth century, Netherlanders
justified their Revolt against Spain most frequently as a conservative
action in defence of their historic 'privileges', or 'liberties'. As Juliaan
Woltjer has pointed out, only some of those privileges had a firm basis in
law or fact, and what they entailed was not always crystal clear. Even the
famous *jus de non evocando*, perhaps the most frequently cited privilege of
all, was capable of varying constructions: while most people agreed that
it guaranteed that a burgher accused of a crime would not be tried by
a court outside his province, opinions differed as to whether it assigned
to local municipal courts sole and final jurisdiction in such cases. Either
way, the privilege conjured up a time when cities and provinces had enjoyed judicial autonomy, and therein lay the true power of the privileges
generally: to evoke an idealised past against which the present could be
judged.[5] However vague their positive content, no one mistook the privileges' negative import as an indictment of, and justification for resistance
to, the Habsburg government's unwelcome initiatives and innovations.
Foremost among the latter were the efforts of Philip II to introduce what
the Dutch, with great effect if little accuracy, called the 'Spanish Inquisition': an institutional structure for suppressing Protestantism, reforming
the Catholic Church, and imposing Tridentine orthodoxy on the people of the Netherlands. Such a programme entailed *gewetensdwang*, the
forcing of consciences, on a massive scale.

But if *gewetensdwang* was new and contrary to the privileges, was its
opposite, freedom of conscience, then part of a hallowed past? That was at
least the vague implication, made more plausible by the fact that believers
in the old Catholic faith as well as converts to Protestantism resisted the
government's religious policies. Still, given that the variety of religious
beliefs spawned by the Reformation was scarcely older than the placards
outlawing them, it took some legerdemain to construe the privileges as
guarantors of freedom of conscience. Nevertheless, a few writers of the
period did so explicitly. Two anonymous pamphlets dating from 1579
appealed to the Joyous Entry of Brabant, the oath taken since 1356 by

---

[5] J.J. Woltjer, 'Dutch Privileges, Real and Imaginary', in J.S. Bromley and E.H. Kossmann
(eds.), *Britain and the Netherlands*, vol. v: *Some Political Mythologies* (The Hague, 1975),
pp. 19–35; James D. Tracy, *Holland Under Habsburg Rule 1506–1566. The Formation of a
Body Politic* (Berkeley, 1990), pp. 147–75.

each new duke of Brabant by which he swore to 'do no violence or abuse to any person in any manner'.

This word *in any manner*, expressly highlighted [*wtstaende*] in the Joyous Entry, excludes any kind of violence or abuse, be it to property, body, or soul, so that the king is bound by virtue of the Joyous Entry to leave every person in possession of their freedom, not only of property or body but also of soul, that is, of conscience.[6]

That this interpretation might seem rather far-fetched did not escape the author of either pamphlet, but in its support both cited a treaty between Brabant and Flanders concluded in 1339 (and published, as a timely reminder, in 1576), in which the vague phrase 'in any manner' is glossed to mean 'in soul, body, or property'. Contrary to what some people think, says one of the pamphlets, it is a wonder to see 'how careful our ancestors always were to preserve and to retain the enjoyment of this right', freedom of conscience, 'which until the arrival of the Inquisition we always enjoyed'.[7] Even more remarkably, both pamphlets go on to equate freedom of conscience explicitly with freedom of worship. Not even the Inquisition could stop people from believing what they wished; the freedom which it took from us, therefore (so the argument went), must have been the right to profess our beliefs publicly and to worship God in accordance with them.

Thus by anachronism religious tolerance took on the aura of an ancient custom. Once gained, that aura did not readily fade. Eighteen years later, Cornelis Pieterszoon Hooft, burgomaster of Amsterdam, thought it entirely plausible to tell his fellow regents that it was 'in accordance with the ancient manner of governing this land and this city' that they 'bear with each others' mistakes in matters of faith and not disturb any person on account of religion'.[8] In 1659, Pieter de la Court represented what he perceived as a decline in religious tolerance as a departure from the 'original maxims' of his province.[9]

Some of its apologists, however, represented the Revolt as a fight not just for specific 'freedoms', plural, but for 'freedom', singular and

---

[6] Anon., *Een goede Waerschouwinghe voor den Borgheren, ende besonder dien vanden leden van Antwerpen/ Datsy hen niet en souden laten verlocken met het soet aengheuen vande bedriechlycke Artijkelen van peyse/ onlancx ghecomen van Cuelen* (n.p., 1579), fo. 15r.

[7] Anon. ('eenen goede[n] liefhebber des vreedts'), *Een Goede vermaninge aen de goede borghers van Bruessele/ dat sy souden blijuen in goede eendracht/ ende niet treden in partijschap teghen malcanderen om eenighe saecken* (Ghent, 1579), fo. 14. Cf. Anon., *Letteren van Verbande tuss. Brabant ende Vlaenderen, ghedaen ende besloten int Jaer 1339* (Delft, 1576); P.A.M. Geurts, *De Nederlandse opstand in de pamfletten 1566–1584* (Utrecht, 1978), pp. 155–6, 250–1.

[8] Gerard Brandt, *Historie der Reformatie, en andre kerkelyke geschiedenissen, in en ontrent de Nederlanden*, 4 vols. (Amsterdam, 1671–1704), vol. I, p. 833.

[9] Pieter de la Court, *The True Interest and Political Maxims of the Republic of Holland* (New York, 1972), p. 69.

abstract. Jacob van Wesembeeke, Pensionary of Antwerp, played a crucial role in developing this argument. In 1566 he described the people of the Netherlands as 'having always been not just lovers, in the manner common to other peoples, but special and extremely ardent advocates, observers, and defenders' of their 'ancient liberty and freedom'.[10] William of Orange, for whom Wesembeeke worked for a time as propagandist, took up the theme, characterising Netherlanders 'as exceptional lovers and advocates of their liberty and enemies of all violence and oppression'.[11] Both men attributed a religious dimension to the liberty so cherished, Wesembeeke speaking reverently, for example, of the 'anchienne liberté au spirituel' of the Netherlands.[12] Thus the Dutch devotion to religious freedom was given a basis in national character as well as custom.

That character took on a sharper profile over the course of the Revolt, especially after the return of the southern provinces to the Spanish fold. Northerners – Hollanders in particular – increasingly appropriated to themselves the special love of freedom once more widely conceded.[13] One way they did so was through the myth of the Batavians, which had been circulating since the 1510s but gained enormous cultural prominence from the 1580s. Histories, dramas, and paintings celebrated this ancient Germanic tribe, known chiefly from the writings of Tacitus, as ancestors of the contemporary Hollanders and founders of their polity. Virtuous, industrious, pious, and clean, paragons of a simple decency, the Batavians appear in works like Hugo Grotius' *Liber de Antiquitate Reipublicae Batavicae* (1610) above all as fiercely independent. The tale of their struggle for autonomy from Rome was taken to prefigure the Hollanders' own struggle with Spain and predict its happy outcome.[14] In another work, the *Parallelon Rerum-Publicarum Liber Tertius* (written around 1601), Grotius compared the formerly Batavian, now Hollandic people to the ancient Athenians and Romans. The former emerge as superior in almost every respect to the paragons of civilisation venerated

[10] Ch. Rahlenbeck (ed.), *Mémoires de Jacques de Wesembeke* (Brussels, 1859), p. 12. Cf. Martin van Gelderen (ed.), *The Dutch Revolt* (Cambridge, 1993), p. xiii.
[11] Quoted in Martin van Gelderen, *The Political Thought of the Dutch Revolt 1555–1590* (Cambridge, 1992), p. 121; cf. Catherine Secretan, *Les privilèges, berçeau de la liberté* (Paris, 1990), p. 28.
[12] Secretan, *Les privilèges*, p. 28.
[13] See E.O.G. Haitsma Mulier and W.R.E. Velema (eds.), *Vrijheid. Een geschiedenis van de vijftiende tot de twintigste eeuw* (Amsterdam, 1999).
[14] Hugo de Groot, *De Oudheid van de Bataafse nu Hollandse Republiek*, ed. G.C. Molewijk (Weesp, 1988); I. Schöffer, 'The Batavian Myth during the Sixteenth and Seventeenth Centuries', in J.S. Bromley and E.H. Kossmann (eds.), *Britain and the Netherlands*, vol. v: *Some Political Mythologies* (The Hague, 1975), pp. 78–101; Simon Schama, *The Embarrassment of Riches. An Interpretation of Dutch Culture in the Golden Age* (New York, 1987), pp. 75–81; Marijke Spies, 'Verbeeldingen van vrijheid: David en Mozes, Burgerhart en Bato, Brutus en Cato', *De Zeventiende Eeuw* 10 (1994), 148–52.

by Renaissance Europe. This experiment in comparative ethnology represents the Revolt as a fight by the Hollanders 'for the freedom of their souls' as well as of their bodies, and exults in the Hollanders' combination of piety and tolerance:

> This [Reformed] religion... we maintain with a rare constancy and we spread it as we extend our territory.... We prescribe it without forcing it on anyone [*zonder hem af te perssen*], and those who take no pleasure in it with us we consider worthy more of pity than of punishment. We have no commands to give to the human heart; we torture no souls. Let each one believe what he can; in this regard too let FREEDOM be inviolate [*ongeschonden*].[15]

The reverse side of such self-congratulation was the anxious xenophobia directed at Calvinist refugees from the southern provinces. This emotion pervaded towns like Leiden and Utrecht, where such refugees comprised one-third or more of the membership of the Reformed Church, but was common enough elsewhere. Southern Calvinists were accused of an intolerance that mirrored that of the Spanish and was equally pernicious. Their opponents said that the Calvinists' form of church government merely replaced the old Spanish Inquisition with a new Genevan one, and that their violent efforts to suppress Catholicism, having fatally undermined the Revolt in the south, now threatened to do the same in the north. The story of Gent's Calvinist theocracy was referred to frequently, in tones of dark foreboding.[16] A famous speech delivered in 1597 by Burgomaster Hooft encapsulates much of this thinking. Occasioned by the excommunication and imprisonment of Goosen Vogelsang, a maker of velvet, it was a tirade against the influence of 'foreigners', by which Hooft meant Calvinist refugees from the south, within the Dutch Reformed Churches. 'The management of affairs', Hooft argued, should be in the hands of 'persons of a prudent, steady, and peaceable disposition, which qualities, I believe, prevail more among the natives than among those who have come here to live from other lands.' These foreign ministers and elders, trying to impose on the natives an alien orthodoxy

---

[15] Hugo Grotius, *Parallelon Rerum-Publicarum Liber Tertius: de moribus ingenioque populorum Atheniensium, Romanorum, Batavorum*, ed. J. Meerman, 3 vols. (Haarlem, 1801–1803), vol. III, p. 146. See also Christian Gellinek, *Hugo Grotius* (Boston, 1983), pp. 65–83; E.O.G. Haitsma Mulier, 'Grotius, Hooft and the Writing of History in the Dutch Republic', in A.C. Duke and C.A. Tamse (eds.), *Britain and the Netherlands*, vol. VIII: *Clio's Mirror. Historiography in Britain and the Netherlands* (Zutphen, 1985), pp. 54–72; H. Kampinga, *De opvattingen over onze oudere vaderlandsche geschiedenis bij de Hollandsche historici der XVIe en XVIIe eeuw* (The Hague, 1917), pp. 14–17, 36–7, 62, 69–73, 80.

[16] Benjamin J. Kaplan, *Calvinists and Libertines. Confession and Community in Utrecht, 1578–1620* (Oxford, 1995), pp. 64–5; Christine Jane Kooi, 'The Reformed Community of Leiden, 1572–1620', PhD thesis, Yale University (1993), especially pp. 155–8; Joke Spaans, *Haarlem na de Reformatie. Stedelijke cultuur en kerkelijk leven, 1577–1620* (The Hague, 1989), p. 110.

and, more importantly, an alien demand for orthodoxy, show that they do not know 'the nature of the land and its people'; Hollanders, declared Hooft, 'are accustomed, like the Bereans, to examine Scripture for themselves'.[17] Hooft ignored the fact that few of the Reformed Churches in the north were ever completely dominated by southerners, and then only briefly. He remained silent about the extremism of some of his own landsmen.

In the seventeenth century, Remonstrants developed further this strategy of branding intolerance a foreign vice and imputing an innate tolerance to the Dutch. In his *Kerckelijcke Historie*, Johannes Wtenbogaert hailed the Revolt against Spain as a fight for the pure Gospel and for freedom of conscience. To these two causes, he suggested, the Dutch had been devoted since the beginning of the Reformation and so remained – especially Hollanders who, 'whatever their persuasion (excepting the Roman and Genevan heretic-hunters and -burners, and those who support them), do not like the burning of books under any circumstances'.[18] Of course, no one needed reminding who the most outspoken champions of religious tolerance were in contemporary Holland. In effect, Wtenbogaert was claiming the Dutch character to be inherently Remonstrant in its religious sensibility. His narrative of the Reformation bolstered such claims by highlighting the continuity between his own party's beliefs and those of the first Dutch reformers.[19]

Other Remonstrant authors adopted the same strategic use of historical narrative, but located the origins of Dutch Protestantism not in the 1550s, as did Wtenbogaert, but earlier, with Erasmus of Rotterdam. It was Grotius who, in his *Ordinum Hollandiae ac Westfrisiae Pietas* (1613), first made the case for the broad popularity of Erasmian piety in the Habsburg Netherlands; he who first represented the Remonstrants as the heirs of this Netherlandish tradition, tracing a continuous chain of influences from the great Christian humanist, via the so-called Libertines of the late sixteenth century, to his own party.[20] As has been shown, the facts

[17] Brandt, *Historie der Reformatie*, vol. I, pp. 818, 820.
[18] Joannes Wtenbogaert, *Kerckelijcke Historie, Vervattende verscheyden Gedenckwaerdige saeken, In de Christenheyt voorgevallen, van Het Jaer vier hondert af, tot in het Jaer sestien hondert ende negentien. Voornamentlijck in dese Geunieerde Provincien* (Rotterdam, 1647), p. 777.
[19] This paragraph is indebted to the insights of Charles H. Parker, 'To the Attentive, Non-partisan Reader. The Appeal to History and National Identity in the Religious Disputes of the Seventeenth-Century Netherlands', *Sixteenth Century Journal* 28 (1997), 57–78. Cf. also D. Nauta, 'De Reformatie in Nederland in de historiografie', in P.A.M. Geurts and A.E.M. Janssen (eds.), *Geschiedschrijving in Nederland*, vol. II: *Geschiedbeoefening* (The Hague, 1981), p. 207.
[20] Hugo Grotius, *Ordinum Hollandiae ac Westfrisiae Pietas*, ed. Edwin Rabbie (Leiden, 1995), p. 151.

of the matter were much more complicated. Erasmus' influence in the Netherlands was as diffuse as it was pervasive, and the inclination to view ethical behaviour as the essence of Christianity did not necessarily owe its inspiration to him. Dirck Coornhert, Hubert Duifhuis, Caspar Coolhaes, and other religious leaders known as Libertines were inspired by spiritualist and Protestant teachings at least as much as by humanist ones. And Jacob Arminius certainly did not derive from Erasmus his position on predestination. By constructing retrospectively such a line of influence, however, Grotius gave his own religious party a venerable genealogy. As a native Hollander, uniquely eminent scholar, and champion of a 'purified' Christianity, Erasmus was the perfect father-figure for a religious movement intent on portraying itself as autochthonous, popular, and distinctly Dutch.[21] Gerard Brandt's *Historie der Reformatie* stands as a masterful elaboration of the same historical schema. It represents Erasmus not just as a bona fide Reformer, but as the wisest and most important in all Europe: 'This man led freedom into the Christian church / . . . / A Rotterdammer teaches the world Reformation.'[22] For Brandt, as for Grotius, the historic popularity of Erasmus in the Netherlands implied that the Remonstrant faith had the sympathy of the Dutch people and the religious tolerance by which it survived their support. By Brandt's day, it also conveyed a message about the legitimacy of the political patrons of tolerance, the pro-States, anti-Orangist party. Remonstrant viewpoints dominated Dutch historiography to the end of the Republic and even

---

[21] G.H.M. Posthumus Meyjes, 'De doorwerking van de Moderne Devotie met name bij de Remonstranten', in P. Bange *et al.* (eds.), *De doorwerking van de Moderne Devotie. Windesheim 1387–1987* (Hilversum, 1988), pp. 81–94; M.E.H.N. Mout, 'Limits and Debates. A Comparative View of Dutch Toleration in the Sixteenth and Early Seventeenth Centuries', in C. Berkvens-Stevelinck, J. Israel, and G.H.M. Posthumus Meyjes (eds.), *The Emergence of Tolerance in the Dutch Republic* (Leiden/New York/ Cologne, 1997), pp. 37–47; Benjamin J. Kaplan, 'Hubert Duifhuis and the Nature of Dutch Libertinism', *Tijdschrift voor Geschiedenis* 105 (1992), 1–29; Kaplan, *Calvinists and Libertines*, chapter 2; Bruce Mansfield, *Phoenix of His Age. Interpretations of Erasmus c. 1550–1750* (Toronto, 1979), chapter 4; J.C.H. Blom and C.J. Misset, ' "Een onvervalschte Nederlandsche geest". Enkele historiografische kanttekeningen bij het concept van een nationaal-gereformeerde richting', in E.K. Grootes and J. den Haan (eds.), *Geschiedenis godsdienst letterkunde. Opstellen aangeboden aan dr. S.B.J. Zilverberg* (Roden, 1989), pp. 226–7; Carl Bangs, *Arminius. A Study in the Dutch Reformation* (Grand Rapids, MI, 1985), pp. 138 *et seq.*

[22] 'Deez' heeft de vrijheit in de Christen' kerk geleidt / . . . / Een Rotterdammer leerdt de werelt Reformeren': Brandt, *Historie der Reformatie*, vol. I, caption to the portrait of Erasmus, between pp. 64 and 65. Cf. Peter Burke, 'The Politics of Reformation History: Burnet and Brandt', in A.C. Duke and C.A. Tamse (eds.), *Britain and the Netherlands*, vol. VIII: *Clio's Mirror. Historiography in Britain and the Netherlands* (Zutphen, 1985), pp. 73–85; S.B.J. Zilverberg, 'Gerard Brandt als kerkhistoricus', *Nederlands Archief voor Kerkgeschiedenis* 49 (1968), 37–58. The historical schema of Remonstrant historian Philip van Limborch was essentially the same; cf. Pieter Jacobus Barnouw, *Philippus van Limborch* (The Hague, 1963), pp. 39–48, 142.

beyond, thanks partly to the influence of the Collegiant Jan Wagenaar's *Vaderlandsche Historie* (1749–59).[23]

Proclaiming themselves the heirs of the original Dutch Reformation and the bearers of a genuinely Dutch Protestantism, Remonstrants found it natural to pray not just for their own welfare but for that of the entire Dutch 'fatherland'. According to Peter van Rooden, the Remonstrants were the first group of dissenters to celebrate the national days of fasting, prayer, and thanksgiving (*bededagen*) decreed by the States-General, adopting the custom as early as 1627. Remonstrant ministers like Simon Episcopius proclaimed that God had bestowed his blessing on the Dutch Republic and allowed it to prosper as a reward for the religious tolerance practised by its government. By the end of the seventeenth century, Mennonite and Lutheran congregations commonly celebrated the same occasions with similar prayers. In the eighteenth century, the different denominations even competed to display the greatest patriotism. All of them attributed the special divine status of the land in part to its tolerance, which allowed their churches to function.[24]

That hundreds of foreigners who visited the Republic remarked on its religious tolerance is well known; indeed, by the late seventeenth century the Netherlands clearly stood for tolerance in the minds of foreigners, just as it does today. From the 1610s, if not earlier, the itinerary of foreign tourists conventionally included a sampling of churches and synagogues; guidebooks, a genre that developed later in the century, pointed them to the same. Like modern tourists, visitors took aesthetic pleasure in the art and architecture; by attending services they satisfied what we would call an anthropological interest in foreign customs and rituals (those of the Jews and Quakers exercised a special fascination, accounts suggest); and, like today's tourist in the red light district, some of them also derived a thrill from exposure to things forbidden at home. Savoured or condemned, religious pluralism featured as a standard topos in their travel accounts, which, in this regard as in others, tended to conflate the Republic as a whole with Holland. Indeed, based sometimes on only a quick visit

---

[23] See G.J. Schutte, ' "A Subject of Admiration and Encomium". The History of the Dutch Republic as Interpreted by Non-Dutch Authors in the Second Half of the Eighteenth Century', in A.C. Duke and C.A. Tamse (eds.), *Britain and the Netherlands*, vol. VIII: *Clio's Mirror. Historiography in Britain and the Netherlands* (Zutphen, 1985), p. 117; L.H.M. Wessels, 'Jan Wagenaar (1709–1773). Bijdrage tot een herwaardering', in P.A.M. Geurts and A.E.M. Janssen (eds.), *Geschiedschrijving in Nederland*, vol. I: *Geschiedschrijvers* (The Hague, 1981), pp. 117–40.

[24] Peter van Rooden, 'Dissenters en bededagen. Civil religion ten tijde van de Republiek', *Bijdragen en Mededelingen betreffende de Geschiedenis der Nederlanden* 107 (1992), 703–12. Although Van Rooden suggests that many Catholics 'probably' celebrated the same *biddagen*, it is unclear whether they expressed (or felt) the same gratitude as did Protestant dissenters for the nation's tolerance.

to Amsterdam, German accounts made sweeping generalisations about Dutch tolerance. In part, this was visitors seeing what they were prepared to see and reporting back what they themselves had read in earlier reports. C.D. van Strien has noted that English authors of travel accounts often borrowed heavily from the travel guides and earlier accounts they had read. Such literature became a vehicle for the circulation of stereotypes. So did the periodical literature of the Enlightenment, which likewise represented the Dutch as an especially tolerant, freedom-loving people.[25]

It was not just foreigners, though, who defined the Dutch as tolerant; rather, as we have seen, the definition originated among groups within the Netherlands for whom it had special, partisan meanings. If it became part of a more widely shared self-definition, it was not because all the Dutch were happy about this characteristic of their society, only that they acknowledged it and saw it as distinctive. Nor should this sense of collective identity be equated with modern nationalism. Scholars have amply documented the ambiguities of the term 'nation' in the early modern period and the continued strength of local and provincial loyalties. As in other spheres, so in the cultural Holland had a disproportionate influence within the Republic and was able to project aspects of its own self-definition on the larger whole. Certain cities, like Haarlem and Gouda, consciously cultivated reputations for tolerance; others, like Dordrecht and Groningen, did not. Only towards the end of the eighteenth century did the notion emerge that each political 'nation' should comprise a single, organically united, culturally and linguistically unique *Volk*. A product of Herder and German Romanticism, the equation of 'nation' and *Volk* gave new power and meaning to the notion of 'Dutch' religious tolerance.[26]

[25] Julia Bientjes, *Holland und der Holländer im Urteil deutscher Reisender 1400–1800* (Groningen, 1967), especially pp. 88–112; Bots, 'Tolerantie of gecultiveerde tweedracht', 668–9; Christian Gellinek (ed.), *Europas Erster Baedeker. Filip von Zesens Amsterdam 1664* (New York, 1988); Marijke Meijer Drees, *Andere landen, andere mensen. De beeldvorming van Holland versus Spanje en Engeland omstreeks 1650* (The Hague, 1997), especially pp. 99–106, 116–31; R. Murris, *La Hollande et les Hollandais au XVIIe et au XVIIIe siècles vus par les Français* (Paris, 1925); C.D. van Strien, *British Travellers in Holland during the Stuart Period. Edward Browne and John Locke as Tourists in the United Provinces* (Leiden, 1993), especially pp. 8–13, 41–9, 131–2, 201–11, 228–9, 322; and Madeleine van Strien-Chardonneau, *Le voyage de Hollande: récits de voyageurs français dans les Provinces-Unies, 1748–1795* (Oxford, 1994), pp. 61–9. See also Herman Meyer, 'Das Bild des Holländers in der deutschen Literatur', in Herman Meyer, *Zarte Empirie. Studien zur Literaturgeschichte* (Stuttgart, 1963), pp. 202–24; and the new anthology, Kees van Strien, *Touring the Low Countries. Accounts of British Travellers, 1660–1720* (Amsterdam, 1998); Schutte, ' "A Subject of Admiration and Encomium" ', pp. 109–31.
[26] F.M. Barnard, *Herder's Social and Political Thought* (Oxford, 1965); Lewis W. Spitz, 'Natural Law and the Theory of History in Herder', *Journal of the History of Ideas* 16 (1955), 459–60.

According to the Romantics and their heirs, every *Volk* had a unique spirit, or character. Generally the qualities attributed in the nineteenth century to the Dutch *volksgeest*, or *volkskarakter*, were the same ones attributed more than two centuries earlier: love of freedom first and foremost, followed by virtue, tolerance, a deep biblical piety, industry, cleanliness, chastity (among women), and certain qualities of moderation and steady temper captured by the term 'phlegmatic' and by Dutch words difficult to translate like *nuchter* and *bedaard* (against these, the most commonly mentioned vices were greed, drunkenness, stupidity, and crudeness). Explanations for these qualities – to the extent that considered ones were offered – shifted a bit more. Early modern scholars had followed the ancient Greeks in pointing to climate and soil as their chief causes. Warm or cold, wet or dry, the environment determined a people's body type and character. While the Dutch, then, shared many traits with other northern peoples, Holland's cold and wetness, it was said, gave its dwellers special 'qualities of soul and of mind'.[27] In the nineteenth century, the great liberal historian Robert Fruin raised two others forces to a level equal with environment: race and 'social conditions'. By the first he meant particularly to distinguish the Germanic from the 'Roman' (that is, romance-language-speaking) *volksaard*; the latter referred to a people's economic activities. Commerce, dominant in the Netherlands, 'demands freedom of movement'; 'it cannot suffer to be regulated or ruled' and has the effect of stimulating love of freedom in all domains, the religious as well as the political. Fruin added cynically that such love did not necessarily translate into 'liberality', a willingness to grant others the freedom you demand for yourself, citing as an example the way the Dutch ruled their colonies. But his was a dissenting opinion, and even he did not pursue the thought consequently. If he had, he might well have cited the Reformation as another example. Instead, he subscribed completely to the Whiggish view of it as a glorious phase in the centuries-long struggle between two great forces, 'centralised tyranny and the spirit of civil and religious liberty', as John Lothrop Motley put it.[28] Both men, along with Bakhuizen van den Brink and other liberal historians of the nineteenth century, projected onto the past the liberal Protestantism of their own age. To them, freedom – religious, civic, economic – was an essential,

---

[27] Grotius, *Parallelon*, vol. I, pp. 17–27; Meijer Drees, *Andere landen, andere mensen*, especially pp. 12–20, 25–56; Kampinga, *De opvattingen over onze oudere vaderlandsche geschiedenis*, pp. 36–7. Among the Renaissance scholars who preceded Grotius in developing this 'climatological theory' was the French political theorist Jean Bodin, unmentioned by Meijer Drees. See the modern translation: Jean Bodin, *Method for the Easy Comprehension of History* (New York, 1945), pp. 85–152.

[28] John Lothrop Motley, *The Rise of the Dutch Republic* (London, 1868), p. 21.

indivisible principle, and necessarily entailed religious tolerance. History was the story of its progress.[29]

Liberal church historians, especially members of the 'Groningen school' of Protestant scholarship, applied the same thinking more specifically to the course of the Dutch Reformation. On the one hand, as a northern Germanic people the Dutch were said to incline naturally to Protestantism, the religion of freedom. On the other, their unique traits were said to give Dutch Protestantism distinctive qualities.[30] Bernard ter Haar wrote of the Reformation in the Netherlands that it 'proceeded entirely from the spirit of the people [*volksgeest*], and took, from its earliest beginning, an independent course that was entirely in accord with the people's character [*volkskarakter*]'.[31] That character was tolerant, confident in human free will, and inclined to view sermon-on-the-mount ethics as the essence of Christianity. Also writing around mid-century, Petrus Hofstede de Groot portrayed Calvinism as a belief system imposed by foreigners on the Dutch people which 'disrupted and disturbed the natural, genuinely Netherlandish development of the Christian spirit here'.[32] In the evolution of that spirit, the Groningen school assigned to Erasmus a very special place. As Barend Glasius put it,

Erasmus's distinctive manner of thinking and acting, with respect to the reformation of the church, had its basis chiefly in his temperament and character as a Netherlander; and ... reciprocally the great influence which he exercised on the supporters of Reformation and the course of Reformation in our fatherland

[29] Robert Fruin, 'Het karakter van het Nederlandsche volk', in Robert Fruin, *Verspreide geschriften*, ed. P.J. Blok, P.L. Muller, and S. Muller, 10 vols. (The Hague, 1900–5), vol. I, pp. 1–21 (on 'liberality', p. 14); Robert Fruin, 'Het antirevolutionnaire staatsrecht van Groen van Prinsterer ontvouwd en beoordeeld', in Robert Fruin, *Verspreide geschriften*, ed. P.J. Blok, P.L. Muller, and S. Muller, 10 vols. (The Hague, 1900–5), vol. X, pp. 158–64; Motley, *Rise of the Dutch Republic*, pp. 21, 49, 131–2, and *passim*; J.W. Smit, *Fruin en de partijen tijdens de Republiek* (Groningen, 1958), especially pp. 26–8, 100–6; John Paul Elliott, 'Protestantization in the Northern Netherlands, a Case Study: The Classis of Dordrecht 1572–1640', PhD thesis, Columbia University (1990), pp. 6–16; Herbert Butterfield, *The Whig Interpretation of History* (London, 1950). While in many ways the liberal historiography of the nineteenth century was a continuation and development of the Remonstrant/*Staatsgezinde* historiographic school of the Republic (represented by historians like Brandt, Van Limborch, and Wagenaar), Smit shows that Fruin departed significantly from this tradition in his appreciation for centralised governmental authority.
[30] B. Glasius and H.M.C. van Oosterzee, *Galerij van Nederlandsche geloofshelden voor de evangelie-waarheid* (Tiel, 1853–4), especially pp. 6–7; Petrus Hofstede de Groot, *De Groninger godgeleerden in hunne eigenaardigheid: toespraak aan zijne vroegere en tegenwoordige leerlingen, na vervulde vijfentwintigjarige hoogleeraarsbediening* (Groningen, 1855), especially pp. 77–8.
[31] Bernard ter Haar, *De geschiedenis der Kerkhervorming, in tafereelen: een leesboek ter bevestiging der protestanten in hun christelijk geloof* (Amsterdam, 1854), p. 241.
[32] Quoted in Nauta, 'De Reformatie in Nederland in de historiografie', p. 215, whose treatment of the nineteenth-century church historians I largely follow.

seems to have resulted from the Netherlanders' natural conformity with their countryman.[33]

Even before Erasmus, though, came Geert Groote, Wessel Gansfort, and the Brothers of the Common Life; for Glasius and the others, these men and the movement with which they were associated, the Modern Devotion, expressed the first distinctly Dutch conception of Christendom and were the true originators of the Dutch Reformation.[34]

In the early twentieth century, the Leiden church historians Fredrik Pijper and Johannes Lindeboom brought a greater scholarly rigour to the study of the Dutch Reformation, but interpretatively they stood directly in the tradition of the Groningen school. To denote the distinctly Dutch religious movement he saw unfolding in the sixteenth century, Pijper coined the label 'national-Netherlandic reform movement' (*nationaal-Nederlandse reformatorische richting*), which Lindeboom later shortened to 'Netherlandic-reformist' (*Nederlandse-reformatorische*) or alternately to 'national-Reformed' (*nationaal-Gereformeerd*). Both men saw the movement as essentially Erasmian in character and continuing in a straight line of influence down to the Remonstrants. They did not celebrate exuberantly, but they did maintain the same pantheon of Dutch reformers as their predecessors, which included such figures as Cornelis Hoen, Anastasius Veluanus, Hubert Duifhuis, and Dirk Coornhert.[35] Lindeboom described the *Niederländisch Frömmigkeitstypus* that these men embodied as oriented towards the Bible (especially in its original languages), optimistic about human nature, and somewhat indifferent to ceremonies; it strives, he said, for apostolic simplicity and for pure behaviour more than pure doctrine.[36] Hendrik Enno van Gelder continued the same historiographic tradition into the 1970s. While dropping the nationalist terminology, he was unabashed in his anachronism: he explicitly presented the same cast of characters as 'the most modern of their time,

[33] Barend Glasius, *Verhandeling over Erasmus als Nederlandsch Kerkhervormer* (The Hague, 1850), p. 5.
[34] Petrus Hofstede de Groot, *Johan Wessel Ganzevoort, op het negende halve eeuwfeest zijner geboorte herdacht* (Groningen, 1871); Ter Haar, *De geschiedenis der Kerkhervorming, in tafereelen*; B. ter Haar, W. Moll, and E.B. Swalue (eds.), *Geschiedenis der christelijke kerk in Nederland, in tafereelen*, 2 vols. (Amsterdam, 1864–9).
[35] Fredrik Pijper, 'Geestelijke stroomingen in Nederland voor de opkomst van het remonstrantisme', in G.J. Heering (ed.), *De remonstranten, gedenkboek bij het 300-jarig bestaan der Remonstrantsche Broederschap* (Leiden, 1919), pp. 37–60; Fredrik Pijper, *Erasmus en de Nederlandsche Reformatie* (Leiden, 1907); Johannes Lindeboom, *De confessioneele ontwikkeling der Reformatie in de Nederlanden* (The Hague, 1946); Johannes Lindeboom, 'Erasmus' Bedeutung für die Entwicklung des geistigen Lebens in den Niederlanden', *Archiv für Reformationsgeschichte* 43 (1952), 1–12; Nauta, 'De Reformatie in Nederland in de historiografie'; Blom and Misset, '"Een onvervalschte Nederlandsche geest"'.
[36] Lindeboom, 'Erasmus' Bedeutung', 7.

unconscious precursors of liberal Protestantism and of modern emancipation from Church supervision, conscious defenders of tolerance, sometimes even of religious freedom'.[37] In *The Two Reformations of the Sixteenth
Century* (1961), Enno van Gelder elevated Erasmian humanism to its ultimate status as not just a bona fide Reformation, but as the 'major'
one of the sixteenth century, exceeding the Protestant Reformation in its
radicalism and long-term impact.[38]

Of course, in every age there have been groups who constructed Dutch
religious identity differently. During the Reformation, the Calvinist minister Reynier Donteclock made the Hollanders out to be natural-born
spiritualists; it was their 'nature and condition', he postulated, 'not to
make a work of religion' – hence their support in great numbers for
his foe, Coornhert.[39] Usually, though, the different religious parties
claimed the Dutch character to incline naturally towards their own beliefs.
The Counter-Remonstrant theologian Jacobus Trigland implied as much
in his *Kerckelycke Geschiedenissen* (1650), the alternate account of the
Reformation he offered as rebuttal to Wtenbogaert's *Kerckelijcke Historie*.
Catholic authors used history similarly, not to claim that the Dutch were
tolerant but to emphasise how ancient and deeply rooted the Catholic
faith was in their land. Such was the overarching purpose, for example, of Hugo van Heussen's *Batavia Sacra, sive Res Gestae Apostolicorum
Virorum, Qui Fidem Bataviae Primi Intulerunt* (1714). In the nineteenth
century, both Calvinist and Catholic historians projected on to the past
their own, confessional visions of the modern Dutch nation. In the twentieth century, some historians have employed a similar essentialism to
explain the historic popularity of Anabaptism and Mennonism in the
Netherlands. Pijper viewed the sixteenth-century Anabaptists as consti-
tuting the 'left wing' of his 'national-Netherlandic Reform movement'.
More recently, William Nijenhuis has declared that Anabaptism was 'a
typically Dutch phenomenon' and 'that two of the [Mennonites'] most
important characteristics were in conformity with the Dutch character:
individualism and a morality which tended towards legalism'.[40]

---

[37] H.A. Enno van Gelder, *Revolutionnaire Reformatie. De vestiging van de Gereformeerde Kerk
in de Nederlandse gewesten, gedurende de eerste jaren van de Opstand tegen Filips II, 1575–1585*
(Amsterdam, 1943), pp. 9–10. Cf. H.A. Enno van Gelder, *Vrijheid en onvrijheid in de
Republiek. Geschiedenis der vrijheid van drukpers en godsdienst van 1572 tot 1619* (Haarlem,
1947), especially p. 262; and H.A. Enno van Gelder, 'Humanisten en libertijnen, Erasmus
en C.P. Hooft', *Nederlands Archief voor Kerkgeschiedenis* 16 (1920), 47, 53.

[38] H.A. Enno van Gelder, *The Two Reformations in the Sixteenth Century. A Study of the
Religious Aspects and Consequences of Renaissance and Humanism* (The Hague, 1961).

[39] Quoted in H. Bonger, *Leven en werk van Dirk Volckertsz. Coornhert* (Amsterdam, 1978),
p. 199.

[40] Pijper, 'Geestelijke stroomingen', pp. 42–5; W. Nijenhuis, 'The Dutch Reformation', in
J.A. Hebly (ed.), *Lowland Highlights. Church and Oecumene in the Netherlands* (Kampen,

It is the liberal vision of Dutch identity, though, that has prevailed in the twentieth century, and still circulates widely. Some theologians continue to find meaningful the notion of a Dutch *theologische volksziel*, which they conceive of as anti-dogmatic, humanistic, and ecumenical.[41] More than a few specialists in religious history continue to explain the tolerance of the Dutch Republic as a product of the unique power of the 'Erasmian spirit' in its progenitor's homeland, and/or in terms of a 'Low Countries tradition'.[42] As for the most popular and widely read historians – Huizinga, Romein, Schama – they all project onto their broad screens variants of the same vision. Even Schama sees the very soul of Dutch national identity as Erasmian, and while he does not credit it directly for the Republic's tolerance, he does represent it as a unifying force that gave people of all religions, from the Catholic painter Jan Steen to the Pietistic Calvinist Jacob Cats, a common ethos. Where Schama departs from his predecessors is that, eschewing essentialism and teleology, he regards 'Dutchness' not as a quality determined by race, climate, topography, or economics, but as a cultural construct, something the Dutch fashioned for themselves in the early years of the Republic. And indeed, that is pre-cisely what they were doing when they defined themselves, among other things, as tolerant.[43]

Recent decades, however, have seen a reaction set in against the cele-bration of 'Dutch' religious tolerance; indeed, some scholars have sug-gested the Dutch Republic was not so tolerant after all. Jonathan Israel has used some of the strongest language. The outlawing of Catholicism and elevation of Reformed Protestantism as the official faith of the Republic in the period 1573–81 entailed the decisive 'rejection of toleration' by the Dutch regent class. What prevailed thereafter and through the

1972), p. 25, critiqued in Otto de Jong, 'How Protestant are Mennonites?', in Alastair Hamilton, Sjouke Voolstra, and Piet Visser (eds.), *From Martyr to Muppy. A Historical Introduction to Cultural Assimilation Processes of a Religious Minority in the Netherlands: The Mennonites* (Amsterdam, 1994), p. 35. See the remark similar to Nijenhuis's in Jan en Annie Romein, *De Lage Landen bij de zee* (Utrecht, 1949), p. 198.

[41] E.g. A. van Beek, 'Het Nederlandse van de Nederlandse theologie', in S.C. Dik and G.W. Muller (eds.), *Het hemd is nader dan de rok. Zes voordrachten over het eigene van de Nederlandse cultuur* (Assen, 1991), pp. 108–20.

[42] For 'Erasmian spirit' see e.g. Samme Zijlstra, ' "Tgeloove is vrij". De tolerantiediscussie in de Noordelijke Nederlanden tussen 1520 en 1795', in Marijke Gijswijt-Hofstra (ed.), *Een schijn van verdraagzaamheid. Afwijking en tolerantie in Nederland van de zestiende eeuw tot heden* (Hilversum, 1989), p. 49; James Tracy, 'Erasmus, Coornhert and the Acceptance of Religious Disunity in the Body Politic. A Low Countries Tradition?', in C. Berkvens-Stevelinck, J. Israel, and G.H.M. Posthumus Meyjes (eds.), *The Emergence of Tolerance in the Dutch Republic* (Leiden/New York/Cologne, 1997), pp. 49–62.

[43] Johan Huizinga, *Dutch Civilization in the Seventeenth Century* (London, 1968), pp. 49–53; Romein, *De Lage Landen bij de zee*, pp. 373 *et seq.*; Schama, *The Embarrassment of Riches*, especially pp. 97, 338. On the modern continuation of this process of cultural construction, see Van Ginkel, *Op zoek naar eigenheid*.

entire seventeenth century was 'an ambivalent semi-tolerance . . . seething with tension'. The case of Amsterdam's Remonstrants exemplifies what Israel sees more broadly as the experience of the dissenting churches: the tolerance granted them was really, in his view, a form of 'concealed intolerance', for by confining them to a single *schuilkerk* it condemned them to the status of a small and marginalised group.[44] Outside the Generality Lands, Catholics, whose number Israel believes has been exaggerated, formed in most places an equally small and tamed minority. In her contribution to this volume, Joke Spaans suggests similarly that 'containment', not tolerance, was the policy of Dutch regents towards the non-Reformed churches. In any event, the true test of tolerance, according to Israel, was not such rival churches at all but radicals who broke with traditional Christianity altogether: Socinians, deists, and especially Spinozists, who enjoyed scant freedom of expression and on occasion suffered direct persecution. Only in the eighteenth century did a genuine tolerance, inspired by the Enlightenment, come to prevail.

Other scholars have denigrated what tolerance did exist by impugning its motives. Sometimes they allow a word or two or a subtly disparaging tone to carry the whole weight of their judgement, as when Marijke Gijswijt-Hofstra uses the phrase *knip-op-de-beurstolerantie*.[45] As she and others point out, by facilitating commerce and immigration tolerance was immensely profitable. Regents saw its utility also in maintaining 'peace' and civil 'order'. Of course, the Dutch themselves advertised the economic benefits of tolerance as early as the sixteenth century, though their more sophisticated discourses tended to bundle tolerance into a broader package of advantageous freedoms.[46] And 'peace' and 'order', it should be recognised, were code words that referred to a specific status quo whose maintenance was neither inevitable nor universally desired. To point out the interests which religious tolerance served is only good history, but to reduce the reasons for its practice to those interests smacks of a reductionism against which all the methodological insights of the last twenty years counsel. Andrew Pettegree goes to an extreme in arguing that tolerance was used 'as ruthlessly and cynically as persecution and intolerance to further particular political ends'. To the magistrates who promoted it, it had no value or meaning in itself; it served merely as a 'weapon' or 'party tool' in their struggle for power with the ministers of the Reformed

---

[44] Jonathan I. Israel, *The Dutch Republic. Its Rise, Greatness, and Fall 1477–1806* (Oxford, 1995), pp. 372, 655, 676, 1033.

[45] Marijke Gijswijt-Hofstra, 'Een schijn van verdraagzaamheid', in Marijke Gijswijt-Hofstra (ed.), *Een schijn van verdraagzaamheid. Afwijking en tolerantie in Nederland van de zestiende eeuw tot heden* (Hilversum, 1989), p. 9.

[46] For an early example see Van Gelderen, *The Dutch Revolt*, p. xiii. De la Court, *The True Interest and Political Maxims of the Republic of Holland*, is the classic exposition.

Church.[47] It seems highly questionable, though, whether the forces of intolerance were themselves always ruthless and cynical, never mind the supporters of tolerance, of whom a majority never served in government. Moreover, if calls for tolerance were merely a stratagem requiring no conviction, one would expect them to come equally from all who would have benefited. Instead, the loudest, most insistent ones came from groups who represented tolerance as one of their core principles: Libertines in the earliest years of the Republic; Collegiants, Waterlander Mennonites, and, above all, Remonstrants later. Pettegree's revisionism would take us from extreme to extreme – from an acceptance of such representations as the whole story to a cynical dismissal of them altogether.

An essay by Gijswijt-Hofstra offers clues to why such revisionism has taken root among historians. It forms the introduction to a volume entitled *Een schijn van verdraagzaamheid* (an 'appearance', or 'false semblance', of tolerance). Gijswijt-Hofstra does not deny the prevalence of religious tolerance in the Republic. She concurs, however, with the paradoxical judgement of Ernst Kossmann that tolerance itself is inherently intolerant, since in the very act of tolerating, a dominant group defines its own behaviour or beliefs as normal and those of the tolerated as deviant.[48] In other words, tolerance comes up far short of the mark when measured against modern standards of equality and non-discrimination. In the second place, Gijswijt-Hofstra expresses great unease with the notion of what she calls '*de* Nederlandse tolerantie', that is, Dutch tolerance in the singular, even when limiting her consideration to the Republic. She argues that religious tolerance was a product largely of 'extensive regional and local autonomy within the Republic', and that so much variation existed in its quality and quantity that to speak of '*the* Republic' as tolerant is in itself misleading. This argument subtly conveys an animus against the nationalism that the notion of 'Dutch tolerance' has come to embody. Finally, she criticises as excessive the sheer amount of attention given to religious tolerance in the Republic. In her view, this fixation perpetuates a myth of the Dutch people as tolerant that obscures the actual intolerance displayed in the modern era, towards ethnic minorities in particular.

These views resonate strongly with values prevalent in modern culture, especially within the academy. Multiculturalism has raised standards of non-discrimination by exposing cultural biases that had gone unnoticed;

---

[47] Andrew Pettegree, 'The Politics of Toleration in the Free Netherlands, 1572–1620', in O.P. Grell and B. Scribner (eds.), *Tolerance and Intolerance in the European Reformation* (Cambridge, 1996), longer quotation from p. 183.

[48] Gijswijt-Hofstra, 'Een schijn van verdraagzaamheid', pp. 20–1. Note that Israel and Kossmann use the term 'tolerance' differently, the former to mean full equality and freedom of public worship.

nationalism has yielded place to anti-nationalism, veneration of the past to the deconstruction of historical myths. Beginning in the sixteenth century, a long succession of groups used the history of religious toleration as a vehicle through which to define and legitimise their own identity. Distorting it through anachronism and teleology, they shaped that history into something quite a-historical, the idea that the Dutch were by nature tolerant. That idea partakes indeed of the mythical.[49] Formerly it invited celebration; today it invites debunking. But, in debunking it, we should remain conscious of the distortions our own ideological commitments might introduce.

Misleading as it was to see in seventeenth-century tolerance the roots of modern liberalism, it would be equally misleading to judge it by modern standards. Ambiguous terminology makes it dangerously easy to do so: today the phrase 'religious tolerance' implies religious freedom, which we define as a basic human right; it entails freedom of worship, religious speech, and assembly, and the legal equality of different religious groups. By contrast, until the Enlightenment to tolerate something meant merely to 'souffrir', or grudgingly concede its existence. Tolerance, by its nature, attributed a basic illegitimacy to what was being tolerated, just as Kossmann says. Thus, to cite but one example, the *Discours sur la permission de liberté*, written in 1579, contrasted tolerance to official sanction; urging that Protestants and Catholics should 'remain in the liberty which they possess either by permission or by connivance and tolerance', it equated tolerance precisely with that *connivence* by which non-Calvinists subsequently were able to worship in the Republic.[50] Adding to the confusion, scholars define tolerance variously as an ideology, attitude, pattern of social behaviour, governmental policy, or legal structure. How much tolerance they find in the Republic seems to depend largely on their choice of definition.

Measuring degrees of tolerance, however, may not be the best way to advance historical understanding. Instead of heaping praise or casting aspersions, I would urge that we adopt, for the time being, a more

---

[49] Kossmann has pointed out the same concerning all representations of the Dutch as a particularly freedom-loving people. E.H. Kossmann, 'Freedom in Seventeenth-Century Dutch Thought and Practice', in Jonathan I. Israel (ed.), *The Anglo-Dutch Moment. Essays on the Glorious Revolution and its World Impact* (Cambridge, 1991), p. 297.

[50] '... demeurent en la liberté de laquelle ou par permission ou par connivence & tolérance ils sont en possession'. Quoted in Catherine Secretan, 'La tolérance entre politique et rhétorique', in C. Berkvens-Stevelinck, J. Israel, and G.H.M. Posthumus Meyjes (eds.), *The Emergence of Tolerance in the Dutch Republic* (Leiden/New York/Cologne, 1997), pp. 99–100. Cf. Philip Benedict, ' "Un roi, une loi, deux foix": Parameters for the History of Catholic-Reformed Co-existence in France, 1555–1685', in Ole Peter Grell and Bob Scribner (eds.), *Tolerance and Intolerance in the European Reformation* (Cambridge, 1996), pp. 67–8.

descriptive approach, and that, instead of continuing to weigh religious fervour against self-interest, we explore the many social and cultural dimensions of confessional co-existence that have never received careful study. In 1995, Simon Groenveld argued provocatively that Dutch society was first *verzuild* ('columnised') not in the late nineteenth century, as usually maintained, but in the seventeenth. By this he meant that Dutch society, in the period 1650–1750, was divided into comprehensive, largely self-contained religious blocks, each one endogamous, with its own norms and values, charitable systems, educational institutions, and business networks.[51] Groenveld's conclusions were based on scant information and premature, to say the least. They raise, however, a host of fascinating questions. How common were religiously mixed marriages? Did Catholics, Calvinists, and Mennonites go to the same schools? Attend each other's weddings and funerals? Read the same books? Play the same music? Did they employ, do business with, give charity to one another? How did confessional co-existence work in practice? And how distinctive really – how unique in time and place – were the accommodations and arrangements by which the different religious groups in the Dutch Republic managed to live together? How 'Dutch', in other words, was 'Dutch' religious tolerance? Ironically, that question remains as unanswered as the others.

---

[51] Simon Groenveld, *Huisgenoten des geloofs. Was de samenleving in de Republiek der Verenigde Nederlanden verzuild?* (Hilversum, 1995).

3 Religious toleration in the United Provinces: from 'case' to 'model'

Willem Frijhoff

The Republic of the Seven United Provinces offers the rather special case of a state which called itself mono-confessional and Protestant while at the same time organising the civic community along the lines of religious toleration; this was sometimes from conviction and at other times from political expediency. The tension between these two aspects of collective life and its representation – confessional co-existence in a state that claimed to be Calvinist – explains the contrasting images of the United Provinces that we find in both contemporary and more recent literature. The variety of solutions adopted in the different provinces, reputed to be autonomous where religion was concerned, adds still more to the opacity of the general picture.

Perceptions of religious diversity

Over the centuries, the Dutch Republic has forged for itself the solid reputation of being a model of religious toleration, in the European historical consciousness.[1] However, on closer observation, we realise that this reputation is based on hindsight, at a time when there was a publicly recognised Church (*publieke kerk*), with its rights and privileges, flanked by confessional groups possessing their own structure but condemned either to a secondary role or even to near-secret worship. At the beginning, the 'Dutch model' was rather an a-typical solution to religious problems that were arising throughout Europe in similar terms. What is more, this model survived the internal evolution of the United Provinces; early in the second half of the seventeenth century the provinces resolutely moved

Several of the paragraphs in this chapter have been published in W. Frijhoff, 'La tolérance sans édit: la situation dans les Provinces-Unies', in J. Delumeau (ed.), *L'acceptation de l'autre de l'Edit de Nantes à nos jours* (Paris, 2000), pp. 86–107. Translated from the French by Mary Robitaille. Translation funded by the Royal Netherlands Academy of Arts and Sciences.
[1] H. Bots, 'Tolerantie of gecultiveerde tweedracht? Het beeld van de Nederlandse tolerantie bij buitenlanders in de zeventiende en achttiende eeuw', *Bijdragen en Mededelingen betreffende de Geschiedenis der Nederlanden* 107 (1992), 657–69.

towards a 'confessionalisation' which had proved its worth in neighbouring countries. The organic link between religious toleration and commercial prosperity was established as early as 1651 in *Les Délices de la
Hollande* printed fifteen times between 1651 and 1728, not to mention
translations – by Jean-Nicolas de Parival from Lorraine, a master of languages, settled in Leiden. It became a cliché, often repeated by later
travellers, from Basnage to Montesquieu, from the Marquis d'Argenson
to Voltaire and Diderot, even while Dutch prosperity was undergoing serious and lasting setbacks.[2] Praise for the 'Dutch model' was then chiefly
used to criticise intolerance at home and to offer an alternative which
seemed to have proved its worth in Holland.

Opinions can obviously diverge as to which term is the most apt to
qualify the religious pluralism that existed in Holland in the seventeenth
century, but the diversity itself was a unanimously established fact, avidly
commented on by contemporaries. However, diversity or pluralism does
not necessarily mean 'toleration', which at the very least is the tacit admission of this diversity as permissible. In fact, several degrees of toleration
can be defined, which cannot easily be distinguished in the modern idiom:
toleration in the active sense of the legal freedom to be different hardly
involved more than freedom of conscience; toleration in the passive sense
of the term was more widespread: in other words, connivance with what
was not allowed (*conniventie* or *toelating*), the non-application of legally
prescribed practice, and the will to turn a blind eye (literally *oogluiking*
in Dutch). It is in this passive sense that toleration usually involved the
freedom of public worship.

But the toleration of dissident cults could go further, provided that the
erring brethren always placed themselves in the same spiritual fraternity
with orthodoxy. As long as the socio-Christian order was not threatened,
even militant Calvinists could put up with certain differences of opinion. Gisbert Voetius (1589–1676), for example, professor of theology at
Utrecht, a defender of Protestant orthodoxy with theocratic leanings,
had several dissertations written on this subject.[3] He made a distinction
between civil toleration (which included *permissio* and *libertas exercitii*)

[2] M. van Strien-Chardonneau, *Le voyage de Hollande: récits de voyageurs français dans les
Provinces-Unies, 1748–1795* (Oxford, 1994), pp. 296–305; R. Murris, *La Hollande et les
Hollandais au XVIIe et au XVIIIe siècles vus par les Français* (Paris, 1925), pp. 215–27;
C.D. van Strien, *British Travellers in Holland during the Stuart Period. Edward Browne and
John Locke as Tourists in the United Provinces* (Leiden/New York/Cologne, 1993); K. van
Strien, *Touring the Low Countries. Accounts of British Travellers, 1660–1720* (Amsterdam,
1998); J. Bientjes, *Holland und der Holländer im Urteil deutscher Reisender (1400–1800)*
(Groningen, 1967). On Parival (*c.* 1605–69), see the article in the *Nieuw Nederlandsch
Biografisch Woordenboek* (Leiden, 1927; reprint Leiden, 1974), vol. VII, cols. 937–40.
[3] G. Voetius, *Selectae disputationes theologicae*, 5 vols. (Utrecht, 1648–69), particularly vol. I
(1648), pp. 487–8, and vol. IV (1667), p. 163.

and ecclesiastical toleration, defined essentially as *moderatio* and *mutua tolerantia, verdraeghsaemheydt* in the idiom of the period. In this form, toleration was considered legitimate as long as peace, concord, and unity among the different Christian confessions remained guaranteed on the basis of mutual understanding.

People have often talked about the late appearance of the term 'toleration' as a concept of political philosophy in the writings of Locke (who in 1689 rigorously divided civil society, to which one is obliged to belong and thus forced to accept its diversity of religious opinions, from religious society, which is purely voluntary), Bayle (whose epistemological scruples separated reason from faith, religion from morals, and wanted to acknowledge 'the rights of the erring conscience'), and Voltaire (who combined both ways of seeing things).[4] In this strong sense of the word, the term 'toleration' seems to have appeared after Holland's political acceptance of religious differences in a situation of legal inequality. However, the medieval origin of the political usage of the concept of *tolerantia* has recently been put forward vigorously, the aim of the concept being to get religious error socially accepted in a context of triumphant and dominating truth; one had to be able to endure evil for the good of public order.[5] It is from these medieval roots that the concept worked its way into humanist thought, beginning with that of Erasmus of Rotterdam. Erasmus was later to exercise a lasting, although somewhat diffuse, influence on the forms of social relations adopted in the civic community of the Low Countries and, through the diffusion of his popular works in schools, on public opinion in general.

However, it was the Revolt against the king of Spain that created a completely new field of political application for the old concept of 'toleration' in the Low Countries – precisely because the new state emerged in co-existence, and as if in interaction, with a complex and fiercely defended religious diversity.[6] This was somehow congenital: it was the right

---

[4] Cf. J. Locke, *Lettre sur la tolérance* [n.p. 1689], ed. P. Vernière (Paris/Geneva, 1995); Voltaire, *Traité sur la tolérance*, ed. J. Renwick (Oxford, 1999); Pierre Bayle, *Commentaire philosophique sur ces paroles de Jésus Christ Contrains-les d'entrer* (Amsterdam, 1686), recently republished as: Pierre Bayle, *De la tolérance. Commentaire philosophique sur les paroles de Jesus-Christ Contrains-les d'entrer*, ed. J.-M. Gros (Paris, 1992).

[5] I. Bejczy, 'Tolerantia: A Medieval Concept', *Journal of the History of Ideas* 58 (1997), 365–84. See also A. Patschovsky and H. Zimmermann (eds.), *Toleranz im Mittelalter* (Sigmaringen, 1998).

[6] J. Israel, 'The Intellectual Debate about Toleration in the Dutch Republic', in C. Berkvens-Stevelinck, J. Israel, and G.H.M. Posthumus Meyjes (eds.), *The Emergence of Tolerance in the Dutch Republic* (Leiden/New York/Cologne, 1997), pp. 3–36. More generally on the different aspects of the question and the discussions in Holland, see Marijke Gijswijt-Hofstra (ed.), *Een schijn van verdraagzaamheid. Afwijking en tolerantie in Nederland van de zestiende eeuw tot heden* (Hilversum, 1989); O.P. Grell and B. Scribner (eds.), *Tolerance and Intolerance in the European Reformation* (Cambridge, 1996): particularly A. Pettegree, 'The Politics of Toleration in the Free Netherlands, 1572–1620',

to religious dissent (the Revolt *religionis ergo*) that justified and at the same time restrained the desire for political liberty (*libertatis ergo*). Had not the leader of the Revolt, William of Orange himself, pleaded for freedom of conscience together with freedom to worship for the various confessions?[7] In spite of the voices that were often raised in Holland to exclude a particular religious group from the political life of the new state (without forgetting the Anabaptists at the beginning of the seventeenth century, we particularly remember the fate of the Catholics from the end of the sixteenth century onwards, of the Arminians at the beginning of the seventeenth century, and of the Socinians a little later on), the principle itself of legitimate differences of opinion was never really challenged. It was not even questioned by the most orthodox and the most demanding Calvinist ministers who were at the height of their power after the Peace of Westphalia which, after all, recognised a state that claimed to be founded on religious dissent. In fact all forms of diversity, of pluralism, and of toleration practised in the Republic of the United Provinces were included in the fundamental principle of freedom of conscience, formulated in article 13 of the Union of Utrecht (1579), which was and remained the philosophical base, as it were, of the new state.

Is it by chance that the subject of one of the first intellectual debates that took place in the new Republic in 1590 was freedom of conscience and was held between two learned men, both opposed to Calvinism, Lipsius and Coornhert? Coornhert won the day. Lipsius (1547–1606), until then professor at Leiden, left in 1591 ostensibly for the southern Netherlands which had become uniformly Catholic again in obedience to the king of Spain. Coornhert (1522–90), neo-Stoic and anti-confessional *perfectist*, was opposed to all forms of forced religious unity; the truth, he said, would establish itself.[8] As early as 1582, Coornhert had published

---

Tolerance, pp. 182–98; and the essential synthesis by J. Lecler, *Histoire de la tolérance au siècle de la Réforme*, 2 vols. (Paris, 1955).

[7] Cf. A.Th. van Deursen and H. de Schepper, *Willem van Oranje. Een strijd voor vrijheid en verdraagzaamheid* (Weesp, 1984), pp. 125–35.

[8] The 'perfectists', in opposition to the Protestants, considered that the grace of God in Jesus Christ was sufficient for man to observe God's commandments during his earthly life. This point of view took no notice of predestination in any of its forms, but was also opposed to the absolute claims of the Catholic Church. In fact it was a-confessional. Coornhert called himself a 'Catholic', not a 'Papist'. Cf. J. Lindeboom, *Stiefkinderen van het christendom* (The Hague, 1929; reprint Arnhem, 1973), pp. 264–77; H. Bonger, *Leven en werk van Dirk Volckertsz. Coornhert* (Amsterdam, 1978), pp. 181–203; H. Bonger, J.R.H. Hoogervorst, M.E.H.N. Mout *et al.*, *Dirck Volckertsz. Coornhert. Dwars maar recht* (Zutphen, 1989); L. Kolakowski, *Chrétiens sans Eglise. La conscience religieuse et le lien confessionnel au XVIIe siècle* (Paris, 1969), pp. 72–7; Th. Wanegffelen, *L'Edit de Nantes. Une histoire européenne de la tolérance du XVIe au XXe siècle* (Paris, 1998), pp. 145–50. For the context see: G. Güldner, *Das Toleranz-Problem in den Niederlanden im Ausgang des 16. Jahrhunderts* (Lübeck/Hamburg, 1968); B.J. Kaplan, 'Hubert Duifhuis and the Nature of Dutch Libertinism', *Tijdschrift voor Geschiedenis* 105 (1992), 1–29.

an apologia for freedom of conscience (*Synodus of Vander Conscientien Vryheit*), which was to have a lasting influence on Dutch political thinking concerning religious peace and the forms it could adopt in the context of a new distribution of religious and secular power. The key-words of his speech were effectively 'permission or tacit connivance' of all religions other than one's own, so that it should profit 'strong concord and benevolent clemency'.[9] Connivance and concord: these are precisely the two pillars of the civil policy of religious peace in the Republic, which we shall come across again throughout this chapter.

By adopting the principle of freedom of conscience, understood not as freedom of religious practice, but as freedom of thought, the United Provinces automatically became a distinctive *case* in the European landscape. Throughout Europe, in fact, territorial or community limitations of religious conscience by the ecclesiastical and civil authorities remained the rule, even in places where edicts of toleration for a particular confession had been issued. The distinctive feature of the Dutch solution was precisely a generalised practice of toleration that had nothing to do with legislation, and which limits were inevitably vague and changeable. It was based on a new and largely implicit relationship between the ecclesiastical and civil authorities, itself based on a new idea of the civic body.[10] The desire for a single Church encompassing all the people was transferred to the secular community which had to be closely knit. By stripping the urban (and rural) landscape of its religious elements, the town itself, in its role as body politic, became the new sacred community, with its own history, its legends, and its symbolism and ritual which ensured a civic peace that went beyond differences of convictions. It was so in Haarlem where the myth of the courage of its crusaders at Damiette, in the days of undivided Christianity, was propagandised among the citizens by the town council to conjure the religious division of the town population.[11]

It is the refusal – to a certain extent sacrilegious – to legislate in the religious domain, while everywhere else divine right was still called upon to impose limitations, which marked out the Dutch Republic in the seventeenth century. Throughout the seventeenth and eighteenth centuries the social arrangements and political procedures, to which religious diversity based on freedom of conscience gave rise, made the Dutch Republic a testing-ground for peaceful co-existence, then for toleration. In the more

---

[9] D.V. [Thierry] Coornhert, *A l'aurore des libertés modernes: Synode sur la liberté de conscience (1582)*, ed. J. Lecler S.J. and M.-F. Valkhoff (Paris, 1979).

[10] On this subject see also W. Bergsma, 'Church, State and People', in K. Davids and J. Lucassen (eds.), *A Miracle Mirrored. The Dutch Republic in European Perspective* (Cambridge, 1995), pp. 196–228.

[11] J. Spaans, *Haarlem na de Reformatie. Stedelijke cultuur en kerkelijk leven, 1577–1620* (The Hague, 1989), pp. 127–30.

or less long term, according to which contemporaries we consult, it was established in Europe as a *model* to be followed. It was not religious diversity itself that marked out the United Provinces in Europe, for it could also be found in England or in Switzerland, nor official toleration, because it was better organised in France (with the Edict of Nantes 1598), in confessionalised Germany, or even in Poland.[12] It is the combination of both these characteristics that made the United Provinces unique: a tacit toleration of religious diversity that was allowed to flourish as long as the necessary concord between believers did not endanger the unity of the body politic and the civic community.

Rather than the concept of unity it is, effectively, that of *concordia*, which was at the centre of the religious policy of the United Provinces; it was moreover written into the motto of the state (*Concordia res parvae crescunt*). Offering solutions of consensus rather than of constraint, of civil pragmatism rather than of religious principles, Holland was to play a major role in the elaboration of the political notion of toleration, despite an obvious decline of religious toleration in Holland in the field of academic theology after the 1670s. It is this pragmatic concept of toleration that provides the supranational political foundation of a socio-religious practice of toleration, already well established in the United Provinces, although it obviously had national outlines. Intellectually, it sometimes went together with Libertinism, sometimes with Irenicism, or even with scepticism.[13] Once it was translated into a notion of political philosophy, this toleration could transcend the Dutch situation and lay the foundations for a new European order, both socio-religious and secular.

For all that, religious diversity was not considered as something positive by all the Dutch people themselves. On the contrary, many voices within the national community denounced the plague of diversity as an attack on the unique rights of truth. Poets and engravers especially vied with each other to produce caricatures of the lack of religious unity, seen as a sign of imperfection, when they did not openly denounce the pervading sectarianism. However, in times of war or oppression, satire was readily transformed into an apologia for pluralism seen as constituent of the identity

---

[12] See O. Christin, *La paix de religion. L'autonomisation de la raison politique au XVIe siècle* (Paris, 1997); B. Cottret, *1598: L'Edit de Nantes* (Paris, 1997).

[13] Cf. R.H. Popkin and A. Vanderjagt (eds.), *Scepticism and Irreligion in the Seventeenth and Eighteenth Centuries* (Leiden, 1993): particularly Th. Verbeek, 'From "Learned Ignorance" to Scepticism: Descartes and Calvinist Orthodoxy', in *ibid.*, pp. 31–45 and E. van der Wall, 'Orthodoxy and Scepticism in the Early Dutch Enlightenment', in *ibid.*, pp. 121–41 (i.e. in the seventeenth century); J. den Tex, 'Locke en Spinoza over de tolerantie', PhD thesis, University of Amsterdam (1926); J. Israel, 'Locke, Spinoza and the Philosophical Debate Concerning Toleration in the Early Enlightenment (c. 1670–c. 1750)', *Koninklijke Nederlandse Academie van Wetenschappen, Mededelingen van de Afdeling Letterkunde*, New Series 62, 6 (1999), 5–19.

of Holland. This is the case in a poem by Jan van der Veen (1578–1656), on the freedom of preaching; he himself had been educated in the Mennonite community with its repeated splits. In his list of groups allowed to express themselves in the Republic, he included not only Catholics with their numerous religious orders each with different tendencies, Lutherans, Mennonites and Arminians, Zwinglians, Puritans and Arians, Libertines and *perfectists*, Socinians and Sophists, but also the lay preachers with flowery names ('Robbert Tobbertsen den Flouwer'), the members of the pietist conventicles ('Jan Taurens in 't Suchtent-huys'), the Rosicrucians, and finally the Turks (maybe Moslems settled in Amsterdam, or Armenian Christians, who had a church there?), Jews and gypsies ('heidens'), not forgetting the violent Anabaptists at the time of the occupation of Munster – but in fact, the latter had fast been excluded from the body politic, and toleration of Jews was, outside Amsterdam, quite insignificant, being limited to only a few towns.[14] Satire, the outlet for tensions which inevitably ran through this society with unequally shared rights, did not, however, hinder the basic general harmony which was the *raison d'être* of the Republic and fast became its international emblem.

The observations of foreigners bear witness to this. As early as the seventeenth century, solutions to the problem of religious diversity adopted by the seven autonomous states, which were reunited in the political union of the Dutch Republic, caused the surprise and sometimes the admiration of travellers and outside observers. Few visitors to the United Provinces made such an accurate assessment of it as Sir William Temple (1628–99) in his *Observations upon the United Provinces of the Netherlands*, published in the year 1673, during the Anglo-Dutch war. In his chapter on religion, Temple clearly described the notable differences he observed, while he was there as ambassador (1688–90), in the treatment and the public status of the different religions present in Holland. But he also stressed what, in his eyes, was the distinctive characteristic of the Dutch Republic: 'the great Care of this State has ever been, To favour no particular or curious Inquisition into the Faith or Religious Principles of any peaceable man, who came to live under the protection of their Laws'.[15]

If despite all this the Catholic religion seemed exempt from the pervading toleration it was because of the suspicion of political treason which

---

[14] The poem's success can be seen in its reprinting in a pamphlet during the Dutch War: *t'Samen-spraeck, Voor-gestelt van vier Persoonen: Twee Hollanders, Pieter en Klaes. Een Fransman. Een Bovenlander* (n.p. 1672), fo. B2r, where the text appears as an apologia for general toleration against the religious intolerance of the invader, the king of France.

[15] W. Temple, *Observations upon the United Provinces of the Netherlands*, ed. G. Clark (Oxford, 1972), p. 103.

had weighed on Catholics since the Revolt. Temple, himself an Anglican, took note of the fact that Catholics apparently formed 'a sound piece of the State and fast joined in with the rest', and that they had never shown any desire for revolution or treason. As for the other religions, Temple insisted on the freedom which existed to practise any religion within private houses, in the private sphere, the so-called *religio domestica* with no danger of being questioned or spied upon. Moreover, he stated,

if the followers of any Sect grow so numerous in any place, that they affect a publique Congregation, and are content to purchase a place of Assembly, to bear the charge of a Pastor or a Teacher, and to pay for this Liberty to the Publique; They go and propose their desire to the Magistrates of the place, where they reside, Who inform themselves of their Opinions, and manners of Worship, and if they find nothing in either, destructive to Civil Society, or prejudicial to the Constitutions of their State, And content themselves with the price that is offer'd for the purchase of this Liberty, They easily allow it; But with the condition, That one or more Commissioners shall be appointed, who shall have free admission at all their meetings, shall be both the Observers and Witnesses of all that is acted or preached among them, and whose testimony shall be received concerning any thing that passes there to the prejudice of the State; In which the Laws and Executions are as severe as against any Civil Crimes.[16]

It is thus the state, namely public order, and not religion, namely the rights of truth or of the faith, which constitutes the supreme criterion of religious toleration in this secularised society. The precocity of this position is the reason why, in the negotiations leading to the Peace of Westphalia, the religious question was only considered, by the Dutch representatives, as regarded Catholics in the recently conquered territories. In the Seven Provinces themselves things were considered as settled.

A lot could be said, of course, about the idyllic image Temple gives us, certainly not without ulterior motives. He let himself be inspired above all by the province of Holland, more liberal than the others. Moreover, his apologia for Catholics, which must have been seen in a certain light in Charles II's England, carefully forgot to mention the repeated clashes between the Catholics who remained faithful to the king of Spain and the authorities.[17] What is more, if Temple deliberately ignored the connivance that several well-placed Catholics had just shown towards the Sun King and the bishop of Munster after their joint invasion of the Republic in June 1672, he could not have known about the remarkable initiative taken by the vicar apostolic Joan van Neercassel (1623–86), who in the eyes of the Dutch Catholics acted as archbishop of Utrecht. On 20 September of

[16] *Ibid.*, pp. 104–5.
[17] Cf. S. Groenveld, 'Trouw en verraad tijdens de Nederlandse Opstand', *Zeeuws Tijdschrift* 36 (1987), 3–12.

the same year, in a letter (which fortunately remained secret, for in times of war it was a flagrant case of high treason), this austere and francophile Oratorian, who had worked and taught in France, asked Louis XIV, on behalf of the whole Catholic population, to establish his authority on the United Provinces permanently in order to guarantee the public re-establishment of the Catholic religion.[18]

Referring to something said by Louis XIV ('J'auray soin de vos catholiques'), the vicar apostolic probably counted on a bi-confessional regime comparable to that which the Edict of Nantes had established in France. For, without wanting to endanger religious pluralism, he simply hoped for a redistribution between the two main public confessions of the buildings for worship, of benefices, of ecclesiastical property, and of jobs to be filled in and by the urban councils. In his eyes, the Catholic Church should retrieve its status as a publicly recognised Church together with the Calvinist Church which, *de facto*, alone had enjoyed it since the adoption of the articles of the Treaty of Utrecht by the different provinces, and *de jure* since the constituent decisions of the 'revised Treaty of Union' (*Naerder Unie*), the result of the Grand Assembly of the States-General held in 1651. In other words, as early as 1672, the native Catholic authority had itself given up the idea of a regime with a single belief system and seemed to want to move towards a French- or German-style confessionalisation. There is no need to point out that this particular direction did not please the central authority of the Catholic Church, and that, together with the Jansenist question, things would soon reach a crisis point.

Despite the obvious limits of his perception, William Temple saw exactly where the remarkable nature of the United Provinces was: in the autonomy of public order and of political reason. The sacred principle of personal and individual liberty, effectively defended by a state that knowingly occupied a purely secular position as regards religion, was violently opposed to any hint of theocracy. It was civic society and more particularly civic peace, Libertine, and republican order that appeared as the yardstick of toleration, not just a religious principle of whatever tendency or order. More than principles, it is what I have elsewhere called the ecumenicity of everyday life (*omgangsoecumene*), this basic civic harmony, on the borderline between public and private, which decided what the measure of religious toleration should be.[19] But in the long term it also led to a new relationship between the group and the individual.

---

[18] M.G. Spiertz, *L'Eglise catholique des Provinces-Unies et le Saint-Siège pendant la deuxième moitié du XVIIe siècle* (Louvain, 1975), pp. 119–21, and the text of the letter, pp. 160–1.

[19] W. Frijhoff, 'La coexistence confessionnelle: complicités, méfiances et ruptures aux Provinces-Unies', in J. Delumeau (ed.), *Histoire vécue du peuple chrétien*, 2 vols. (Toulouse, 1979), vol. II, pp. 229–57; W. Frijhoff, 'Le seuil de tolérance en Hollande au XVIIe siècle', in *Homo religiosus. Autour de Jean Delumeau [Avant-propos d'Alain Cabantous]*

In particular it permitted the emergence of religious individualism and therefore was a real danger for the Churches, who forbade it. If on the one hand the state wanted to maintain a public privileged Church as a guarantor of civic order, since the unfortunate times of partisan and fratricide struggles around the Synod of Dordt (1618–19), it still refused to adopt a doctrinal point of view or to cede the exclusivity of the regulation of conscience and public opinion to any religious group, not even to the Calvinist Church itself. It was only later that this toleration was set up as a philosophical principle, then as a legal one.

There was, however, a limit to this freedom. Faced with the pluralism of religious ideas, only two options caused the state to hesitate; these were Unitarianism that refused the divinity of the Saviour, and philosophy without God. This was the case for the concept that was taking shape in the Libertine circle around Spinoza, or for the anti-Trinitarianism of the Socinians and of the Polish Brethren – two spiritual temptations which, as they were considered as sacrilegious movements, risked undermining the Christian order and disrupting society, even the authority of the state itself. In 1651–3 the Socinians, who had chosen the Republic as land of asylum since the arrival in Amsterdam in 1598 of Ostorodt and Wojdowski, were banned from several provinces. In 1669, the Spinozist Adriaen Koerbagh was condemned to an unusually severe and cruel punishment on account of his 'blasphemous speeches', that were supposedly atheist – but he died in prison before serving the whole of his sentence.[20] Hobbes' *Leviathan* and Spinoza's *Theologico-Political Treatise* (*Tractatus Theologico-Politicus*) were both the object of political censure in 1674 – which was rather ironic when we consider that it was precisely in this work, so dependent on the social reality of the Netherlands, that Spinoza had laid the theoretical foundations for generalised toleration.[21] But it is true that toleration according to Spinoza was based on a *libertas philosophandi* from which – unlike the traditional *libertas prophetandi* of the Arminian theologian Episcopius – all religious reference was eliminated: it claimed entire freedom of thought and expression, the radical position of which

(Paris, 1997), pp. 650–7; W. Frijhoff and M. Spies, *1650: Bevochten eendracht* (The Hague, 1999), pp. 50–1, 179–82, 358–59.

[20] P.H. van Moerkerken, *Adriaan Koerbagh (1633–1669). Een strijder voor het vrije denken* (Amsterdam, n.d.).

[21] I. Weekhout, *Boekencensuur in de Noordelijke Nederlanden. De vrijheid van drukpers in de zeventiende eeuw* (The Hague, 1998), pp. 88–107; cf. C. Secrétan, 'La réception de Hobbes aux Pays-Bas au XVIIe siècle', *Studia Spinozana* 3 (1987), 27–46; M.J. Petry, 'Behmenism and Spinozism in the Religious Culture of the Netherlands, 1660–1730', in K. Gründer and W. Schmidt-Biggemann (eds.), *Spinoza in der Frühzeit seiner religiösen Wirkung* (Heidelberg, 1984), pp. 111–47; W. van Bunge and W. Klever (eds.), *Disguised and Overt Spinozism around 1700* (Leiden, 1996); W. van Bunge, 'On the Early Dutch Reception of the Tractatus Theologico-Politicus', *Studia Spinozana* 5 (1989), 225–51.

contrasted strongly with what were after all moderate forms of toleration propagated by John Locke or even Pierre Bayle. Because of this it
constituted a formidable threat to the Christian order.

In his study *Amsterdam au temps de Spinoza*, Henri Méchoulan has insisted on the links that existed in Holland among the political control of
religion, the regime of freedom, and the lure of gain.[22] Effectively, the
venality of magistrates was so patent that it even runs through William
Temple's analyses. But, written into the very heart of the relation between
public service and the modern state, it must not make us forget the novelty of the structure that the state of the Netherlands built up over a very
long period; the circumstantial nature of its religious policy is especially
surprising. Built in part on a refusal of Catholic monopoly, then on the
refusal of any religious monopoly, the state placed itself under the banner of freedom of conscience. Written into the Union of Utrecht, this
remained the genuine touchstone of the state edifice. While fulminating
against the liberties taken by Papists and in demanding a severe repression
of all the expressions of Catholic *worship*, both in public and in private,
the strict Calvinists themselves did not dare attack the fundamental law
of freedom of individual *conscience*. It is thus a redistribution between the
public and private spheres, and a redefinition of the domains to which
this distinction applied, which were at the heart of the Netherlands 'case'
as a testing-ground for toleration in Europe.

Pluralism and diversity: the Dutch 'case'

Let us now look at this case more closely. What exactly were the conditions
of religious freedom in the United Provinces? They can be summarised in
four points: individual freedom of conscience, religious sociability from
the bottom up, a culture made up of debate and civic participation, and a
social ideal of real co-existence.[23] These characteristics, which historical
analysis finds deposited beneath the culture of the Netherlands, did not
necessarily coincide with the image that foreign observers built up for
themselves. Generally speaking, in the seventeenth century three images
structured the religious perception of the United Provinces abroad: the
English Puritans considered the Republic, with its dominant Calvinist
Church, as a Protestant paradise; the persecuted Protestants saw it as the
great Ark of the fugitives (according to Pierre Bayle's formula, himself
a refugee in Rotterdam); and the numerous travellers in turn praised
or criticised the religious toleration that reigned there. These images

[22] H. Méchoulan, *Amsterdam au temps de Spinoza: argent et liberté* (Paris, 1990).
[23] These characteristics are put forward in: Frijhoff and Spies, *1650: Bevochten eendracht*.

overlapped and succeeded one another, while at the same time occasionally contradicting one other. To understand their meaning and impact, we must look back at their evolution.

The distinctive position of the Reformed Church in the Dutch Republic is closely linked to the evolution of the Dutch state itself.[24] In 1579 the Seventeen Provinces which since 1548 constituted the Burgundian-Habsburg territory of the Low Countries split into two, forming the southern Union of Arras faithful to the sovereign (6 January 1579) and in the north that of Utrecht (23 January 1579) which abjured the king on 22 July 1581. The stakes involved in the separation of the northerners were twofold: political freedom (*libertatis ergo*), and religious freedom (*religionis ergo*). That was right at the beginning of the Revolt – for after the religious peace decreed by the States of Holland during their rebel assembly held at Dordt on 20 July 1572, the balance was again thrown into question by the union of Holland and Zeeland concluded at Delft in 1575 under pressure of war. The Pacification of Ghent negotiated between the rebel provinces in 1576 only provisionally confirmed a very precarious religious status quo. Although still only slightly affected by Calvinism, the Northern Provinces pushed by Holland into the hands of the rebels put forward the ideology of Reformation for political reasons, as the only way of rallying the hard-and-fast Calvinists who were so numerous, especially in the Southern Provinces. But they knew quite well that the united front against the king was henceforth founded on an ambiguity; a large part of the population of the north was not automatically won over to Calvinism, not even to the Protestant Reformation. They simply wanted freedom, either to maintain the specific federative organisation that characterised the political structure of the Low Countries, or to be able freely to exercise a form of religion whose ecclesiastical or doctrinal outlines did not necessarily correspond to the religious order favoured by the Protestants.

The ambiguity is found yet again in the articles of the Union of Utrecht – the final draft of which owed much to the young Oldenbarnevelt (1547–1619), by then the pensionary of the town of Rotterdam, the future Grand Pensionary who was to die on the scaffold in May 1619, notably for having remained faithful to his principles of religious toleration and freedom of conscience. Article 13 of the Treaty of Union stipulated that the United Provinces should fully recognise individual freedom of conscience but left each individual province free to do as it wished within its frontiers concerning religious affairs. There was only one restriction: article 2 explicitly opposed the re-establishment of Catholicism

---

[24] A. Duke, *Reformation and Revolt in the Low Countries* (London, 1990).

as the only religion.[25] As early as 1580, the public practice of Catholicism was forbidden for political reasons. For two centuries, the articles of Union had to take the place of a constitution in the Dutch Republic. They established freedom of conscience, allowed basic religious diversity (which could embrace a form of *devotio domestica*), and justified the intervention of the public authorities in the religious affairs of the province or of the city. In their choices in favour of particularism – the acknowledgement of the sovereignty of each of the confederate provinces – and of locally established religion, they at the same time hindered the constitution of a national Reformed Church with an unvarying political and administrative regime for all the provinces.[26] Because of this delay the application of the Presbyterian-synodal model was curtailed. In spite of a unified socio-political ideology expressed in the metaphor of the New Israel, and of a few high-flown appeals in favour of Protestant union on a national scale, the provincial Synods continued to support their specific rulings and followed their own political lines. Even the appointment of ministers was subject to procedures that were different according to the provinces.[27] The national Synod of Dordt, which condemned the Arminians and established Reformed orthodoxy, prudently respected this provincial autonomy.[28] Moreover, this was the last national Synod before the nineteenth century.

Thirty years later, in 1648, the Peace of Westphalia put an end to the war. It brought with it the recognition of the United Provinces as an independent state having fixed frontiers and freed it from the Holy Roman Empire. The question of religion was already formally settled in the Republic, the only thing left to determine being the status of the conquered

[25] J.C. Boogman, 'The Union of Utrecht, its Genesis and Consequences', *Bijdragen en Mededelingen betreffende de Geschiedenis der Nederlanden* 94 (1979), 5–35.

[26] B.J. Kaplan, 'Dutch Particularism and the Calvinist Quest for "Holy Uniformity"', *Archiv für Reformationsgeschichte* 82 (1991), 239–56.

[27] W. Frijhoff, 'Inspiration, instruction, compétence? Questions autour de la sélection des pasteurs réformés aux Pays-Bas, XVIe-XVIIe siècles', *Paedagogica Historica* 30, 1 (1994), 13–38.

[28] J. van den Berg, 'The Synod of Dort in the Balance', *Nederlands Archief voor Kerkgeschiedenis* 69 (1989), 176–94; W. van 't Spijker *et al.*, *De Synode van Dordrecht in 1618 en 1619* (Houten, 1987). In a context of political opposition, the Synod settled the conflict over predestination (election to eternal life) between the partisans of Jacobus Arminius (1560–1609), closer to the Catholics, and those of Franciscus Gomarus (1563–1641), more austere and closer to the Puritans, in favour of the Gomarists. According to the happy turn of phrase of A.Th. van Deursen: 'for the Arminians election was the fruit of faith, for the Gomarists faith was the fruit of election'. Cf. C. Bangs, *Arminius: A Study in the Dutch Reformation* (Nashville, TN, 1973); A.Th. van Deursen, *Bavianen en slijkgeuzen. Kerk en kerkvolk ten tijde van Maurits en Oldenbarnevelt* (Assen, 1974); by the same author, *Plain Lives in a Golden Age. Popular Culture, Religion and Society in Seventeenth-Century Holland*, trans. M. Ultee (Cambridge, 1991).

territories (particularly northern Brabant). Ignoring the Spanish proposals, the States-General managed to impose and immediately apply the principle of forced Calvinisation on these territories, at the same time stumbling against deep-rooted Catholicism, locally regenerated by the Counter-Reformation and managing to survive thanks to priests and religious working in the independent enclaves around these territories.[29] Only the town of Maastricht, under a co-seignorial regime, kept the German-style bi-confessional regime that some would have liked to extend to the whole of the Republic, after its conquest in 1632.[30] In a few districts around Maastricht, the *simultaneum* (the officially established use of one church building by several confessions in turn) was instituted. Everywhere else, however, the Reformed Church remained the only legally recognised confession, even if here and there Lutheranism managed, thanks to its support in commerce and the army, to obtain permission to maintain semi-public worship, of which a few big Lutheran churches opened after 1633 in Amsterdam and elsewhere are proof.

As soon as the Peace was signed, however, the Reformed Church of the United Provinces made one last effort to ensure for itself the status of a State Church. The violently anti-Papist province of Zeeland, bordering Catholic Flanders and champion of strict Calvinism, became the protagonist of this wish.[31] Above all, it was the fear of a compromise with the Catholics, suspected of secret agreements with the enemy and conspiracy against civil order, that led the Zeelanders to go as far as refusing the ratification of the Peace of Westphalia itself. It was only thanks to one of those subterfuges of the sort known only to the political organisation of the United Provinces, that the unanimity required for peace was obtained; in the temporary but intentional absence of the Zeeland representative, the unanimity of the deputies present was noted. When the Grand Assembly of the States-General was held in 1651 at the Hague, bringing together all the political authorities in order to settle once and for all the affairs of the Union which had been in abeyance during the war, provincial idiosyncrasies prevented any new common decision concerning religious matters, whether for or against a dominant Church. By

---

[29] P.H.A.M. Abels and A.P.F. Wouters (eds.), *Acta conventus Sylvae-Ducensis extraordinarii 1648, uijt alle provintien der Verenigde Nederlanden tesamen geroepen...*, 2 vols. ('s-Hertogenbosch, 1985); G. Rooijakkers, *Rituele repertoires. Volkscultuur in oostelijk Noord-Brabant 1559–1853* (Nijmegen, 1994), pp. 127–32; M.P. Christ, *De Brabantsche saecke. Het vergeefse streven naar een gewestelijke status voor Staats-Brabant 1586–1675* (Tilburg, 1984).

[30] P.J.H. Ubachs, *Twee heren, twee confessies: de verhouding van staat en kerk te Maastricht 1632–1673* (Assen, 1975).

[31] J.H. Kluiver, *De souvereine en independente staat Zeeland. De politiek van de provincie Zeeland inzake vredesonderhandelingen met Spanje tijdens de Tachtigjarige Oorlog tegen de achtergrond van de positie van Zeeland in de Republiek* (Middelburg, 1998).

the treaty renewed at the Hague on 21 August 1651, the provisions of the Union of Utrecht and of the Synod of Dordt were merely confirmed, each province promising to maintain the 'true Reformed Christian religion' taught in 'the public churches of these provinces' and confirmed by the Synod of Dordt. A promise was made to stop 'sects and denominations' from spreading further, as long as they only enjoyed mere 'connivance' rather than 'public protection'. Finally, placarding against Catholics was revived, but soon the deliberate (and sometimes reasoned) laxity of the civil authorities got the upper hand, and everything stayed as it was.[32]

In fact, as early as the second quarter of the sixteenth century the northern Low Countries had been worked on by numerous religious movements: Catholics, Lutherans, and Calvinists formed as many confessional groups, variable in number, which could have very different conformations locally, not to mention the different and sometimes antagonistic tendencies within these communities, reinforced by political opposition.[33] The radical Reformation was still numerically important at the beginning of the seventeenth century. Its three branches made themselves known continually throughout the period, if only by their noisy internal quarrels: the pacifism or millenarianism of the Mennonites (the non-violent Anabaptists), the rationalism of the Socinians and disciples of Spinoza, the spiritualism of the Visionaries. The tendency towards repeated splits among the Mennonites was proof of a marked individualism, while at the same time the divisions were preparing the ground for an effective toleration of different opinions.[34] Since the middle of the seventeenth century, the Mennonite community had dramatically declined in number, but thanks to the practice of *connubium* that ensured the

[32] Frijhoff and Spies, *1650: Bevochten eendracht*, pp. 351–432; F.G.M. Broeyer, 'IJkpunt 1650 – "Andre gezintheden met tollerantie getolereert"', in C. Augustijn and E. Honée (eds.), *Vervreemding en verzoening. De relatie tussen katholieken en protestanten in Nederland 1550–2000* (Nijmegen, 1998), pp. 35–67.

[33] W. Nijenhuis, 'Variants within Dutch Calvinism in the Sixteenth Century', *Acta historiae Neerlandicae* 12 (1979), 48–64; J.J. Woltjer, 'Stadt und Reformation in den Niederlanden', in Franz Petri (ed.), *Kirche und gesellschaftlicher Wandel in deutschen und niederländischen Städten der werdenden Neuzeit* (Vienna, 1980), pp. 155–67; A. Duke, 'The Ambivalent Face of Calvinism in the Netherlands, 1561–1618', in M. Prestwich (ed.), *International Calvinism 1541–1715* (Oxford, 1985), pp. 109–34; A. Jelsma, *Frontiers of the Reformation. Dissidence and Orthodoxy in Sixteenth-Century Europe* (Abingdon, 1998). Two case studies: W. Bergsma, 'Calvinismus in Friesland um 1600 am Beispiel der Stadt Sneek', *Archiv für Reformationsgeschichte* 80 (1989), 252–85, and W. Bergsma, *Tussen Gideonsbende en publieke kerk. Een studie over het gereformeerd protestantisme in Friesland, 1580–1650* (Hilversum, 1999); A.Ph.F. Wouters and P.H.A.M. Abels, *Nieuw en ongezien. Kerk en samenleving in de classis Delft en Delfland 1572–1621*, 2 vols. (Delft, 1994).

[34] I.B. Horst (ed.), *The Dutch Dissenters. A Critical Companion to Their History and Ideas* (Leiden, 1986); A. Hamilton, S. Voolstra, and P. Visser (eds.), *From Martyr to Muppy. A Historical Introduction to Cultural Assimilation Processes of a Religious Minority in the Netherlands: The Mennonites* (Amsterdam, 1994).

cohesion of the group and knit together its elites while preventing their fortunes from being scattered, it remained very influential at the end of the eighteenth century.[35] The intellectual and social quality of its members, and their spirit of initiative in the political, economic, and social fields made these dissidents the social and political avant-garde of the revolutionary period.

Moreover, we now know that initially quite a large number of Christians formed intermediate groups that pleaded in favour of a policy of compromise (*accommodatie*).[36] Some of them had lost all confidence in the Churches and refused to support them, while at the same time practising a sort of basic religion: they met together in lay communities (*conventikels*) to read the scriptures and discuss the affairs of the faith.[37] The local nature of this intermediate sector, very probably still important around the year 1600, took many decades to disappear.[38] Throughout the seventeenth century we come across manifestations of it in the radicalism of the *collegiants* (those who met in colleges or *conventicles* to discuss matters among themselves, without an ordained minister).[39] It was moreover the only form of discussion in which women could participate on an equal footing, although still under the distrustful eye of the consistories.[40] The basic forms of popular pietism, with its lay preachers tracked down by the ecclesiastical authorities, sometimes drew on these groups, and a fraction of the large number of 'amateurs' (*liefhebbers*) of the Reformed

[35] On the *connubium* after 1650, see S. Groenveld, *Huisgenoten des geloofs. Was de samenleving in de Republiek der Verenigde Nederlanden verzuild?* (Hilversum, 1995), pp. 32–41.

[36] This is the thesis defended by J.J. Woltjer, *Tussen vrijheidsstrijd en burgeroorlog. Over de Nederlandse Opstand 1555–1580* (Amsterdam, 1994); J.J. Woltjer, 'Political Moderates and Religious Moderates in the Revolt of the Netherlands', in P. Benedict, G. Marnef, H. van Nierop, and M. Venard (eds.), *Reformation, Revolt and Civil War in France and the Netherlands 1555–1585* (Amsterdam, 1999), pp. 185–200. For a very detailed local study, see B.J. Kaplan, *Calvinists and Libertines. Confession and Community in Utrecht, 1578–1620* (Oxford, 1995).

[37] F.A. van Lieburg, 'Het gereformeerd conventikelwezen in de classis Dordrecht in de 17e en 18e eeuw', *Holland* 23 (1991), 2–21; for Rotterdam, see J. Zijlmans, *Vriendenkringen in een discussiecultuur. Particuliere verenigingsvormen van het culturele leven in de zeventiende-eeuwse Republiek* (The Hague, 1999).

[38] J. Pollmann, *Religious Choice in the Dutch Republic: The Reformation of Arnoldus Buchelius (1565–1641)* (Manchester, 1999), has just made a superb presentation of the long and complex itinerary of a member of Utrecht's intellectual elite, from militant Catholicism to orthodox Calvinism.

[39] A.W. Fix, *Prophecy and Reason. The Dutch Collegiants in the Early Enlightenment* (Princeton, NJ, 1991).

[40] Cf. M. de Baar, 'Van kerk naar sekte: Sara Nevius, Grietje van Dijke en Anna Maria van Schurman', *De Zeventiende Eeuw* 7, 2 (1991), 159–71; L. Geudeke, 'Mannenbastion of vrouwenbolwerk? De positie van vrouwen in de gereformeerde kerk, 1566–1650', in M. Cornelis et al. (eds.), *Vrome vrouwen: betekenissen van geloof voor vrouwen in de geschiedenis* (Hilversum, 1996), pp. 67–86; F.A. van Lieburg, 'Vroomheid kent geen sekse: piëtistes in de achttiende eeuw', in *Vrome vrouwen*, pp. 109–28; Zijlmans, *Vriendenkringen*, chapter 4.

religion could be found there. The term *liefhebbers* referred to those who admitted an interest in the Reformed religion without making the confession necessary to be recognised as full members of the Church.[41] Their noncommittal position allowed them to avoid the constraints of church life, in particular the exercise of moral censure, and of discipline. Those whom Leszek Kolakowski thought he could call 'Christians without a Church' were often, above all, Christians immune to all ecclesiastical authority and practising a basic religiosity, better still a religious sociability at a basic level.[42] This was perhaps the real innovation of the young Republic in religious matters. It was to mark political attitudes towards the established Churches for a long time.

It was only after 1650, when Dutch society left its expansive phase and started a long period of consolidation, that the Churches managed bit by bit to incorporate these undecided or stubborn people and to give themselves a solid social structure embracing the whole confessional group. Thus the popular pietism of the laity,[43] somewhat hesitant towards the ecclesiastical authorities, more or less disappeared in favour of a powerful and structured pietist movement within the Churches and under the leadership of the ministers themselves who, moreover, provided them with the essential part of their spiritual writings. This movement of Christian renewal, which later received the title 'Further Reformation' (*Nadere Reformatie*), became at that time more and more closely linked to the great European pietist movement.[44]

It is precisely in the phase of ecclesiastical formation of Dutch Calvinism before 1650 that the religious landscape is at its richest and most colourful. This pluralism was appreciated to different degrees, both within the country and by foreign visitors, but there is no doubt about its reality. We recall Jean-Baptiste Stouppe's famous question: 'Is this really a Protestant country that we have occupied?' in his apologia *La Religion*

---

[41] Van Deursen, *Bavianen en slijkgeuzen*, pp. 134–5; Wouters and Abels, *Nieuw en ongezien*, pp. 259–64.

[42] Kolakowski, *Chrétiens sans Eglise*.

[43] Cf. W. Frijhoff, *Wegen van Evert Willemsz. Een Hollands weeskind op zoek naar zichzelf 1607–1647* (Nijmegen, 1995), especially pp. 351–88 and 875–80.

[44] F.E. Stoeffler, *The Rise of Evangelical Pietism* (Leiden, 1965); M.H. Prozesky, 'The Emergence of Dutch Pietism', *Journal of Ecclesiastical History* 28 (1977), 29–37; J. van den Berg and J.P. van Dooren (eds.), *Pietismus und Reveil. Der Pietismus in den Niederlanden und seine internationale Beziehungen* (Leiden, 1978); T. Brienen *et al.*, *De Nadere Reformatie en het gereformeerde piëtisme* (The Hague, 1989); J.R. Beeke, *Assurance of Faith. Calvin, English Puritanism, and the Dutch Second Reformation* (New York, 1991); J. van den Berg, 'Die Frömmigkeitsbestrebungen in den Niederlanden', in M. Brecht *et al.* (eds.), *Der Pietismus vom siebzehnten bis zum frühen achtzehnten Jahrhundert* (Göttingen, 1993), pp. 57–112; F.A. van Lieburg, 'From Pure Church to Pious Culture: The Further Reformation in the Seventeenth-Century Dutch Republic', in W.F. Graham (ed.), *Later Calvinism: International Perspectives* (Kirksville, MO, 1994), pp. 409–29. A case study: F.A. van Lieburg, *De Nadere Reformatie te Utrecht ten tijde van Voetius* (Rotterdam, 1989).

des Hollandois (1673), written for his compatriots who were worried about his participation in a war officially destined to repress, if not to wipe out, Protestantism in Holland. He was a Swiss Calvinist, commanding the town of Utrecht for the invader, the king of France. Surprised by the very great number of sects, confessions, and religions existing in the Republic, he wrote:

Les Etats donnent une liberté illimitée à toute sorte de Religions, lesquelles y ont une liberté entière de célébrer leurs mystères et de servir Dieu comme il leur plaist. Vous saurez donc qu'outre les Réformés il y a des Catholiques Romains, des Lutheriens, des Brounisted, des Independants, des Arminiens, des Anabaptists des Sociniens, des Ariens, des Enthousiastes, des Quacquiers ou des Trembleurs, des Borrélistes, des Arméniens, des Moscovites, des Libertins et d'autres enfin que nous pouvons appeler des Chercheurs parce qu'ils cherchent une Religion et qu'ils n'en professent aucune de celles qui sont établies. Je ne vous parle point des Juifs, des Turcs et des Persans.

['The States give unlimited freedom to all sorts of religions, which are completely at liberty to celebrate their mysteries and to serve God as they wish. You will therefore know that besides the Protestants there are Roman Catholics, Lutherans, Brounisteds [Congregationalist followers of Robert Browne], Independents, Arminians [Remonstrants], Anabaptists [Mennonites], Socinians, Arians, Enthusiasts, Quakers or Shakers, Borelists [partisans of the collegiant Adam Boreel, who tended towards prophetism], Armenians, Moscovites, Libertines, and others whom we can call Seekers because they are seeking a Religion and they do not profess any of those established. I do not say more about Jews, Turks, and Persans']

before getting carried away against the free-thinking Spinoza, whom he called 'neither Jew nor Christian': the obvious disbelief of the self-made-philosopher did not fit into the colonel's view of the world.[45] His violent antisemitism was, moreover, refuted by another French-speaker, the minister Jean Brun, in his *Véritable religion des Hollandais* (Amsterdam, 1675).

Stouppe forgot to enumerate the linguistic variants that existed among the Protestants. These increased still further the number of churches in the towns and sometimes the number of the dogmatic or spiritual currents. This was true of the Protestant Walloons, tormented by the Arminian temptation, of the English, close to the Puritans, of the Scots, and of the Germans.[46] Besides this extraordinary hive of spiritual

---

[45] J.B. Stouppe, *La Religion des Hollandois* (Cologne [=Leiden?], 1673), pp. 32, 79. For these tendencies, see Lindeboom, *Stiefkinderen van het christendom*; C.W. Roldanus, *Zeventiende-eeuwse geestesbloei* (Utrecht/Antwerp, 1961); Kolakowski, *Chrétiens sans Eglise.*

[46] G.H.M. Posthumus Meyjes, 'Les rapports entre les Eglises Wallonnes des Pays-Bas et la France avant la Révocation', in *La Révocation de l'Edit de Nantes et les Provinces-Unies 1685. Colloque international du Tricentenaire, Leyde, 1–3 avril 1985* (Amsterdam/Maarssen, 1986),

activity, it is the freedom of conscience guaranteed by the state that struck people. This fundamental right would have had but little effect had it not been associated in everyday life with a great permissiveness on the part of the local authorities. It is true that this was a venal attitude, for the councillors and other magistrates were richly paid for the connivance they showed towards semi-public practices of those who were not Protestants: churches that were hardly hidden, organs, songs and procession inside houses, night-time pilgrimages.[47] For the religious minorities – although Catholics, and perhaps even the Mennonites, remained more numerous than the Protestants until the middle of the seventeenth century – it was a religious regime that one could describe as 'tempered liberty'.[48]

Legitimisation of diversity, figures of unity

Political connivance could count on the intellectual understanding of a part of the population. The intellectuals who were protagonists of a certain degree of toleration were numerous in Holland: the humanist Coornhert, the first great theorist of freedom of conscience; the jurist Gerard Noodt (1647–1725) with his stirring rectorial speech on religious toleration delivered in Leiden on 8 February 1706 under the title *De religione an imperio iure gentium libera?*;[49] texts by Grotius and the *Commentaire philosophique* (1686) by Pierre Bayle;[50] John Locke's resounding *Epistola de tolerantia* (1689) published on his return from Holland; the patiently corrosive work of the Remonstrants around Philippus à Limborch and Jean Le Clerc taking up Simon Episcopius' *libertas prophetandi*;[51] the blows

pp. 1–15; K.L. Sprunger, *Dutch Puritanism. A History of English and Scottish Churches of the Netherlands in the Sixteenth and Seventeenth Centuries* (Leiden, 1982).

[47] H. Roodenburg, ' "Splendeur et magnificence". Processions et autres célébrations à Amsterdam au XVIe siècle', *Revue du Nord* 69, 274 (1987), 515–33; P. Raedts, 'Le Saint Sacrement du Miracle d'Amsterdam: lieu de mémoire de l'identité catholique', in P. den Boer and W. Frijhoff (eds.), *Lieux de mémoire et identités nationales* (Amsterdam, 1993), pp. 237–51.

[48] H.A. Enno van Gelder, *Getemperde vrijheid. Een verhandeling over de verhouding van kerk en staat in de Republiek der Verenigde Nederlanden en de vrijheid van meningsuiting in zake godsdienst, drukpers en onderwijs, gedurende de 17e eeuw* (Groningen, 1972).

[49] On Noodt: F. Lomonaco, *Tolleranza e libertà di coscienza. Filosofia, diritto e storia tra Leida e Napoli nel secolo XVIII* (Naples, 1999), pp. 5–66; J. van Eijnatten, 'Gerard Noodt's Standing in the Eighteenth-Century Dutch Debate on Religious Freedom', *Dutch Review of Church History* 79, 1 (1999), 74–98.

[50] C. Berkvens-Stevelinck, 'La tolérance et l'héritage de P. Bayle en Hollande dans la première moitié du XVIIIe siècle. Une première orientation', *Lias* 5, 2 (1978), 257–72.

[51] H. Bots and J. de Vet, 'La notion de tolérance dans la *Bibliothèque ancienne et moderne* (1714–1727) [by Jean Le Clerc]', *Lias* 10 (1983), 123–9; L. Simonutti, *Arminianesimo e tolleranza nel Seicento olandese. Il carteggio Ph. van Limborch-J. Le Clerc* (Florence, 1984); J. van Eijnatten, *Mutua Christianorum Tolerantia. Irenicism and Toleration in the Netherlands: The Stinstra Affair 1740–1745* (Florence, 1998).

dealt by Spinoza and his Dutch disciples.[52] Relying on the freedom of the press and supported by the international book trade that had its centre in Holland, theorising on the different forms of Irenicism or of civil and religious toleration could allow itself free rein in the Dutch Republic.[53] Religious diversity, however, was not always seen as an ideal. On the contrary, much thought was given to the question of knowing how to restore unity of faith, to bring believers together, or to obtain the reunification of Churches.[54] In fact, the struggle for the unity of the Church and Irenicism continued for a long time to divide even the Protestants themselves. From the beginning of the Dutch Republic, there was the same clash of two opinions that we keep finding throughout the modern era under different names. Justus Lipsius had maintained that the state should impose religious unity for the benefit of public order. His opponent Coornhert objected that, on the contrary, truth would always emerge and that it was therefore useless for the state to get mixed up in it for political reasons.[55]

The course of this discussion shows to what extent the United Provinces were an exception in Europe. While everywhere else the tolerance of Libertinism had to give way before political rigour for reasons of state, the opposite happened in Holland. Lipsius left his Chair at the University of Leiden for that of Louvain and converted back to Catholicism, closer to his politico-religious convictions. These convictions did not, however, disappear from the United Provinces. They remained the prerogative of the theocratic reform movement, without ever managing to force their way into the structure of the state.

At the end of the sixteenth century Coornhert, for his part, clearly reflected the opinion of the majority of Dutch people. Even the first pietists themselves, who were more concerned with the authority of the Bible than that of any Church, remained vigilant as regards all attempts to enforce unification beyond the rights of the individual conscience. Did

---

[52] H.J. Siebrand, *Spinoza and the Netherlanders. An Inquiry into the Early Reception of his Philosophy of Religion* (Assen, 1988); cf. Popkin and Vanderjagt (eds.), *Scepticism and Irreligion*.

[53] D. Nobbs, *Theocracy and Toleration. A Study of the Disputes in Dutch Calvinism from 1600 to 1650* (Cambridge, 1938); E.H. Kossmann, 'Freedom in Seventeenth-Century Dutch Thought and Practice', in J.I. Israel (ed.), *The Anglo-Dutch Moment. Essays on the Glorious Revolution and its World Impact* (Cambridge, 1991), pp. 281–98. An important clarification has been made in A. Rotondò, *Europe et Pays-Bas. Evolution, réélaboration et diffusion de la tolérance aux XVIIe et XVIIIe siècles* (Florence, 1992).

[54] G.H.M. Posthumus Meyjes, 'Protestants irenisme in de 16e en eerste helft van de 17e eeuw', *Nederlands Theologisch Tijdschrift* 36 (1982), 205–22; C. Berkvens-Stevelinck, J. Israel, and G.H.M. Posthumus Meyjes (eds.), *The Emergence of Tolerance in the Dutch Republic* (Leiden/New York/Cologne, 1997); Méchoulan, *Amsterdam au temps de Spinoza*.

[55] F. de Nave, 'De polemiek tussen Justus Lipsius en Dirck Volckertsz. Coornhert (1590): hoofdoorzaak van Lipsius' vertrek uit Leiden (1591)', *De Gulden Passer* 48 (1970), 1–39.

not the Protestant Reformation stem from the conviction that reformation of faith and customs should come from man's inner self with no outside compulsion? Although in fact we know very little of the *religion vécue* (the religious experience) in the first decades of the Dutch seventeenth century, one obvious trait is the ambient pietism that penetrated all religious groups like a powerful socio-cultural current going beyond confessional frontiers: the Protestants, the Mennonites, the collegiants, and the Lutherans themselves were all part of it.

Only the Catholics, traumatised by the loss of their freedom to worship and their eviction from public life, seemed to escape it, if we do not take into account their evident propensity for miracles and religious catastrophism, linked to historical circumstances.[56] But the attraction exercised on a fraction of Catholics by the dissident spirituality of one Antoinette Bourignon (1616–80)[57] or that of the 'nomad' Jean de Labadie (1610–74), to quote Michel de Certeau,[58] shows that they did not remain insensitive to forms of mysticism that had their roots in a basic practice of life and in readings. In so far as it stressed the importance of direct contact with the scriptures and of devotional experience, Jansenism itself was a catalyst of practical spirituality for the elites.[59]

After the formal introduction of the Confession of Heidelberg as the 'dominant' religion in the last quarter of the sixteenth century, the militant Calvinists were not long finding out that, for many of their compatriots attracted to their Church, religious life remained just as much an outside show as in the days of Catholicism. So the Protestant elites themselves formulated a dual obligation. First the new doctrine had to be imposed publicly by making the Reformed Church a real State Church; this was the Genevese model of the *civitas Dei*, where the Church dominates the state, as opposed to the pluralist Evangelical model, where the state dominates the Church. At the same time it was necessary to reform the life of the community by a new practice of piety. *Reformatio vitae* and *praxis pietatis* were henceforth the key words of the efforts at Christianisation. Quite rapidly, however, the Reformed Church had to

---

[56] W. Frijhoff, 'La fonction du miracle dans une minorité catholique: les Provinces-Unies au XVIIe siècle', *Revue d'Histoire de la Spiritualité* 48 (1972), 151–78.

[57] While waiting for Mirjam de Baar's thesis, 'De Nieuwe Eva: Antoinette Bourignon (1616–1680) als spiritueel leidster', forthcoming 2002, we have only the somewhat dated work by M. van der Does, *Antoinette Bourignon, 1616–1680. La vie et l'œuvre d'une mystique chrétienne* (Amsterdam, 1974).

[58] M. de Certeau, *La fable mystique, XVIe–XVIIe siècle* (Paris, 1982), pp. 374–405: 'Labadie le nomade'; T.J. Saxby, *The Quest for the New Jerusalem. Jean de Labadie and the Labadists, 1610–1744* (Dordrecht/Boston/Lancaster, 1987).

[59] Th. Clemens, 'La répercussion de la lutte entre jansénistes et antijansénistes dans la littérature de spiritualité depuis 1685 jusqu'à la fin du XVIIIe siècle', in E.J.M. van Eijl (ed.), *L'image de C. Jansénius jusqu'à la fin du XVIIIe siècle* (Louvain, 1987), pp. 203–29.

recognise the clear refusal of theocratic desires on the part of the authorities. The latter were quite happy with a popular Church, marked by Protestantism, but with only very few confessions. However, they did not want a theocracy under the control of ministers. The publicly recognised Church certainly enjoyed privileges but no longer lived in symbiosis with the state as State Churches in the proper sense of the term did elsewhere in Europe. While continuing to defend its point of view in the pulpit, the Reformed Church had in fact to resign itself to a position of limited power and a reduced number of members. It therefore gave up its ambition to form a great popular Church, co-extensive with the nation in the way the medieval Church had been before. The new idea of a Church for the Saved, an *Ecclesia purior*, was like the dogma that was taking shape (the predestination of a limited number of chosen people) and like the disciplinary practice which preferred a small perfect community easy to control rather than a religiosity of 'sociological Christians' interested only in the rites of passage and the social ministry of the diaconate.

This ideal profited from the religious migrations of the First Refuge in the years from 1585 to 1625.[60] Figures vary, but the immigrants from the southern Netherlands alone can be estimated at some 100,000 or even, according to J. Briels, at 150,000: in other words between 7 and 10 per cent of the total population of the Republic around 1600.[61] Towns like Haarlem, Leiden, or Middelburg saw their populations double; Amsterdam, Gouda, and Rotterdam populations increased by a good one-third. The demographic, economic, cultural, and religious contribution of these immigrants was so considerable that according to the picture that we have today, Dutch society was completely transformed in less than half a century.[62] The tremendous impact of these migrations is essentially attributed to their religious character, which made it instrumental in a certain confessionalisation.[63] From this point of view it did not matter whether the immigrants fled their country for religious reasons or for economic or political reasons; although some of the refugees kept to their dissenting faith or even to Catholicism,

[60] P. Dibon, 'Le Refuge wallon précurseur du Refuge huguenot', *XVIIe Siècle* 76–77 (1967), 53–74; reprinted in *Regards sur la Hollande du Siècle d'Or* (Naples, 1990), pp. 315–41; W. Frijhoff, 'Migrations religieuses dans les Provinces-Unies avant le Second Refuge', *Revue du Nord* 80, 326–7 (1998), 573–98.

[61] J. Briels, *Zuid-Nederlanders in de Republiek 1572–1630. Een demografische en cultuurhistorische studie* (Sint Niklaas [Belgium], 1985); J. Briels, 'De Zuidnederlandse immigratie 1572–1630', *Tijdschrift voor Geschiedenis* 100 (1987), 331–55.

[62] J.I. Israel, *The Dutch Republic. Its Rise, Greatness, and Fall 1477–1806* (Oxford, 1995), pp. 307–18.

[63] Cf. H. Schilling, 'Nationale Identität und Konfession in der europäischen Neuzeit', in B. Giesen (ed.), *Nationale und kulturelle Identität. Studien zur Entwicklung des kollektiven Bewusstseins in der Neuzeit* (Frankfurt, 1991), pp. 192–252; here, pp. 216–21.

finally they all rallied to a conception of Calvinism which had become the emblem of their origins and of their culture. The northern Low Countries thus found their more-or-less definitive confession, Calvinism of strict observance that had developed from the austere Calvinism (dictated by circumstances) of the mass of immigrants, and in permanent tension between the theocratic ambitions of the Reformed Church and the secular political reason of the public authorities. Without the weight of immigration, the United Provinces might have stayed with just an 'Arminian' Reformation, a 'third' and more liberal or open-minded road, and perhaps closer to pre-Tridentine Catholicism.

Seen from this angle, Christian humanism and political moderation collapsed simultaneously half a century after the beginning of the Revolt, the one at the Synod of Dordt, the other on the scaffold of the Grand Pensionary, Oldenbarnevelt, executed on 13 May of that same year 1619. The militants of the First Refuge entered a territory where relations between the confessions were still to be defined. Through the combined efforts of their great number, the role of religion (in particular the theology of exile, *Exulantentheologie*) in the process of social and cultural assimilation, and its liberating character, these militants were able to influence the religion and the culture of the host country profoundly, and to help unify it culturally. They could, after all that, literally feel at home.[64] This process worked both ways. Certainly the refugees adapted themselves, but because of their great number and the intensity of contacts the host populations, too, changed their perceptions, values, and even their religious practices. So in a way the Dutch became Flemish, as we can clearly see in the painting of the period. At the end of it all, a new society took shape which combined the features of the north and the south in a 'Dutch Calvinism' shared by all, with its austerity, its individualism, its tendency to be shut in on itself, its fundamental sense of equality, and its eschatological certitude of being elected, all of which have asserted themselves more strongly since then.

A century later, during the Second Refuge, numerically less important it is true (probably 35,000 rather than the 50,000, or even the 70,000, French that used to be suggested), the Dutch Republic proved to be far less receptive.[65] Certainly, in 1685 it remained 'the great Ark for exiles'. But from being a young community seeking its way, the United Provinces had become an adult society with well-oiled wheels, having nothing left to learn concerning relations between Church and state. Although they were

[64] Frijhoff, 'Migrations religieuses dans les Provinces-Unies'.
[65] H. Bots, 'La migration huguenote dans les Provinces-Unies, 1680–1715. Un nouveau bilan', in Ph. Henry and M. de Tribolet (eds.), *In dubiis libertas. Mélanges d'histoire offerts au professeur Rémy Scheurer* (Hauterive, 1999), pp. 271–81.

welcomed with open arms, the Huguenots managed only with difficulty to become familiar with the host society on which they made hardly any lasting impact.[66]

The sixteenth-century Revolt had tipped the balance of central political power towards the territorial states. Centres of decision-making were scattered. The towns and provinces took their fate into their own hands, the local 'regents' (co-opted councillors, burgomasters, aldermen) considered themselves as bearers of sovereignty and so created a political ideology that was tinged within Libertarian Republicanism.[67] They formed only a small oligarchy; some two thousand for a population of two million. The decisive weight of the town was felt even in the inner provinces where traditionally the nobility carried the most weight in politics. This swing to a federal power put the Churches at the mercy of the masters of the day, not only the semi-tolerated dissident communities, but even the publicly recognised Church. This can be seen clearly in the politico-religious factions, like those in Amsterdam around the rigid burgomaster Reinier Pauw in the 1620s. In Rotterdam, a Homeric struggle broke out in 1622 between the orthodox Protestants and the Liberals concerning the great bronze statue of Erasmus which the town, controlled by the Arminians, had put up in the great market place. Could one honour a man, however great a scholar, while it was forbidden to represent even the biblical saints themselves? Above all, did it really have to be Erasmus, who had for the orthodox become a symbol of everything they abhorred in their relation with the world: a politician, a Liberal and an Irenicist, critical certainly of Rome, but just as critical of the Reformers?[68]

Dutch society, in constant danger of splitting up, needed symbols of unity to stay together. It was the Reformed Church that, better than any other, stood out as a centralising and unifying element. More than the civil power with its tendency to particularism, it was the Church that fed and nurtured the newborn national feeling. Among the religious models of unity, the notion of the New Israel, or of 'Dutch Israel' was particularly important.[69] Many Protestants, horrified by the atrocities

---

[66] *La Révocation de l'Edit de Nantes et les Provinces-Unies*, 1685.

[67] H. Schilling, 'Der libertär-radikale Republikanismus der holländischen Regenten', *Geschichte und Gesellschaft* 10 (1984), 498–533.

[68] J. Becker, *Hendrick de Keyser: Standbeeld van Desiderius Erasmus in Rotterdam* (Bloemendaal, 1993), pp. 56–76; L. Visser-Isles, *Erasmus and Rotterdam* (Rotterdam, n.d. [1993]), pp. 78–82.

[69] G. Groenhuis, 'Calvinism and National Consciousness: The Dutch Republic as the New Israel', in A.C. Duke and C.A. Tamse (eds.), *Britain and the Netherlands*, vol. vii: *Church and State since the Reformation* (The Hague, 1981), pp. 119–33; C. Huisman, *Neerlands Israël. Het natiebesef der traditioneel-gereformeerden in de achttiende eeuw* (Dordrecht, 1983); S. Schama, *The Embarrassment of Riches. An Interpretation of Dutch Culture in the Golden Age* (New York, 1987), pp. 94–100; G.J. Schutte, *Het calvinistisch Nederland* (Utrecht,

of the *Conseil des Troubles* with its at least 7,000 victims, had seen the struggle against Spain as the combat of God himself against the enemies of His children. New images of evil, introduced during the sixteenth and seventeenth centuries, such as that of the Antichrist, assimilated to the Roman Pontiff, of the massacre of Saint Bartholomew's Day, prototype of Catholic treachery, of the Inquisition or of tyrannicidal Jesuits, could not but reinforce this sentiment of being saved, beyond the frontiers of the state that God Himself had fixed.

The central notion was well and truly that of being chosen; Israel being the chosen people of God, the new Israel was the instrument that God had recently chosen to realise his kingdom on earth and spread his message. The community argument here joined the theological argument of predestination, which also implied a certainty of being saved and brought with it an obligation to sanctification.[70] Since the Revolt, which was seen as a war of independence just like the struggles of the Jewish people, the Protestants had got into the habit of comparing themselves with biblical heroes, particularly those of the Old Testament.[71] The Prince of Orange had become the new Moses, Gideon or David, the enemy being the Spanish Sennacherib (Philip II) or the French Nebuchadnezzar (Louis XIV), both descendants of Cain. The very existence of the Dutch Republic was literally a miracle for many.[72]

The popular pietist writers (particularly ministers such as Teellinck, Udemans, and Lodensteyn) constantly drew parallels. In *Pascha*, a play by Joost van den Vondel (1587–1679) – the prince of poets from Amsterdam, even though he was a Liberal who became a Catholic in 1641 – the Dutch people in search of liberation are explicitly assimilated to the Jewish people in their long crossing of the desert and search for a country. The identification of the United Provinces with Israel, Canaan, or Jerusalem became still more insistent during the second half of the seventeenth century, in particular with orthodox ministers such as Abraham van der Velde (1614–77) or Herman Witsius (1636–1708). They interpret Dutch history as a prelude to the heavenly Jerusalem; it is the Dutch who must be the driving force in its coming. Thus the need for the permanent conversion of the Dutch people who, by sanctification, must show themselves worthy of being saved. A whole political theology was derived from these

1988); R. Bisschop, *Sions vorst en volk. Het tweede-Israëlidee als theocratisch concept in de Gereformeerde Kerk van de Republiek tussen ca. 1650 en ca. 1750* (Veenendaal, 1993).

[70] M.A. Hakkenberg, 'The Predestinatarian Controversy in the Netherlands 1600–1620', PhD thesis, University of California at Berkeley (1989).

[71] Cf. M.Th. uit den Bogaard, *De gereformeerden en Oranje tijdens het eerste stadhouderloze tijdperk* (Groningen/Djakarta, 1954).

[72] K.W. Swart, *The Miracle of the Dutch Republic as seen in the Seventeenth Century* (London, 1967), p. 18.

metaphors. The community of the Saved was the hub of society, 'the city on the mountain', as the minister Streso stated in his sermon before the Grand Assembly in 1651. The state, which had to ensure the best conditions for the effective sanctification of the people of Saints, was at its service, and not the other way round.

But Witsius did not for all that urge religious division; for him the choice of the people of God transcended the doctrinal conflicts in the Reformed Church, showing him to be a forerunner to a greater intra-Christian tolerance which was defended more and more eloquently during the eighteenth century. However, the different confessions resisted this tendency. The position of power and of moral responsibility that the publicly recognised Church had meanwhile obtained in national life now had them caught. Thus the *mutua Christianorum tolerantia* suggested in 1745 by the Protestant Cocceian theologian Johannes van den Honert (1693–1758) in a noisy debate with the minister Johannes Stinstra (1708–90), remained contained within the limits of orthodoxy and the established order.[73] In any case, the timid overtures made by the Reformed Church towards other confessions continued to exclude Catholics. Although their presence as a confession was legally recognised by the 1730s with the public recognition of priests, the opposition of the Protestant Churches was even more emphatic, which did not promise well for the future, as the confessional divisions of the country in the nineteenth and twentieth centuries have proved.[74]

It is the permanent tension between this figure of unity, centred on Calvinist ideology and its secular derivatives on the one hand, and the model of religious toleration that was always threatened by a split in the social order on the other, that explains the deep ambiguity of the image the Low Countries enjoyed in the world from the end of the sixteenth century, just like the deeply rooted uncertainty about its collective destiny that has always marked its national feelings.

---

[73] Van Eijnatten, *Mutua Christianorum Tolerantia*; for the different conceptions of religious unity in the eighteenth century, see J. van Eijnatten, 'The Debate on Religious Unity in the Eighteenth-Century Netherlands: The German Connection', in H. Duchhardt and G. May (eds.), *Union - Konversion - Toleranz. Dimensionen der Annäherung zwischen den christlichen Konfessionen im 17. und 18. Jahrhundert* (Mainz, 2000), pp. 325–48.

[74] Th. Clemens, 'IJkpunt 1750. Op zoek naar nieuwe grenzen in het politiek-religieuze landschap van de Republiek', in Augustijn and Honée (eds.), *Vervreemding en verzoening*, pp. 69–101.

4 The bond of Christian piety: the individual practice of tolerance and intolerance in the Dutch Republic

Judith Pollmann

Dutch society in the Golden Age presents a Janus-faced image. On the one hand, people at all levels of Dutch society were, according to foreign observers, intensely engaged with religion. A huge pamphlet literature permanently highlighted confessional differences, and preaching – in all confessions – made a high priority of attacking the doctrines of other Churches.[1] On the other hand, this was also a society that became proverbial for religious toleration and where religiously inspired violence was rare. Scholars have come up with a range of different explanations for this phenomenon. One solution is to assume that believers of different confessions tried to avoid each other as much as possible, under the guidance of a state that exerted itself to contain potential conflict. In the late 1970s, A.Th. van Deursen concluded that Golden Age believers of all denominations 'over the fortifications of their church walls, could only see heretics and never fellow Christians of another confession'.[2] According to this line of argument, it was through a form of social and cultural apartheid, more or less in the style of Dutch society between 1880 and 1960, that these divisions did not lead to open violence.

There is indeed little doubt that all Churches were aiming for segregation. Every Church promoted education, charity, and marriage within the boundaries of its own confession. Although acknowledging that the implementation of this policy was a slow process, S. Groenveld argued a few years ago that by 1650 segregation had become a fact and had created a society that was *verzuild*, with each individual living and working

Part of this chapter is based on my *Religious Choice in the Dutch Republic: The Reformation of Arnoldus Buchelius (1565–1641)* (Manchester, 1999) and on a chapter called 'Public Enemies, Private Friends. Arnoldus Buchelius' Experience of Religious Diversity in the Early Dutch Republic', in Arthur Wheelock and Adele Seeff (eds.), *The Public and Private in Dutch Culture of the Golden Age* (Newark/London, 2000), pp. 181–90. I am grateful to Manchester University Press and the Associated University Presses for their kind permission to use material from both book and article in this volume.

[1] A.Th. van Deursen, *Mensen van klein vermogen. Het kopergeld van de Gouden Eeuw* (Amsterdam, 1993), pp. 263–351.
[2] *Ibid.*, p. 338.

within the boundaries of his or her own denomination.[3] Yet at the very time when Groenveld expounded on the existence of *verzuiling* in the seventeenth-century Netherlands, new research had begun to question whether the ideal of confessional segregation, however high on the agenda of the Churches, had ever materialised in practice. Groenveld acknowledged that confessionalism made only very slow progress in society after the Revolt. J. Spaans had been the first to show that by 1620 about half the Haarlem population did not belong to a Church at all, and, since then, the work of others on this period has shown that Haarlem was no exception.[4] Groenveld was aware of this, but argued that we had to put the moment of *verzuiling* at a later date, around 1650. That argument, however, depended heavily on the assumption that by 1650 almost everyone in the Dutch Republic belonged to a confession.[5] The figures on which he based that assumption now seem fundamentally unreliable. Using the population survey of 1809, J. de Kok had calculated that almost the entire Dutch population was at that time affiliated to a Church, and extrapolated that this had been the case since about 1650.[6] As J.J. Woltjer has pointed out, however, the population survey of 1809 had categorised believers according to the Church in which they had been baptised.[7] What De Kok had not taken into account is that in fact it took more than baptism to be a member of the Reformed Church in the Netherlands. As Van Deursen demonstrated in 1974, the membership of the Reformed Churches consisted of those adults who had made a formal declaration of their faith and had been accepted as a member by the consistory of their Church. Membership brought the privilege of access to communion, yet it also implied that one would be subject to church discipline, the control over doctrine, morals, and life exerted by the consistories.[8] Whether

---

[3] S. Groenveld, *Huisgenoten des geloofs. Was de samenleving in de Republiek der Verenigde Nederlanden verzuild?* (Hilversum, 1995). The term *verzuiling* is sometimes translated into English as 'pillarization'.

[4] Joke Spaans, *Haarlem na de Reformatie. Stedelijke cultuur en kerkelijk leven* (The Hague, 1989), p. 104. Similar conclusions can be drawn for Delft from A.P.F. Wouters, *Nieuw en ongezien. Kerk en samenleving in de classis Delft en Delfland, 1572–1621*, 2 vols. (Delft, 1994), vol. I, pp. 234, 242–3, and for Utrecht from Benjamin J. Kaplan, *Calvinists and Libertines. Confession and Community in Utrecht, 1578–1620* (Oxford, 1995), pp. 117, 255, 277–8. Wiebe Bergsma, *Tussen Gideonsbende en publieke kerk. Een studie naar het gereformeerd protestantisme in Friesland, 1580–1650* (Hilversum, 1999), pp. 96–150, proposes similar figures for Friesland, Groningen, and Drenthe.

[5] Groenveld, *Huisgenoten des geloofs*, pp. 18–19.

[6] J. de Kok, *Nederland op de breuklijn Rome-Reformatie. Numerieke aspecten van protestantisering en katholieke herleving in de noordelijke Nederlanden, 1580–1880* (Assen, 1964).

[7] J.J. Woltjer, 'De plaats van de calvinisten in de Nederlandse samenleving', *De Zeventiende Eeuw* 10 (1994), 19.

[8] A.Th. van Deursen, *Bavianen en slijkgeuzen. Kerk en kerkvolk ten tijde van Maurits en Oldenbarnevelt* (Assen, 1974), pp. 128–34.

many people found that this was too high a price to pay, or because they lacked interest in communion, it is quite clear that many people who had been baptised in the Reformed Churches never became members of the Church. Woltjer pointed out that this was as true in 1809 as it had been around 1620. Subsequently, W. Bergsma has shown that in Friesland, Groningen, and Drente, at least, a very considerable proportion of the population remained unaffiliated throughout the seventeenth and eighteenth centuries.[9] Confessionalism, it now seems, only ever flourished in a part of early modern Dutch society.

The more aware we are that membership of a Church ususally meant that one belonged to a minority, the more important it is to understand how members of these minorities co-existed with those of other faiths. Even if confessional culture impinged on fewer Dutch believers than we used to think, that does not rule out that it did indeed create formidable cultural boundaries between believers of different confessions. Yet recent research points to a culture of co-operation and tolerance, rather than to the confessional apartheid which Groenveld was describing. In her study of the Reformation in Haarlem, Spaans argued that the town council tried to counter the potentially explosive effects of religious pluralism by essentially Christian but not denominationally bound policies that stressed civic unity, while it firmly curbed attempts by the Reformed Church to impose its own ideals on society as a whole. Although she noted problems over religious divisions within families, the citizens continued to live and work together with people of other denominations without any problems, and other social bonds and conventions often outweighed religious differences. The citizens were encouraged to celebrate a common Christianity that united them, rather than their doctrinal differences.[10] In his study on Utrecht, B. Kaplan has taken this thesis one step further and argued for the continued existence of a pious but non-confessional Christian culture that united Utrecht's citizens of different confessions, not just because the authorities wanted it that way, but because there was broad support for it within the population itself.[11] Recent findings of L. Bogaers and W. Bergsma have confirmed this, and W. Frijhoff has begun to develop a theory on the unwritten codes that guided such contacts.[12]

[9] Bergsma, *Tussen Gideonsbende en publieke kerk*, pp. 96–150, 186.
[10] Spaans, *Haarlem na de Reformatie*, pp. 195–9, 121, 238.
[11] Kaplan, *Calvinists and Libertines*, pp. 291–4.
[12] L.C.J.J. Bogaers, 'Geleund over de onderdeur. Doorkijkjes in het Utrechtse buurtleven van de vroege Middeleeuwen tot in de zeventiende eeuw', *Bijdragen en Mededelingen betreffende de Geschiedenis der Nederlanden* 112 (1997), 336–63; Bergsma, *Tussen Gideonsbende en publieke kerk*, pp. 334–43; Willem Frijhoff, 'Dimensions de la coexistence confessionelle', in C. Berkvens-Stevelinck, J. Israel, and G.H.M. Posthumus Meyjes (eds.), *The Emergence of Tolerance in the Dutch Republic* (Leiden/New York/Cologne, 1997), pp. 213–37.

Increasingly, scholars have begun to ask whether it was really possible for believers to practise the separation from the 'children of the world' that their Churches preached. In the Dutch Republic the decision to join a Church was a voluntary one and was often taken individually. As a consequence, Protestants who were converts of the first generation all had kinsmen who had not joined the Church. For them it seemed neither practicable nor particularly religious to break off family bonds for confessional reasons. A Swiss delegate to the Synod of Dordt in 1618 had probably not witnessed an exceptional situation when he reported that he stayed with a family of which the mother and the daughter were Calvinist, the father and the son were Catholic, the grandmother was Mennonite, and an uncle was a Jesuit.[13] For believers of the second and third generation, maintaining confessional unity in the family became a practical possibility, yet it was not necessarily a priority. It seems that the number of mixed marriages may have remained much higher than was previously supposed. Recent research on Utrecht and Bergen op Zoom certainly suggests this, and even late in the seventeenth century foreign observers continued to comment on the apparent ease with which Dutch families sustained confessional difference.[14] As late as the 1680s the English traveller Ellis Vereyard noted that 'it is very ordinary to find the man of the house of one opinion, his wife of another, his children of a third and his servant of one different from them all; and yet they live without the least jangling of dissension'.[15]

The gender balance – or rather imbalance – within the Reformed Church also suggests that within families religious uniformity was not seen as essential. About two-thirds of the Reformed membership appear to have been women.[16] Even if we account for a large number of spinsters and widows among them, this suggests that quite a few women may

---

[13] Wiebe Bergsma, ' "Uyt christelijcken yver en ter eeren Godes". Wederdopers en verdraagzaamheid', in Marijke Gijswijt-Hofstra (ed.), *Een schijn van verdraagzaamheid. Afwijking en tolerantie in Nederland van de zestiende eeuw tot heden* (Hilversum, 1989), p. 84.

[14] R. Rommes, *Oost, west, Utrecht best? Driehonderd jaar migratie en migranten in de stad Utrecht (begin 16e – begin 19e eeuw)* (Amsterdam, 1998), pp. 190–1; Charles de Mooij, *Geloof kan Bergen verzetten. Reformatie en katholieke herleving te Bergen op Zoom, 1577–1795* (Hilversum, 1998), pp. 578–83.

[15] Cited in C.D. van Strien, *British Travellers in Holland during the Stuart Period. Edward Browne and John Locke as Tourists in the United Provinces* (Leiden, 1993), p. 203.

[16] Van Deursen, *Bavianen en slijkgeuzen*, pp. 134–5; Wouters, *Nieuw en ongezien*, pp. 261–4. About the position of women, see L. Geudeke, 'Mannenbastion of vrouwenbolwerk? De positie van vrouwen in de gereformeerde kerk, 1566–1650', in Mirjam Cornelis *et al.* (eds.), *Vrome vrouwen. Betekenissen van geloof voor vrouwen in de geschiedenis* (Hilversum, 1996), pp. 67–86, and Judith Pollmann, 'Women and Religion in the Dutch Golden Age', *Dutch Crossing* 24 (2000), 162–82.

have been married to men who did not choose to join the Church.[17] These men may have been among the *liefhebbers*, or sympathisers, of the Reformed Church, that is to say the category of believers who regularly attended services but who did not join the Church.[18] Yet it was clearly not necessary for the family to present a totally united front.

Of course confessional differences often caused bitter strife within families and marriages.[19] But whereas the Reformed mathematician Isaac Beeckman may have been truly appalled when his sister wanted to marry a Remonstrant, he was on the best of terms with his brother-in-law after the marriage had become a fact.[20] Outside families, too, contacts with the unaffiliated and members of other Churches was, in many ways, hard to avoid. In civic militia companies, guilds, and *gebuurten* (neighbourhood organisations) one would have to deal with those of other faiths, and there is little to suggest that Church members shunned such contacts, immensely important as these were for civic culture. Bogaers, for instance, counted zealous Calvinists as well as Arminians and Catholics participating in Utrecht's *gebuurten*.[21]

The question, however, is how we can match this picture of everyday interconfessional bliss with the 'other face' of Dutch society. There may be plenty of evidence for good interconfessional relationships, but there is equally abundant evidence for the aggressive defence of confessional difference. Violence, certainly, was quite rare. Yet the vitriolic pamphlet literature, the great interest in religion, and the obvious zeal with which many Dutch Church members proselytised and defended their beliefs, and gave political expression to them, should also be fitted into the picture. The more we stress that in everyday life religious differences could be overcome, the harder it becomes to explain this intolerance and insistence on confessional difference. It would be simplest, of course, if we could demonstrate that some groups were tolerant, and others were not. In his analysis of the situation in Utrecht, Kaplan has been arguing, for instance, that the confessionalising instincts of the Calvinist minority clashed with the a-confessional, conservative, and

---

[17] For some figures see Bergsma, *Tussen Gideonsbende en publieke kerk*, pp. 337, 370, and Pollmann, 'Women and Religion'.

[18] Van Deursen, *Bavianen en slijkgeuzen*, pp. 128–34.

[19] See e.g. Luuc Kooijmans, *Vriendschap en de kunst van het overleven in de zeventiende en achttiende eeuw* (Amsterdam, 1997), pp. 210–16; Van Deursen, *Bavianen en slijkgeuzen*, pp. 152–4.

[20] Klaas van Berkel, *Isaac Beeckman (1588–1637) en de mechanisering van het wereldbeeld* (Amsterdam, 1983), pp. 109, 142.

[21] Bogaers, 'Geleund over de onderdeur'. See also Gabrielle Dorren, 'Communities within the Community: Aspects of Neighbourhood in Seventeenth-Century Haarlem', *Urban History* 25 (1998).

communalist Christian notions of Libertines, Mennonites, Collegiants, and the unaffiliated.[22]

Yet when we take a closer look at the behaviour of individual people, it proves quite difficult to make a clear distinction between the tolerant and the intolerant in Dutch society. On the basis of a case-study concerning the Utrecht lawyer and diarist Arnoldus Buchelius, I shall argue here that Dutch Church members could and did participate *both* in the intolerant discourse of confessionalism *and* in the a-confessional religious culture that Kaplan identified. Through an analysis of Buchelius' tale, I shall try and suggest how and why they did so.[23]

Arnoldus Buchelius was born in 1565 as the illegitimate child of an Utrecht canon and a printer's daughter from Kampen. He was raised in a Catholic tradition that was 'Erasmian', had little time for monks and friars, and focused strongly on practical and personal piety rather than ritual. Yet it was a Catholic tradition that was on its last legs. By the time Buchelius was fifteen, Catholic worship was prohibited in the Republic, whilst in the Catholic world it was rapidly being replaced by the new Catholicism of the Counter-Reformation. Between 1584 and 1586, when Buchelius studied in Douai and spent almost a year in Paris, he got a taste of this new Catholicism, but he was not impressed by its stress on ceremony and ritual, the power it assigned to the clergy, and the social discipline that it promoted.[24] Caught between the outdated religious tradition of his childhood, and the unfamiliar Catholicism of the Counter-Reformation, he effectively found himself without a confessional homeland.

The young Buchelius deeply deplored the Dutch Revolt and the religious fragmentation. Like many others he saw the political and religious divisions as a punishment that was sent by God to chastise the Dutch for their sins.[25] He associated the Revolt and Protestantism with chaos, sedition, and the destruction of social hierarchy, and in angry poems he reviled this world-turned-upside-down where 'weavers and women'

[22] Kaplan, *Calvinists and Libertines*, pp. 47–51, 292–304.
[23] See for a more extensive version of what follows, and on Buchelius in general, Pollmann, *Religious Choice*.
[24] E.g. Arnoldus Buchelius, 'Acta diurna in itinere Gallico et Italico', Ms. 1640, fo. 9v (19 August 1584), fo. 23v (1 January 1585), fo. 26v (10 April 1585), fo. 96v (April 1586), fo. 98r (9 April 1586), University Library Utrecht.
[25] E.g. Katharina Boudewyns, 'Een ander [schoon liedeken]', in Gerrit Komrij (ed.), *De Nederlandse poëzie van de 12de tot en met de 16de eeuw in 1000 en enige bladzijden* (Amsterdam, 1994), pp. 1186–8; *Dagboek van Broeder Wouter Jacobsz*, ed. I.H. van Eeghen, 2 vols. (Groningen, 1959–60), vol. 1, pp. 3–4, 8, 14–17; Wiebe Bergsma, 'Adliger im exil: Johan Rengers ten Post', in Hajo van Lengen (ed.), *Die 'Emder Revolution' von 1595* (Aurich, 1995), pp. 19–20; Wiebe Bergsma, *De wereld volgens Abel Eppens: een Ommelander boer in de zestiende eeuw* (Groningen, 1988), pp. 146–8; Hendrik Spieghel, *Lieden op 't Vader Ons*, ed. Gilbert de Groote (Zwolle, 1956), p. 134.

interpreted the Bible and 'millers' ruled.[26] The Calvinist coup in Utrecht in 1586 and the ensuing years of militant Calvinist rule did nothing to abate his suspicions. It was only after Holland had helped to restore Utrecht's old 'Libertine' elite to power, in 1588, that he became reconciled to the existence of the Dutch Republic. A trip to Germany, in the meantime, had increased his knowledge of the Protestant tradition, even if it by no means tempted him to join their ranks. Rather, as he learned more about Protestantism, and as he began to believe that Protestantism and political orderliness were not mutually exclusive, he decided to make up his own mind about religious issues. By the late 1580s he had, to all extent and purposes, become one of the 'unaffiliated'. He relied on Christian ethics and his own reading of Scripture, not on confessional resources, to solve a major personal crisis, and now adopted that casual attitude to confessional difference that was so typical for many Dutch, but which clergy of all denominations found deeply disturbing.[27] He was praying to the saints one moment, attending a Reformed service the other, being godfather to a Catholic child one day, and discussing Coornhert the next.[28] Yet it was not a position which was a matter of principle for him. Soon after his marriage in 1593 to Claesje van Voorst, whose family had strong links with Utrecht Libertinism, Buchelius became affiliated to Utrecht's 'Libertine' Reformed Church.[29]

But it was not only marriage that prompted this move. Having grown up in the chaotic world of the Revolt, Buchelius had always been immensely concerned about the religious fragmentation of his society. In a remarkable text from the mid-1590s, written soon after he had joined the Church, he argued that confessional differences did not matter:

Since we all gaze at the same stars, and all aim for the same goal of eternity, what does it matter by which knowledge each man seeks the truth, by which road he has reached the end of his course? He was right [who said] that it is not possible to arrive at such a great mystery by one route only, but one goal is set for all, and one door is open to those who hasten towards it. We seek Christ and Him

---

[26] See e.g. Arnoldus Buchelius, 'Farrago poematum juvenilium/Epistolarum farrago', Ms. 836, fo. 45r, fo. 48v, University Library Utrecht; Pollmann, *Religious Choice*, pp. 39–40, 49, 52–3.

[27] Kaplan, *Calvinists and Libertines*, p. 80; Woltjer, 'De plaats van de calvinisten', 18; W. Bergsma, 'Calvinisten en libertijnen. Enkele opmerkingen n.a.v. Benjamin Kaplan, *Calvinists and Libertines. Confession and Community in Utrecht*', *Doopsgezinde Bijdragen*, New Series 22 (1996).

[28] Arnoldus Buchelius, 'Commentarius rerum quotidianarum, in quo, praeter itinera diversarum regionum, urbium, oppidorumque situs, antiquitates, principes, instituta, mores, multa eorum quae tam inter publicos quam privatos contingere solent, occurrent exempla', Ms. 798, vol. II, fo. 111v (23 September 1589), fo. 132v (10 October 1589), fo. 144r (16 June 1591), fo. 155v (August 1591), University Library Utrecht.

[29] On this Church see Kaplan, *Calvinists and Libertines*.

we follow, albeit along different roads; and the man who resolves upon this aim cannot go astray.[30]

This passage can be read as a plea for tolerance, but it is also a plea for concord, and hence for conformity. Its implication is not that the proliferation of doctrinal disputes is harmless. In fact, it is extremely dangerous, because it diverts people from the goal that truly matters, Christ, and from the service that man owes Him, in the form of *pietas*. To Buchelius' mind, there was apparently no possibility of disagreement over the meaning of *pietas* itself. It is the respect due to God and His commandments, respect for tradition, respect for one's past, that expressed itself in virtuous and charitable behaviour. Although the type of Christian doctrine that was followed ultimately did not matter, Buchelius measured its value through its ability to further *pietas*. The incessant religious changes had demonstrated that people were only too likely to 'fashion their own Gods' and make this an excuse for introducing novelty and sedition. Although the old Church was in many ways much better suited to protect *pietas* in his society, conformity was the only answer to the threat of strife, godlessness, and impiety that threatened to overwhelm the Dutch.

Gradually, he became more and more committed to the Church he had originally seen as a second-best alternative, and this expressed itself in a growing sense of confessional superiority. By the mid-1590s he actively criticised Catholicism for its 'reliance on external matters' and he supported the suppression of Catholic worship at the ruins of former Churches.[31] In the meantime, the Utrecht Reformed Church began to shed more and more of its 'Libertine' characteristics, but Buchelius did not deplore this development and in fact hardly noticed it. Still, it is somewhat surprising to see that Buchelius developed into an orthodox Counter-Remonstrant Calvinist. Since his religious development during the Twelve Years' Truce and the great Arminian–Gomarist conflict about predestination is not very well documented, it is not altogether clear how he ended up in the Counter-Remonstrant camp. We can, however, identify a number of good personal and political reasons which may have driven him to this stance. Personal contacts, anxiety about Holland's domination in the Union, a dislike of the Truce, and deep contempt for Gillis van Ledenberg, Oldenbarnevelt's powerbroker in Utrecht, all steered him into the camp of the winners of 1618.[32]

Yet such sound political reasons for supporting the Gomarists did not detract from the seriousness of his commitment to the Counter-Remonstrant cause, from which he – incidentally – did not reap much

---

[30] Buchelius, 'Commentarius', vol. I, fo. 44v.
[31] Buchelius, 'Commentarius', vol. II, fo. 200r (July 1595), ff. 233r–v (August 1598).
[32] Pollmann, *Religious Choice*, pp. 104–37.

political or material profit himself. The journals and letters he wrote after 1618 show that Buchelius was now a very committed Reformed believer, a pillar of the Church, and a fully-fledged participant of Calvinist culture at its most confessionalised. In 1622 he became an elder of Utrecht's Reformed Church. He was to serve two terms, campaigning vigorously for Reformed education and for discipline in the Church and lamenting the authorities' lack of commitment to the Reformed cause.[33] In the 1630s he was an ardent supporter of Gisbertus Voetius, who for decades was one of the most outspoken proponents of Calvinist orthodoxy in the Republic, and he was hotly in favour of the latter's appointment to the Reformed ministry in Utrecht.[34]

Although there was good reason for the Reformed Church to feel that there was still much progress to be made in Utrecht, it may seem peculiar to find that Buchelius considered its position to be highly precarious. Yet it is his complete absence of a sense of victory that turns Buchelius into a clear representative of the Counter-Remonstrant victors of 1618.[35] An extraordinary siege mentality dominated much Reformed discourse after 1618, in Utrecht as elsewhere, and both Buchelius' journals and many of his letters, from 1619 until his death in 1641, express acute disappointment, anger, and anxiety about the state of Dutch society and the 'moderation' that threatened to overwhelm the Reformed Church.

Since the 1590s Buchelius' commitment to the war with Spain had grown enormously. By the 1620s, he was talking of the Spanish as the 'hereditary foe' and the 'natural enemy' of the Netherlands, and the struggle had gained mythical proportions as well as intense religious significance for him. Although he never made any references to this being the fight of a Dutch Israel, each development in the war, to him, reflected the workings of divine providence. In this titanic struggle with Spain, the presence of Arminians and Catholics was a security risk. After the Spanish attack on Cadzand in 1630, he noted gloomily that this was a triumph for the 'Romish, . . . these pests of our fatherland and the Republic in our midst'.[36] And when in 1623, after the discovery of the conspiracy against Stadholder Maurits, some Arminian canons in Utrecht

[33] See especially the journals he kept of his activities as an elder, i.e. 'Observationes ecclesiasticae sub presbyteratu meo (1622–1626)', Collectie Eysinga, EVC 1323a, Rijksarchief Friesland; and 'Ecclesiastica Ultraiectina (1626–1638)', Ms. 1053, University Library Utrecht.

[34] Buchelius, 'Ecclesiastica', fo. 113r (1636).

[35] J.L. Price, *Holland and the Dutch Republic in the Seventeenth Century. The Politics of Particularism* (Oxford, 1994), p. 202.

[36] *Notae Quotidianae van Aernout van Buchell*, ed. J.W. van Campen. Werken uitgegeven door het Historisch Genootschap, 3rd Series, vol. LXX (Utrecht, 1940), p. 14 (September 1630).

decided it was safer to put in an appearance at the Dom, Buchelius commented:

I hope that others whose conscience is not as yet completely branded and in whose hearts there still remains some love for their fatherland will follow them, so that thus united we may thank the Almighty God, and through God's grace may employ ourselves with the more industry to the welfare and protection of the country.[37]

Even if the clandestine Churches were not actually assisting the Spanish, they were clearly out to destabilise the Republic, whilst their disobedience itself contributed to the 'confusion' that to Buchelius had always been a sign of evil. After the controversial imprisonment of the Utrecht Arminian, Abraham Halinck, in March 1627, Buchelius and minister Bernhard Bushof explained to a worried Church member that men like Halinck were 'pests in a Republic and poison in the community, whatever appearance of godliness they were feigning'.[38]

Yet it was, above all, the moral influence of Arminians and Catholics that threatened society and which made it imperative to curb their activities. The Catholics, of course, were breaking God's commandments and were thus soliciting divine wrath. Buchelius noted how their conventicles promoted 'scandalous idolatry and a denial of the only sacrifice made by Christ on the Cross, and would therefore do nothing but aggravate the wrath of God towards our lands'.[39] Still, Buchelius seems to have been lamenting the blindness and stupidity of Catholics rather than their wickedness. Schools in Utrecht's former convents still inhabited by 'former' nuns, he lamented in 1624, were 'seminaries' of 'all horrors, so openly in conflict with the will of God, exercised so stubbornly, and supported with such mistaken zeal by wandering, blind people'.[40]

Matters were undoubtedly much more serious when it came to the Arminians. Buchelius was convinced that their doctrines were not just wrong, but were actively contributing to the decay of the Christian fibre of society. Some Counter-Remonstrant propagandists, like the minister Festus Hommius whom Buchelius admired, had long claimed that behind the five Remonstrant articles there lurked infinitely more sinister doctrinal aberrations, akin to Libertinism, Socinianism, or even atheism.[41] Buchelius lent a willing ear to such associations. In 1638 he heard about the findings of the spies that the Utrecht theology professor and Reformed minister, Gisbertus Voetius, sent to Remonstrant services,

[37] Buchelius, 'Observationes', fo. 68v (16 February 1623).
[38] Buchelius, 'Ecclesiastica', fo. 16v (5 March 1627).
[39] Buchelius, 'Ecclesiastica', ff. 70r–v (6 April 1628).
[40] Buchelius, 'Observationes', ff. 139v–140r (28 July 1624).
[41] Van Deursen, *Bavianen en slijkgeuzen*, pp. 288–9.

where their 'rabbis', as he called them, preached a doctrine that was near to Socinianism: 'They rob our Holy Savior Jesus Christ of his divinity. Eternity, merit, baptism and Holy Communion are held in small esteem by them.'[42] When reconciliation with an Arminian member of the Church seemed to fail in March 1623, Buchelius noted that in his opinion the Church could achieve little with these people and was exposing itself to danger in the process: 'For once they [i.e. the Church] have let in Libertinism – that is, opened the window to atheism – they can be very easily driven by the slightest wind from one thing to another, under the specious label of moderation.'[43]

Buchelius' conviction that Arminianism steered its adherents from bad to worse was based on the idea that Arminians could easily develop into a type of *perfectists*. Their assertion that election is the fruit of faith, granted and foreseen by God, but potentially to be forfeited by those who reject this gift, to Buchelius' mind had transformed itself into a doctrine that asserted that man could attain perfection and justification under his own steam.[44] Such a doctrine tempted human sinners into trusting themselves rather than God, and would inevitably steer them away from His commandments towards living for their own human desires.

In Buchelius we can thus recognise a type of Calvinist that is only too familiar, deeply anxious and very intolerant. To him, the Church could not simply be a righteous island in a society of sinners. It was the task of both the Church and the authorities to root out godlessness. Failure to do so would inevitably provoke the anger of the Almighty, and lead to the destruction of the Republic. As he put it in a speech to the consistory in 1626,

The examples are fresh, our neighbours are our mirrors, in whose agony and destruction we may see our future misery should we not seek to improve our lives . . . [And we pray to God almighty] that he will move the hearts of our authorities and move us all to true repentance and shame over our past failings.[45]

Yet when we come to look at how this conviction affected his actual behaviour towards individuals of other faiths, the picture suddenly changes completely. Buchelius wrote some of his most emotive and personal statements about his faith, not to one of his brethren in the Church, but to one of those he supposedly considered a 'pest of the Republic'. Caspar Barlaeus, an Arminian theologian whose career had been wrecked by Buchelius' own Church, was told by Buchelius to rest assured that God would preserve him.

---

[42] *Notae Quotidianae*, pp. 69–70 (July 1638).
[43] Buchelius, 'Observationes', fo. 72r (20 March 1623).
[44] See e.g. Buchelius, 'Ecclesiastica', fo. 16v (5 March 1627).
[45] Buchelius, 'Observationes', fo. 141r (28 July 1624).

Buchelius' friendship with Caspar Barlaeus was, in fact, only one of the many contacts he had and continued to make with people of different denominations throughout his life. He maintained an old friendship with the Catholic nobleman Johannes de Witt until the latter's death in 1622.[46] He had worked together intensively with the Mennonite engraver Crispijn de Passe, and he was a lifelong friend and admirer of the Catholic painter Abraham Bloemaert.[47] His antiquarian friends Petrus Scriverius and Gerardus Vossius both had Arminian sympathies, while his much younger friend and the future editor of his work, Gijsbert Lap van Waveren, was a devout Catholic.[48] During a short spell in the Amsterdam chamber of the United East India Company, he was a staunch champion of his fellow-Utrechter, the Catholic admiral Steven van der Haghen.[49] But it is in his friendship with Barlaeus, which is exceptionally well documented, that we can best see how Buchelius combined his hard-line public principles with warm private contacts with those whose beliefs he did not share.

Buchelius was first introduced to Caspar Barlaeus in 1626. Between 1612 and 1619 Barlaeus had been a tutor at the Statencollege – the theological college – and later Professor of Logic at Leiden. He had supported the Arminian theologians at the Synod of Dordt, had written bitter pamphlets against the Gomarists, and was the personal friend of many of the Arminian leaders. As an ordained minister he was forced to sign the *Akte van Stilstand*, promising that he would no longer preach or publish on religious issues, and he was dismissed from his position at Leiden. After his dismissal, he had studied medicine in France, but discovered that he hated practising it and supported his family by teaching privately in Leiden. Although his sympathy remained with the Remonstrants, he did

[46] J.B.M.M. Sterk, 'Johannes de Wit Stevenszoon', *Jaarboek Oud-Utrecht* (1974), 108–62; A. Hulshof and P.S. Breuning, 'Brieven van Johannes de Witt', *Bijdragen en Mededelingen van het Historisch Genootschap* 60 (1939), 87–208.

[47] On the relationship with De Passe, see Pollmann, *Religious Choice*, p. 127; Ilja Veldman, 'Keulen als toevluchtsoord voor Nederlandse kunstenaars (1567–1612)', *Oud Holland* 107 (1993), 47–51. On the relationship with Bloemaert, see Marten-Jan Bok, 'Abraham Bloemaert', in Albert Blankes and Leonard J. Slatkes (eds.), *Nieuw licht op de Gouden Eeuw. Hendrick ter Brugghen en tijdgenoten* (Utrecht, 1987) pp. 208–12; Marten-Jan Bok, 'Biographies and Documents', in Marcel G. Roethlisberger, *Abraham Bloemaert and his Sons. Paintings and Prints* (Doornspijk, 1993).

[48] On Lap, see H.M.J. Müter, 'Gijsbertus Lap van Waveren. Historicus te Utrecht, 1596–1647', *Archief voor de Geschiedenis van de Katholieke Kerk in Nederland* 1 (1959), 169–229. On Vossius, C.S.M. Rademaker, *Life and Work of Gerardus Johannes Vossius (1577–1649)* (Assen, 1981). On Scriverius, the anonymous 'Het leven van Petrus Scriverius', in *Gedichten van Petrus Scriverius, Benevens een Uuytvoerige Beschrijving van het Leeven des Dichters*, ed. S. Doekes (Amsterdam, 1738), pp. 37–8.

[49] 'Verweerschrift gesteld door A. van Buchel ten behoeve van Steven van der Haghe', *Utrechtse Volks-Almanak* 31 (1867), 170–81; M.A.P. Meilink-Roelofsz, 'Steven van der Haghen', in L.M. Akveld et al. (eds.), *Vier eeuwen varen* (Bussum, 1973), pp. 26–49.

not dare to act as an Arminian minister himself. He did, however, remain close to the Arminian leadership, particularly to Simon Episcopius, and made no secret of his friendship with them.[50]

Buchelius and Barlaeus maintained a typical Humanist correspondence in the genre of 'familiar letters', in which every subject was allowed as long as it was discussed with scholarly elegance. The basis of their friendship was an interest in the *studia humanitatis*. They had many friends in common, and kept each other up to date about the publication of new books and academic gossip. Buchelius also tried to be of practical help to Barlaeus, and solicited information about a fund which Barlaeus hoped might benefit his son. After a few years, the men became closer and started to touch on more personal matters, like Buchelius' approaching death and Barlaeus' attacks of melancholy.

It was as citizens of the *Respublica literaria* that the men had met and had become friends, but they did not ignore the fact that there were higher loyalties. After all, as Barlaeus reminded his friend, 'as guests on earth our abode is in heaven; we are colonists of the one Republic, but citizens of the other'.[51] But although God is indeed omnipresent in their correspondence, Buchelius and Barlaeus took great care not to make any mention of the doctrinal and church political issues that divided them. They showed a clear and great appreciation for each other's piety. Barlaeus admired Buchelius' combination of *eruditio*, *pietas*, and *simplicitas*, and dedicated several religious poems to his friend. He contrasted 'the type of learned man which this age, barren of virtue as it is, produces' with Buchelius' approach: 'More wisely, you take your morals from the teaching itself, and by the bond of Christian piety have joined a large number of excellent virtues to yourself.' He hoped that his *Hymnus in Christum* would serve Buchelius as David's harp had served to alleviate the melancholy of Saul, would lighten the sadness of his old age, and chase away Buchelius' fears of death by reminding him that 'there is no condemnation for those who are in Christ'.[52]

Buchelius, in his reply, praised Barlaeus' *Hymnus* as coming from 'a true prophet and theologian' who had spoken beautifully about the mysteries of religion, and he thanked him warmly for his 'admonishment'.

---

[50] J.A. Worp's biography, 'Caspar van Baerle', *Oud-Holland* 3 (1885), 241–65; *ibid.* 4 (1886), 24–40, 172–89, 241–61; *ibid.* 5 (1887), 93–126; *ibid.* 6 (1888), 87–102, 241–76; *ibid.* 7 (1889), 89–128, remains the best general study. On Barlaeus' depressions, see F.F. Blok, *Caspar Barlaeus. From the Correspondence of a Melancholic* (Assen, 1976), and on his later conflicts with the Contra-Remonstrants, F.F. Blok, 'Caspar Barlaeus en de Joden. De geschiedenis van een epigram', *Nederlands Archief voor Kerkgeschiedenis* 57 (1977), 179–209, and *ibid.* 58 (1978), 85–108.

[51] Barlaeus to Buchelius, 8 May 1627 (ns), in Caspar Barlaeus, *Epistolarum liber*, ed. G. Brandt (Amsterdam, 1667), no. 57, p. 188.

[52] Barlaeus to Buchelius, 7 January 1629 (ns), in Barlaeus, *Epistolarum liber*, no. 104, p. 267.

He said that the contemplation of his own sins often deeply depressed him, but that

the words of Him who cannot deceive bring consolation: 'I do not desire the death of the sinner, but that he be converted and live'. I acknowledge my frailty and recognise the hardness of my heart. I seek and await a remedy from the One God and know that He will not reject the supplicant. The spectacles and crimes of human life which I see urge me more towards the thought of eternal matters. . . . I have now rightly come to despise this vile age and to hanker after the coming joys of blessedness. May the greatest Knower of Hearts grant these to us, He who will preserve you and me and all good men for salvation.[53]

This letter, probably the most pietist in style that Buchelius was ever to write, shows how much his Calvinism had influenced his piety, but simultaneously makes it overwhelmingly clear that Buchelius thought Barlaeus at least as likely to be saved as himself. For Buchelius, the elect were clearly not just to be found within the Church. Neither Barlaeus' ongoing close association with the Arminian camp, nor Buchelius' militant Calvinist sympathies, hampered their friendship. There was controversy over the founding of the Athenaeum Illustre in Amsterdam by the Arminian Amsterdam magistracy in 1631, and the appointment of both Barlaeus and Vossius did nothing to alleviate Counter-Remonstrant suspicions.[54] Yet there was not a hint of suspicion in Buchelius, who rejoiced in his friend's good fortune, although he pitied him for having to live amongst the mercenary Amsterdammers.[55] And even when Barlaeus, a few years later, came under attack from Buchelius' own party, this did not affect their friendship.

Early in 1635, Barlaeus had written an epigram for *De creatione problemata*, a treatise by the Amsterdam rabbi Menasseh Ben Israel. He had apparently not realised that this might involve him in the debate about the toleration of Jews which since 1633 had been raging between the Reformed minister Nicolaus Vedelius and the Remonstrant Simon Episcopius. With a little effort one could read into Barlaeus' poem the notion that both Judaism and Christianity revered the same God, precisely the point on which Vedelius and Episcopius disagreed. More than a year after its publication, Vedelius decided to take Barlaeus to task for his epigram. Martin Schoock, one of Voetius' favourite pupils and tutor of rhetoric at Utrecht, joined the attack. By the autumn of 1636,

53 Buchelius to Barlaeus, 26 January 1629, Ms. 985, University Library Utrecht.
54 Chris L. Heesakkers, 'Foundation and Early Development of the Athenaeum Illustre at Amsterdam', *Lias* 9 (1982), 5–6; P. Dibon, *La Philosophie néerlandaise au Siècle d'Or*, vol. i, *L'Enseignement philosophique dans les universités à l'époque précartesienne (1575–1650)* (Paris, 1954), pp. 224–5.
55 Buchelius to Barlaeus, 22 June 1631, Ms. Pap. 2, University Library Leiden.

Barlaeus found to his horror that his poem was being used as proof of the dangerous Judaising and atheistic tendencies of the Remonstrants. There even circulated a rumour that he was to be officially charged with Socinianism.[56]

Behind the scenes, it was none other than Gisbertus Voetius, Buchelius' hero, who led the campaign against Barlaeus. Voetius often made use of others, particularly Schoock, to do his polemical dirty work for him, and Barlaeus and his friends knew very well that Voetius was behind it. Deeply worried, Barlaeus wrote an angry refutation of his critics, and sent a copy to Buchelius.[57] Buchelius hastened to read Barlaeus' apology and sent him a subtle reply, expressing total confidence in his friend, but also hinting that he based this on his knowledge of Barlaeus rather than on total disagreement with his critics.

He knew, he said, that Barlaeus' critics claimed he had become such an avid friend of Menasseh, this 'adversary of Christianity, who (as they say) openly proclaims that Christ Himself is an impostor', that Barlaeus had come to share his religious convictions. Buchelius thought Barlaeus had explained very well 'how different it is, on the one hand, to keep company with someone in a political or civic context and to discuss profane subjects (it is stated nowhere that Christians are prohibited to do so with Turks, Jews and barbarians) and, on the other hand, to worship the same sacred things with him'. Barlaeus' whole life was, in fact, proof that his commitment to Christ and God was strong enough not to be overturned by civil contacts with a Jew. What had unfortunately lent credibility to the slander of his critics, however, was that there were indeed people who had come to the dangerous conclusion that Turks and Jews had the right to exercise their religion, 'which I consider to be alien to a true Christian and see as an attack on the truth and as going completely astray from the faith of those who founded our religion with their blood'. In any case, he said that he had such ample experience of Barlaeus' 'piety towards God and sincerity towards men' that he could never suspect his friend of fostering such ideas.[58] This argument enabled Buchelius to argue on the one hand that there was need to fight the ideas Barlaeus was accused of promoting, and on the other to maintain that Barlaeus himself was not guilty of harbouring these. Interestingly, Barlaeus himself used a similar approach. In his reaction to Buchelius' letter, Barlaeus contrasted the behaviour of his critics, who had not had the charity to ask him what

[56] See on this affair, Blok, 'Caspar Barlaeus en de Joden'.
[57] Caspar Barlaeus, *Vindiciae Epigrammatis viri clarissimi Casparis Barlaei, philosophiae in illustri Amstelodamensium gymnasio professoris, adversus improbas theologi cuiusdam anonymi criminationes* (Amsterdam, 1636).
[58] Buchelius to Barlaeus, 17 September 1636, Ms. Pap. 2(9), University Library Leiden.

he meant by the poem before they attacked him, with the attitude of his friend: 'It is sweeter, my Buchelius, to speak with you, to whom pious old age dictates better words and whose mind it has bent to all civility, grace and love towards me.'[59]

The exchange provides interesting insights into the strategies that could be employed to avoid the souring of a personal friendship by the bitter animosity between the camps in which they stood. Not only did they have no problems in communicating in a civil or political context, they also managed to find a way to worship the same sacred things, by each rigorously restricting these to the tangible, experienced piety they detected in the other. The Dutch Confession stated that the 'marks' by which one could recognise those Christians who truly were of the Church were 'faith, and [that] when they have accepted the one Redeemer Jesus Christ, [they] flee sin and seek justice, love the true God and their neighbours, do not verge to the left or the right, and crucify their flesh with His works'.[60] Buchelius obviously detected these marks in Barlaeus, despite the fact that his friend had not done what the Confession stated all humans ought to, that is, 'separate themselves from those who are not of the Church and join this gathering'.[61]

Both Buchelius' intolerant stance towards Catholics and Arminians as abstract categories, and his tolerance of private individuals, were genuine. But why did he see no conflict between the two? The answer to this question seems to be that as far as Buchelius was concerned religion was to a large extent about tangible, visible piety. Buchelius became obsessed by confessional orthodoxy, but not because he had withdrawn into splendid confessional isolation. If one looks at the reasons Buchelius gave for the importance of discipline and purity within the Church, one cannot escape the paradoxical conclusion that ultimately these did not so much concern the Church itself as society at large. Moderation in the Church, he said, was so dangerous because 'it would disturb the community, attract many to Popery, bring many to Libertinism, because they do not have anything firm to lean on'.[62] It was precisely this function of the Church, to give people something to lean on, that had attracted him to its membership in the 1590s. The chaos of the 1580s and 1590s had led him to exclaim that 'Christian religion is withering and is disappearing in the divergence of opinions, so that it is on its way to becoming the laughing-stock of

---

[59] Barlaeus to Buchelius, 25 October 1636 (ns), in Barlaeus, *Epistolarum liber*, no. 345, pp. 685–6.

[60] 'Nederlandse geloofsbelijdenis (1619)', in J.N. Bakhuizen van den Brink (ed.), *De Nederlandse belijdenisgeschriften in authentieke teksten met inleiding en tekstvergelijkingen* (Amsterdam, 1976), art. XXIX.

[61] *Ibid.*, art. XXXVIII.   [62] Buchelius, 'Ecclesiastica', fo. 85v (23 April 1629).

the common people.'[63] He had looked for a force that could clearly and firmly guide people towards *pietas*, an awe of God and of His order in society, rather than trust in their own opinions and desires.

From very early in his life, Buchelius had diagnosed human presumption and pride as the main diseases of his society. The pestiferous influence of both Arminianism and Catholicism, let alone Libertinism and atheism, according to Buchelius, had its roots in the illusory role they reserved for the works of man, the illusion that man by himself or his works could be, or become, perfect. Such illusions could but lead to one thing, to a society where human concerns, and thus human sins, ruled – a society in chaos. Greed, ambition, sedition all fed on human presumption and pride. And these sins, as he repeated over and over again, were certain to elicit divine punishment. The Church was thus to have an exemplary, guiding function for society as well as for its own members. This, in turn, made it imperative for the Church itself to be exemplary in its zeal for piety, something that to Buchelius – probably as a result of the Gomarist–Arminian controversy – had come to imply that it could not compromise.

But Buchelius' conception of the Church's role did not of course rule out the possibility that people outside it could be pious, as pious indeed as the people within it. Whether they preached that piety was the *expression* or the *means* of salvation, both Protestant and Catholic Churches stressed that the Christian should be seen to be pious. Yet if a good Christian would be recognisable as a good person, it was hard to deny that when someone was a good person, he or she was also likely to be a good Christian. Buchelius' ideas on what it meant to be pious changed remarkably little in the course of his life and remained rooted in general Christian notions rather than confessional norms. In judging his fellow humans, Buchelius looked towards their 'piety towards God, and sincerity towards men'. When he saw these in evidence, there was no reason not to interact with them.

He also seems to have avoided personal confrontations. Buchelius' aggression towards those of other faiths was rarely vented in public. The one known occasion at which he was involved in an open religious quarrel, in 1623, was when he was approached by an acquaintance who insisted on discussing a new work by Hugo Grotius with him. He gave his opinion, yet when the discussion became too heated he quickly took his leave, rather than to prolong the argument.[64] Even in his role as an elder, he rarely directly confronted those whom he criticised, or drew confrontations to

---

[63] Buchelius, 'Commentarius', vol. II, fo. 166r (19 December 1591).
[64] Buchelius, 'Observationes', fo. 74v (1 April 1623).

their bitter end. When he and a minister accidentally encountered an Arminian minister who was sought by the authorities, they rebuked him but did not hand him over.[65] Back in the consistory chamber, of course, they bitterly complained that the authorities were not acting with more resolve against the Arminians.

These last examples to some extent bear out Willem Frijhoff's interesting suggestion that there were spaces that were, and spaces that were not, appropriate for expressing confessional sentiments and opinions.[66] Yet perhaps we can take it a step further, and distinguish two religious modes, not only appropriate for different spaces, but also for different social roles. In private contacts, Buchelius applied the rules and norms of an a-confessional Christianity. When it came to the needs of society and the Church that had to keep it in check, however, he adhered to a confessional worldview that related to the collective fate of society. Thus, he did not hesitate to write a friendly Latin caption for a portrait of a former Arminian minister in Utrecht.[67] But as an elder he did refuse to readmit the man to communion.[68] Buchelius was not unique in this, nor was it an attitude that was typical for the Reformed alone.[69] Concerning the poet Joost van den Vondel, who had converted to Catholicism and did everything to spread it amongst his friends, it was said that 'he considered non-Catholics to be heretics, but he had a very high opinion of his [Mennonite] grandfather Kranen, and, because of his simple piety, expected the best for him, despite the fact that he had died a non-Catholic.'[70] Like Buchelius, Vondel thus operated in two religious modes, one connected with confessional religion, the other based on an a-confessional concept of piety. It is these modes, too, which Gilbert Burnet, who lived in the Netherlands for a long time in the 1680s, seems to be describing when he explains what he had learned there: 'I saw so many men of all persuasions that were, as far as I could perceive, so truly religious, that I never think the worse of a man for his opinions.'[71] In the Netherlands

---

[65] *Ibid.*, fo. 76r (3 April 1623).

[66] Frijhoff, 'Dimensions de la coexistence', pp. 228–34.

[67] In Henricus Caesarius, *Staet van regeringhe, nae den wijsen raedt van Iethro priester in Midian tot Moses sijnen swager/Exod. 18.21.22, voor-gestelt alle overheeden hooge ende leege als coningen, princen, staten ende heeren, soo oock alle andere magistraten ende ampt-draghende persoonen over haere onderdaenen* (Utrecht, 1625), p. [5].

[68] Buchelius, 'Ecclesiastica', fo. 41v (12 August 1627), ff. 42v–43r (14 August 1627), fo. 43r (19 August 1627), fo. 44r (2 September 1627), fo. 62v (2 March 1628).

[69] Note e.g. the views of the diarist Lodewijck van der Saen later in the century. See Donald Haks, 'Een wereldbeeld uit de "middelmaetigen stant". De aantekeningen van Lodewijk van der Saen, 1695–1699', *Tijdschrift voor Sociale Geschiedenis* 24 (1998), 113–37.

[70] Geeraardt Brandt, 'Het leven van Joost van den Vondel', in Joost van den Vondel, *Poëzy, of Verscheide Gedichten*, 2 vols. (Franeker, 1682), vol. II, p. 76.

[71] Cited in Van Strien, *British Travellers*, p. 203.

a culture of 'persuasion' (or confessional allegiance and doctrinal purity) co-existed with one of 'religion' (or a-confessional Christian piety). Believers were able and willing to participate in both these cultures. However, few of them were prepared to go as far as Burnet in accepting the principle of religious diversity. Even if private, social, bonds often prevailed over confessional enmity, we cannot ignore that people like Buchelius and Vondel also found confessional differences important enough to think of the collective, abstract 'other' as a danger. It was not just their society that was Janus-faced, it was individual Dutch believers, tolerant and intolerant at one and the same time.

5 Religious policies in the seventeenth-century Dutch Republic

Joke Spaans

There is a general and long-standing agreement among historians that the Dutch Republic was tolerant on the issue of religion. Still, it is not at all easy to determine how this celebrated toleration actually worked out in practice. It is evident that religious toleration was a hotly debated issue. Jonathan Israel has recently mapped out these discussions and the shifts in their focus.[1] This makes religious toleration an obvious object of study in the history of ideas. The leap from these ideas and discussions to the practicalities that ruled interconfessional relations in the Dutch Republic is seldom attempted, partly because our knowledge of toleration in practice, and why it worked the way it did, is still highly impressionistic.

Toleration as a topic in Dutch historiography

This gap in our understanding of the place of religion in Dutch society, and how this society coped with religious diversity, is mainly a product of historiographical trends in the past. Religious toleration has long been, and still is, an item of national pride, and historians have not been really interested in the particulars of its legal basis and the policies that gave it its characteristic form. Historiographically religious toleration is embedded in the nineteenth-century contest over Dutch national identity that resulted in the famous *verzuiling* or 'pillarization'. Two strands of argument have to be mentioned here. The first puts toleration in the context of an ongoing struggle between intolerant ministers and humanist magistrates, between Calvinists and Libertines. Ministers are portrayed as a party that was set on moulding society after their theocratic ideals, but ran into increasing opposition of tolerant magistrates unwilling to have their own lifestyles censured by the Church. This view, that still has its defenders,[2]

---

[1] Jonathan Israel, 'The Intellectual Debate about Toleration in the Dutch Republic', in C. Berkvens-Stevelinck, J. Israel, and G.H.M. Posthumus Meyjes (eds.), *The Emergence of Tolerance in the Dutch Republic* (Leiden/New York/Cologne, 1997), pp. 3–36.

[2] The measure in which determined Calvinists attempted to force and succeeded in forcing Reformed Protestantism upon society at large is discussed around the so-called

owes much to the rivalries between Liberal and neo-orthodox Protestants in the nineteenth century. The former created a tolerant past, in an Erasmian spirit that closely fitted their ideal of a general national-Protestant Christianity pervading public life. The latter evoked a national history dominated by an almost theocratic Calvinism, favouring their creation of a sectional culture in which neo-orthodox Protestants, now freed from the constraints of Libertine *regenten*, could live their entire lives according to their own confessional norms.[3]

A second topic relevant to historical views of toleration under the Republic is the position of the Catholics. Here a liberal tradition argues that full citizens' rights were withheld and that some financial extortion took place by regrettably venal government officials, but that on the whole Dutch Catholics enjoyed remarkable freedoms compared with religious minorities elsewhere in early modern Europe. Catholic authors have countered that being systematically treated as second-rate citizens, denied access to the most prestigious areas of public life, and being the occasional victims of extortion as well is nothing to be cavalier about. Here again, Liberals saw the Republic as essentially tolerant – in fact exemplary according to early modern standards – whereas Catholic authors, set on underpinning Catholic emancipation, stressed the structural intolerance of the confessional state towards religious minorities.[4] Liberal Protestants, neo-orthodox Protestants, and Catholics each claimed to reflect the true national religious tradition, based on their partisan interpretation of religion in general and of the position of the public Church under the Republic in particular.

Each of these interpretations focuses mainly on Holland, where diversity was most pronounced. All are mainly concerned with the decades from the beginning of the Revolt to around the middle of the seventeenth century. Until recently religion in the seventeenth and eighteenth

---

'protestantiseringsthese' by L.J. Rogier, *Geschiedenis van het katholicisme in Noord-Nederland in de zestiende en zeventiende eeuw*, 3 vols. (Amsterdam, 1945–7); P. Geyl, 'De protestantisering van Noord-Nederland', in P. Geyl, *Verzamelde opstellen*, 4 vols. (Utrecht, 1978), vol. I, pp. 205–18; H.A. Enno van Gelder, 'Nederland geprotestantiseerd?', *Tijdschrift voor Geschiedenis* 81 (1968), 445–64. See also the use of the opposition Calvinists versus Libertines, for example by Andrew Pettegree, 'The Politics of Toleration in the Free Netherlands, 1572–1620', in Ole Peter Grell and Bob Scribner (eds.), *Tolerance and Intolerance in the European Reformation* (Cambridge, 1996), pp. 182–98, and, with more justification, in the exceptional case of Utrecht by Benjamin J. Kaplan, *Calvinists and Libertines. Confession and Community in Utrecht, 1578–1620* (Oxford, 1995).

[3] A reflection of these discussions in Dutch Church history appears in Peter van Rooden, *Religieuze regimes. Over godsdienst en maatschappij in Nederland, 1570–1990* (Amsterdam, 1996), pp. 147–68.

[4] The liberal view is presented in W.P.C. Knuttel, *De toestand der Nederlandsche katholieken ten tijde van de Republiek*, 2 vols. (The Hague, 1892–4); its Catholic opposite first and foremost in Rogier, *Geschiedenis van het katholicisme in Noord-Nederland*.

centuries was of little interest to historians. Developments after 1650 remain particularly unclear. This is changing now, but toleration is still hardly a favourite topic for historical research in this later period. It is more or less taken for granted. The emphasis is rather on the various ways Catholics, Lutherans, Mennonites, and Jews, once a modicum of acceptance was achieved, managed to build new religious communities and devise markers of communal identity to go with them.[5] In addition there is a growing interest in conviviality within confessionally mixed guilds, fraternities, and neighbourhoods and the concomitant ideology of civic republicanism.[6] In this way the question of how the officially Calvinist state treated its minorities and how this may have changed over time, in theory and in practice, is not systematically addressed.

Our understanding of toleration in the Dutch Republic thus remains impressionistic. The general idea is that it was there. The northern provinces of the Low Countries that rebelled against their Spanish overlord had written freedom of conscience into the Union of Utrecht (1579), the document that would come to function as a sort of constitution for the Republic. Persecution for, and inquisition into, religious convictions were officially rejected, and interconfessional relations were fairly harmonious. Membership of the public Reformed Church was voluntary, although members of dissenting Churches were barred from public office. The

---

[5] For example W.Th.M. Frijhoff, 'De paniek van juni 1734', *Archief voor de Geschiedenis van de Katholieke Kerk in Nederland* 19 (1977), 170–233; W.Th.M. Frijhoff, 'Katholieke toekomstverwachting ten tijde van de Republiek: structuur, en grondlijnen tot een interpretatie', *Bijdragen en Mededelingen betreffende de Geschiedenis der Nederlanden* 98 (1983), 430–59; Xander van Eck, *Kunst, twist en devotie. Goudse schuilkerken 1572–1795* (Delft, 1994); Marc Wingens, *Over de grens. De bedevaart van katholieke Nederlanders in de zeventiende en achttiende eeuw* (Nijmegen, 1994); Marit Monteiro, *Geestelijke maagden. Leven tussen klooster en wereld in Noord-Nederland gedurende de zeventiende eeuw* (Hilversum, 1996); an exceptional interest in the formal rules of tolerance in Theo Clemens, 'IJkpunt 1750. Op zoek naar nieuwe grenzen in het politiek-religieuze landschap van de Republiek', in C. Augustijn and E. Honée (eds.), *Vervreemding en verzoening. De relatie tussen katholieken en protestanten in Nederland 1550–2000* (Nijmegen, 1998), pp. 69–101; Alastair Hamilton, Sjouke Voolstra, and Piet Visser (eds.), *From Martyr to Muppy. A Historical Introduction to Cultural Assimilation Processes of a Religious Minority in the Netherlands: The Mennonites* (Amsterdam, 1994); C.Ch.G. Visser, *De Lutheranen in Nederland tussen katholicisme en calvinisme, 1566 tot heden* (Dieren, 1983); R.G. Fuks-Mansfeld, *De Sefardim in Amsterdam tot 1795. Aspecten van een joodse minderheid in een Hollandse stad* (Hilversum, 1989); Miriam Bodian, *Hebrews of the Portuguese Nation: Conversos and Community in Early Modern Amsterdam* (Bloomington, IN, 1997).

[6] Willem Frijhoff, 'La coexistence confessionnelle: complicités, méfiances et ruptures aux Provinces-Unies', in Jean Delumeau (ed.), *Histoire vécue du peuple chrétien*, 2 vols. (Toulouse, 1979), vol. II, pp. 229–57; and Willem Frijhoff, 'Dimensions de la coexistence confessionnelle', in C. Berkvens-Stevelinck, J. Israel, and G.H.M. Posthumus Meyjes (eds.), *The Emergence of Tolerance in the Dutch Republic* (Leiden/New York/Cologne, 1997), pp. 213–37.

Republic became a haven for those persecuted elsewhere in Europe. Toleration had its limits, but even though the penal laws against Catholics, and from the 1620s also against Arminians, were occasionally enforced, and Catholics were vulnerable to extortion, things could have been worse. Moreover, as time progressed, discrimination seems to have abated. Supposedly toleration, such as it was, found a soulmate in the emergent Enlightenment. In the eighteenth century, although dissenters remained excluded from public office, they could worship more or less openly and extortion was no longer considered appropriate. Under pietist influence the notion developed among Protestants from various confessional backgrounds that the confessional boundaries might not be absolute.

The Dutch Republic among confessional states

All this adds up to a general impression of a harmonious, almost spontaneous growth of religious toleration in the Dutch Republic. If this impression were true, that would make the country unique in early modern Europe.

Early modern Europe was made up of confessional states. Recent research by Heinz Schilling and Wolfgang Reinhard, Ronnie Hsia, and Jonathan Clark has considerably deepened our understanding of this phenomenon. The Reformation changed the relationship between Church and state, both in Protestant and in Catholic polities. The new arrangement derives its name 'confessional state' from the fact that rulers made extensive use of the possibilities organised religion offered to strengthen their power over their subjects, whether they ruled kingdoms, principalities, or cities. All regimes maintained and protected one official Church. They expected these Churches to help forge a communal identity and strengthen internal cohesion. A shared religion was supposed to weld rulers and subjects together under the Divine Protection that depended on an orderly religious life regulated by true doctrine, a well-ordered church organisation, decent public worship, and pious public conduct.

It is thus no coincidence that Reformation and the confessional period in religious history overlap state formation and absolutism in political history. There appears to be some difference of opinion on the chronological boundaries of the period of confessional states. For Schilling the period seems to end around 1675, with the appearance of formally accorded toleration. Hsia extends the period to around the middle of the eighteenth century, which suggests that Enlightened policies superseded the old order. For Clark the confessional state in England lasted until the late 1820s when finally the laws that limited the civil rights of Protestant dissenters and Catholics were repealed.[7] The confessional state was the early modern answer to the problem of religious diversity. Religious unity among the ruled was the ideal, but in many areas diversity was a fact of life. At best dissenters enjoyed some measure of protection under a religious peace or an official edict of toleration. In the worst case they suffered persecution and expulsion.[8] Whatever the degree of freedom allowed to tolerated faiths in practice, confessional states were always, by their very nature, intolerant towards religious dissent. Mark Goldie has lucidly and compellingly set forth how religious intolerance could be defended politically, ecclesiologically, and theologically. In political theory religious diversity was seen as a danger to political stability, a theory abundantly confirmed by the religious wars of the sixteenth and early seventeenth centuries. The ecclesiological argument ran that uniformity in religion, exercised in a state-backed national Church, guarantees the decency of worship and public piety on which divine favour depends. Theologically it was argued, mainly on the basis of the letters of the church father Augustine, that the state has a pastoral duty not only to protect the true Church, but also to take disciplinary measures against dissent. This is a pastoral duty, because forcing dissenters, both the wilfully obstinate and the honestly misled, into the Church is ultimately for their own good. Instead of tolerating error, the state should use its strong arm to make the dissenters listen to the instruction of the official Church.[9] Goldie's focus is on Restoration England, but this logic of intolerance was practically all-pervading. Confessional states all show a disciplinary approach to religious dissent. There is ample scope for variation here, but essentially the limited toleration of the English Toleration Act and the fierce persecution of Huguenots leading up to and

---

[7] Overview in: Heinz Schilling, 'Confessional Europe', in Thomas A. Brady, Heiko A. Oberman, and James D. Tracy (eds.), *Handbook of European History 1400–1600, Late Middle Ages, Renaissance and Reformation*, vol. II: *Visions, Programs and Outcomes* (Leiden, 1995), pp. 641–81; R. Po-Chia Hsia, *Social Discipline in the Reformation. Central Europe 1550–1750* (London, 1989); J.C.D. Clark, *English Society, 1688–1832. Ideology, Social Structure and Political Practice during the Ancien Régime* (Cambridge, 1985); J.C.D. Clark, *The Language of Liberty 1660–1832. Political Discourse and Social Dynamics in the Anglo-American World* (Cambridge, 1994), pp. 141–217; see also Clark's discussion with Joanna Innes in *Past and Present* 115 (1987), 165–200, and *ibid.* 117 (1989), 195–207.

[8] A concise overview in Wiebe Bergsma, 'Church, State and People', in Karel Davids and Jan Lucassen (eds.), *A Miracle Mirrored. The Dutch Republic in European Perspective* (Cambridge, 1995), pp. 196–228.

[9] Mark Goldie, 'The Theory of Religious Intolerance in Restoration England', in Ole Peter Grell, Jonathan Israel, and Nicholas Tyacke (eds.), *From Persecution to Toleration. The Glorious Revolution and Religion in England* (Oxford, 1991), pp. 331–68.

following on the Revocation of the Edict of Nantes stem from the same religio-political world view.

Coping with diversity

Did the rulers of the Dutch Republic ignore this early modern logic that they could allow their minorities steadily greater freedoms, or had they found a superior solution to the problem of religious diversity? No, they had not. They too held 'disciplinary' views about religious dissent. Only the location of these diverged from the pattern we know from other European countries.

Let us look at the concrete situation in the Republic and the changes over time. Initially the Revolt showed the characteristics of a religious war. Protagonists of the Revolt strongly identified with Calvinism, its most determined opponents with Catholicism. As soon as the actual warfare shifted from Holland and Zeeland, the heartland of the Revolt, to the borders, the religious situation behind the frontlines was stabilised.[10] From 1572 to 1594 the individual provinces, each of them bearers of sovereignty, all decided on the Reformed Church as the public Church. The option of religious peace, under which Protestants and Catholics would have the right to public worship alongside each other, attempted in Holland in the years 1572 and 1573 and proposed for the other provinces in 1578–9, proved shortlived. The basis for the religious configuration up to the separation of Church and state in 1796 was to be and to remain the Union of Utrecht with its proclamation of freedom of conscience and its rejection of inquisition into, and persecution for, religious conviction.

It bears pointing out that the first attempt to deal with religious diversity was religious peace. For this the young Republic could find inspiration and models in Switzerland, Germany, and France. There, repeated outbreaks of religious war ended each time with a succession of peace treaties in the course of the century between the Peace of Kappel in 1531 and the Peace of Westphalia in 1648. Religious peace treaties were meant to end open hostility between factions of opposing religious adherence. They allowed those of both opposing religions more or less equal rights, or, more commonly, an amount of freedom that reflected their actual political strength. In a number of cases this resulted in attempts at geographical separation between faiths. As it turned out that among Dutch Catholics some groups remained steadfastly loyal to the Catholic Habsburg regime

---

[10] In fact three clearly differentiated areas emerged, each with its own religio-political order: Van Rooden, *Religieuze Regimes*, pp. 20–2, 169–72.

78   *Joke Spaans*

which the Northern Provinces were in Revolt against, religious peace soon proved not to be a realistic option. Instead, from 1581 penal laws excluded Catholics from full citizens' rights and hampered their organisation as a religious community.[11]

The other staple solution to religious diversity was comprehension. Here England led the way. The Anglican Church combined a Protestant theology with a highly traditional form of liturgy. The express intention was to keep the country united in one faith that would be acceptable both to Reformers and traditionalists.[12] Although initially it did show promise, in the end this attempt would fail spectacularly. In the Dutch Republic, however, comprehension was doomed from the start. Both the character of the Reformed Church as a gathered rather than a national Church, and the decentralised structure of the secular power, made a comprehensive Protestant Church illusory, even though the ideal was strongly present. It became acute in the near-civil war during the Twelve Years' Truce (1609–21). The party that had advocated comprehension was crushed, and at the Synod of Dordt the Reformed Church affirmed its exclusive Calvinist character. The Arminian wing of the Reformed Church that had been closely associated with the losing party in this conflict, seceded from the Reformed Church as the Remonstrant Brotherhood. Penal laws were immediately issued against the Remonstrants, laws that show a marked similarity to those issued earlier against the Catholics. Both were formally denied all forms of religious organisation and church services in all but the most private settings because of the potentially political character of their organisations.[13]

So religious peace and comprehension were both impracticable. Still, that did not condemn the state to Libertarian laxity. Received wisdom has it that the secular authorities in the Republic paid lip-service only to the officially Calvinist confessional identity of the state, and left their subjects largely to their own convictions, conniving at religious organisation of nonconformists for purely pragmatic reasons. Tolerance was after all conducive to the trade interests of the merchant elite that ruled the cities and eventually the state itself, and was in accordance with the Erasmian humanism prevalent in this period.

[11] Olivier Christin, *La paix de religion. L'autonomisation de la raison politique au XVIe siècle* (Paris, 1997); Philip Benedict, ' "Un roi, une loi, deux fois": Parameters for the History of Catholic-Reformed Co-existence in France, 1555–1685', in Ole Peter Grell and Bob Scribner (eds.), *Tolerance and Intolerance*, pp. 65–93; Joke Spaans, *Haarlem na de Reformatie. Stedelijke cultuur en kerkelijk leven 1577–1622* (The Hague, 1989), pp. 64–8.
[12] Christopher Haigh, *English Reformations. Religion, Politics and Society under the Tudors* (Oxford, 1993), pp. 235–50.
[13] Jonathan Israel, *The Dutch Republic. Its Rise, Greatness and Fall 1477–1806* (Oxford, 1995), pp. 421–77; cf. Israel, 'The Intellectual Debate about Toleration', pp. 9–13.

The solution they found was indeed humanistic, but not in the spiritualist tradition that ran from Erasmus to Coornhert, in which the unknowability of true doctrine made toleration of confessional diversity a compelling necessity.[14] Rather, it appears that, in true humanist fashion, they looked for inspiration to Roman Civil Law. Here they found a set of rules that allowed religions other than the official State Church limited rights. Roman Law permitted voluntary societies without corporate identity whose sole aim was religious worship. They remained, however, *collegia illicita*. They were not allowed any organisation beyond regular devotional meetings and were denied communal possessions in order to prevent higher, more specifically political, aspirations. The supposition made here that Dutch policy towards religous diversity was informed by Roman Law needs further research, but some evidence can be presented.

Roman Laws on religious dissenters were invoked in Hugo de Groot's proposal for an ordinance on the admission of Jews. His argument was that as long as Jews remained a voluntary society, strictly separated from the Christian public sphere and its avenues of power and patronage, without corporate identity and thus without the means to amass communal property or funds, they could be allowed synagogues for public worship. Jews were attractive immigrants, commanding valuable trade networks that promised profits to the cities that received them. Allowing Jews official toleration under the provisions proposed by De Groot could, however, be construed as a precedent for allowing other dissidents, most importantly the politically suspect Catholics, similar freedom of worship. It is probably for this reason that De Groot's propositions never made it into formal law, although a number of cities admitted Jewish communities under regulations not unlike his.[15] In fact all dissenting communities, as long as they were considered politically dependable, often enjoyed the limited freedoms allowed to *collegia illicita* under Roman Law, while the strict penal laws were enforced only when tolerated communities or their clergy were suspected of political untrustworthiness.

Around the end of the seventeenth century the Roman Law code was again referred to in the development of jurisprudence around the position of other dissenting groups. In this period tolerated Churches were given responsibility over the relief of their own poor. Originally public welfare

---

[14] James D. Tracy, 'Erasmus, Coornhert and the Acceptance of Religious Disunity in the Body Politic: A Low Countries Tradition?', in C. Berkvens-Stevelinck, J. Israel, and G.H.M. Posthumus Meyjes (eds.), *The Emergence of Tolerance*, pp. 49–62, even suggests a close relation between this concept of tolerance and Dutch corporate traditions.

[15] Hugo de Groot, *Remonstrantie nopende de ordre dije in de landen van Hollandt ende Westvrieslandt dijent gestelt op de Joden*, ed. Jaap Meijer (Amsterdam, 1949), especially the legal appendix, p. 132.

had supported the locally settled poor irrespective of religion, except the full members of the Reformed Church, who could apply for welfare to the *diaconie* of their Church. In a number of places the Reformed *diaconie* was amalgamated with the local public welfare fund, in which case this joint welfare board supported all the locally settled poor, including Reformed Church members. In the second half of the seventeenth century, however, urban magistrates urged all Churches to provide for their poor members. This was hardly feasible without allowing these Churches to amass property in the accustomed way of poor-funds, that is by regular collections among Church members for daily expenses and by inviting donations and bequests that could be invested in bonds and real estate. The invested capital rendered long-term dependable revenues, acted as a reserve for incidental large expenses and in times of dearth, and also gave the administrators of poor-funds access to short-term credit. Legal difficulties were immediately presented, bringing up again the stipulations of the Roman Law code that permitted religious dissidents, as *collegia illicita*, no freedom of organisation beyond communal worship. Ultimately these were tacitly ignored, and in the eighteenth century tolerated religious communities were allowed corporate identity in all but name.[16]

To all appearances these Roman legal principles provided the basis for the differentiated treatment of religious groups outside the public Church even though they were never explicitly codified in Dutch laws or regulations. Their simple existence in the Roman Law code that was at the basis of government and administration sufficed. Following their rule of thumb Mennonites and Lutherans were generally allowed to worship in private, as they were considered to have no ulterior political motives, while same freedom was denied to Catholics and Arminians, among whom these motives were assumed.

---

[16] This development has been reconstructed both for Haarlem and Frisia: Joke Spaans, 'Katholieken onder curatele. Armenzorg als ingang voor overheidsbemoeienis in Haarlem in de achttiende eeuw', *Trajecta* 3 (1994), 120–2, and Joke Spaans, *Armenzorg in Friesland 1500–1800. Publieke zorg en particuliere liefdadigheid in zes Friese steden: Leeuwarden, Bolsward, Franeker, Sneek, Dokkum en Harlingen* (Hilversum, 1997), pp. 240–58, 272–86. For a specific case: See Joke Spaans, 'Gereformeerden en doopsgezinden: het proces over het Marcelis Goverts Gasthuis te Leeuwarden 1687–1688', in S. Zijlstra *et al.* (eds.), *Vroomheid tussen Vlie en Lauwers* (Delft, 1996), pp. 141–5. The texts referred to are: *Codex Iustinianus* I, 5: De haereticis et manichaeis et samaritis, par. 4,22 (excluding heretics from financial transactions, including bequeathing and inheritance); *Codex Iustinianus* I, 6: Ne sanctum baptisma iteretur, par. 3 (applying these rules to Anabaptists); and *Digesta* XXXIII, 2, par. 16–17 (this text was used in the sixteenth and seventeenth centuries to deflect legacies and bequests illegally made in favour of tolerated Churches, not to the legal successors, but to the local Reformed *diaconie*). In a way this practice was a convergence towards the similar obligations of the Jewish communities towards their poor earlier in the seventeenth century, see the article of Peter van Rooden in this same volume.

These simple basic principles were adapted and embellished over time to fit local circumstances. The local nature of these adaptations needs to be stressed: there was considerable variation in the degree of toleration of dissenting groups from one province or town to another. An obvious example is the permission granted to the Amsterdam Jews and Lutherans to build public places of religious worship in the 1630s. No one who has ever seen the Portuguese Synagogue or the Lutheran Church on the Spui or the somewhat later one on the Singel, can mistake these for examples of *schuilkerken*, the private places of worship to which tolerated groups were restricted. These are very visible buildings, in the most sumptuous of seventeenth-century architectural styles. Permission to build so publicly was limited to the Amsterdam Jews and Lutherans: elsewhere their co-religionists did not share the privilege. The Amsterdam communities owed their liberties to the fact that they counted among their membership a number of wealthy, well-connected merchant families of foreign origin. These communities could therefore be treated as the 'nations', or foreign merchant communities, that had traditionally been accorded special privileges by trade centres, and also for the organisation of their religious worship.[17]

Just as important as legal rules for our understanding of the workings of religious toleration in the Dutch Republic, but even less obvious, were the religious policies of secular governments, both on the provincial and local levels, to incorporate dissident religious communities into the fabric of the body politic. The pervasive historiographical models mentioned at the beginning of this chapter leave little room for the assumption that there was such a thing as a religious policy. Toleration of dissent seems a rather passive attitude, refraining from persecution or too much harassment, or ignoring the claims of the Reformed Church to cultural hegemony. I would argue, on the contrary, that there were several, overlapping religious policies.

A consistent policy among magistrates everywhere was to divide and rule, to suppress the more disaffected elements in dissident groups and to favour those more loyal to the existing regime. This assumes of course that the Calvinist magistrates closely monitored dissident communities. We know that they did so from the early years of the Revolt. They kept themselves informed of the comings, goings, and doings of dissident

[17] So in Venice: See Bergsma, 'Church, State and People', pp. 209–10; but also, see for example, the Lutheran German merchant community in Amsterdam before it introduced the Reformed Church: Visser, *De Lutheranen in Nederland*, pp. 17–18. The same goes for exile Churches, such as the Dutch in Emden: Andrew Pettegree, *Emden and the Dutch Revolt. Exile and the Development of Reformed Protestantism* (Oxford, 1992), pp. 36–7; and the French in Geneva: See Jeannine E. Olson, *Calvin and Social Welfare. Deacons and the Bourse Française* (Selinsgrove, PA, 1989).

clergy. These were expected to preach obedience to lawful authorities, civic morality, and the virtues of social harmony. Criticism of the political *status quo*, demanding bizarre devotions or causing schism and unrest within their communities, could, and usually did, get dissident clergy banished. When schisms or conflicts occurred within tolerated communities local magistrates often arbitrated to restore the peace.[18]

A common preference of magistrates everywhere was for indigenous clergy. Not only were those of foreign birth considered to be less suitable than those originating from the same province, or at least from the Republic itself, but so were those educated abroad. Minimising the number of foreign missionaries and of regular priests under the authority of superiors residing in Catholic countries is a recurrent theme in the history of the Dutch Catholic community. The repeated bans of the States of Holland against 'foreign' vicars apostolic can be read as an active policy of secular authority to push the *Missio Hollandica* into a more national course. The secession of the Jansenist-influenced Old Episcopal Clergy as a separate, national Catholic Church, legitimate successor to the medieval Church, with indigenous bishops and its seminary in Amersfoort, could have been invented by the States themselves. Unfortunately for them the Old Episcopal Clergy never thrived. In the course of the eighteenth century protocols were devised according to which Catholic priests could be officially admitted, provided they presented an oath of loyalty to the government of the Republic. Discussions over foreign-born and foreign-educated clergy also played a part among the Lutherans. In the second half of the seventeenth century opposition grew against German ministers who clung to the orthodoxies taught at the Wittenberg theological faculty, and a 'Dutch school' of Lutheran ministers gained the ascendancy. As magistrates only allowed dissident clergy to function in their jurisdictions after their explicit approval had been secured, they had considerable leverage in this respect.[19]

The second half of the seventeenth century also shows another very remarkable course of action, initiated by city magistrates, in redefining religious communities and the role of religion in society. This was achieved by the reorganisation of poor relief along the confessional lines mentioned earlier. This reorganisation made Churches into something like mutual insurance societies. Members lapsing into poverty had henceforth to be supported by their fellow Church members. At the same time

---

[18] See examples in Spaans, *Haarlem na de Reformatie*, pp. 75–82, 99, 103, 200–3; see also Spaans, 'Unity and Diversity as a Theme in Early Modern Dutch Religious History: An Interpretation', in R.N. Swanson (ed.), *Unity and Diversity in the Church* (Oxford, 1996), pp. 221–34.

[19] Spaans, 'Katholieken onder curatele', 120–2; Visser, *De Lutheranen in Nederland*, pp. 77–86.

this reorganisation strengthened the position of prominent laymen in each Church.

In all different religious groups in the Republic, among Jews, Catholics, and Lutherans, as among Mennonites and Reformed, the clergy wielded spiritual authority only. All Churches had lay boards of elders, procurators or wardens, recruited from the local social elite, who were responsible for the election of clergy, church finance, and keeping the peace within the community. In the tolerated Churches they were the ones who were held responsible by local governments for the proper conduct of their religious community as a whole. They were called to account when clergy overstepped the boundaries set by public authority, or when the activities of the Church encroached upon the public sphere. These lay administrators had held positions of power in their communities from the moment these had developed some internal organisation. Now they were made welfare officers as well, which in many cases meant a heavy burden of administration and a constant concern to make ends meet, but at the same time always increased their authority among their co-religionists. From now on they were not only expected to keep their communities in the place allotted to dissenters under a confessional state: they also had to discipline their poorer members. Any disaffection among their poor with established authorities could no longer be deflected to secular magistrates, but had to be met by the lay leadership of the Church.

As the local Churches were themselves responsible for the support of poor co-religionists, the delegation of responsibility for poor relief also gave the Churches a compelling interest in discouraging poor people to join their congregations. Especially Catholic, Lutheran, and Jewish communities in this period seem to have grown mainly from German immigrants, looking for a better life in the Republic. Congregations of co-religionists offered obvious channels of entrance. Making the Churches bear the burden of support for poor newcomers strengthened existing policies to allow only the immigration of skilled or otherwise valuable persons, and to reject the poor.

For the new system to work efficiently, exact criteria had to be devised to determine which of the poor belonged to which welfare office and, consequently, under this new regime, who belonged to which Church. Local magistrates claimed and exercised the authority to lay down the rules to determine, for the practical purpose of support, the confessional status of the poor in dubious cases. This was a complicated matter. The burden of support for spouses in mixed marriages could be shared by two *diaconieën*, or *diaconieën* could agree upon relief of families on the basis of the confessional status of the husband or the head of the household in general. But what was to be done with orphans who were too young to be considered members of a Church? Or with orphans living in the households of grandparents who were themselves on welfare from their Church but who professed a different confession from that of the deceased parents? And could a religious community be burdened with the support of people who had been born in that particular confession, but no longer participated in its worship or were excommunicated for flouting its religious precepts? By assuming authority to decide these matters city magistrates in fact set the borders of their local Churches, decided who was and who could not become a member. Congregations could, and did, use these rulings in order to keep their membership within the limits of their financial possibilities.

All this resulted in strictly defined religious communities the sum of which was nowhere completely co-extensive with the local population. A number of inhabitants would be neither full members of the public Church nor of one of the tolerated Churches. These people without Church affiliation were defined as Reformed, although they could in fact be non-practicing or excommunicated Catholics, Mennonites, or Jews. The term 'Reformed' refers only to the fact that they were members of an officially Reformed society. If they did not belong to any other confession, what else could they be but Reformed? But if they happened to be poor, the *diaconie* of the public Church would not be responsible for them. The *diaconie* catered for full members only. The suggestion that the public Church used its welfare funds in order to lure the poor into its fold will not stand close scrutiny. For charity, poor people without a claim on any Church had to rely on the public system of poor relief.

All of these ways in which the magistrates were involved in the tolerated Churches – monitoring clergy, arbitration in case of schisms, defining confessional constituencies – tended in one direction. The arrangement implied a certain recognition of all Churches as legitimate parts of the social and religious order, and accorded them a measure of freedom to organise their own religious affairs within given limits. These limits varied, sometimes considerably, from place to place, but these differences were differences of degree. Penal laws became superfluous, since the social elites of tolerated groups were found willing to discipline their coreligionists, and this usually included their clergy.

It can be taken for granted that these policies, taken together, were consciously aimed at stabilising the religious order and the relations between different confessions. Some of them are evident from the very beginning of the Dutch Republic, others developed at a later date. By the beginning of the eighteenth century they had resulted in a social order made up of several recognised and sharply defined religious communities, each controlled by the civil magistrates through their lay elders. A last, important characteristic of this social order was that, by this time, religious differentiation had also come to mirror social stratification. This socio-religious differentiation has been noted and described earlier by Willem Frijhoff.[20] The key to the development of this stratification is, in my opinion, the reform of poor relief along the confessional lines described above. Those Churches that made the highest demands in the field of godly conduct tended to shrink in numbers and to move upwards on the social ladder. In a number of cases they appear to have used their moral demands in tandem with the criteria devised by local governments according to which the poorer sort could be kept out. At the end of the eighteenth century the Mennonites, the Old Episcopal Clergy (or Jansenists), and the French-speaking Walloon Reformed were small and highly elitist Churches. Catholic, Lutheran, and Jewish communities which, with the exception of Amsterdam, were mostly made up of immigrants, were undemanding and poor. The Reformed held a social position between the elitist and the poor Churches, but they were the only ones eligible for public office.[21]

A tolerant Republic?

The religious policies described here are not very evident even in the existing historical sources. These present a chaotic jumble of arrangements made at the local level and without a clear periodisation. While Lutherans in Amsterdam enjoyed their beautiful churches, their co-religionists in Leeuwarden had a hard time getting permission to worship in a private house and were never allowed public worship until the end of the *ancien régime*. Holland officially admitted Catholic priests in 1730, Friesland did not do so until 1776.

Two main causes were at the root of this diversity. They are both well known. First, the Dutch Republic was highly decentralised. Arrangements were concluded at a local, rather than at a central, level. Secondly, as the Reformed Church insisted on its exclusive character, the civil magistrate was reluctant to insist on a national, comprehensive Church. Membership of the Dutch Reformed Church probably never encompassed a clear majority of the population. This made the Reformed Church an ambiguous partner of the political power in the construction of a confessional state. While elsewhere state and public Church jointly devised policies on religious minorities, in the case of the Dutch Republic relations were somewhat more complicated. Local or provincial

---

[20] Frijhoff, 'La coexistence confessionnelle', pp. 242–5.
[21] Spaans, *Armenzorg in Friesland*, pp. 305–14.

authorities confronted both the public Church and the other religious communities.

However, there were religious policies. Their overall result was to divide the population into strictly defined religious communities, leaving a surplus category of those who were not members of any community. Each of these religious communities, including their clergy, was under the strict discipline of a body of lay elders. The obligation to support poor members and the freedom to exercise religious discipline, and so accommodate or limit membership, allowed the development of a social hierarchy among them. For those outside the organised Churches, a category that probably should be equated with the poor and unsettled, secular mechanisms of control were devised.[22] All this made for a society which was very stable and by contemporary European standards harmonious, but at the same time highly authoritarian. The strict discipline that accompanied the much-praised freedom of Dutch society, and perhaps which made it possible, has been noted by Jonathan Israel.[23] In line with his view of a society that was free and ordered, I would argue that it was not Erasmian tolerance or magisterial laxity, but a rather strict disciplinarian regime and a considerable amount of social engineering that produced public recognition and relative freedom for dissident groups.

---

[22] *Ibid.*, pp. 258–62.   [23] Israel, *The Dutch Republic*, pp. 677–99.

6   Paying off the sheriff: strategies of Catholic toleration in Golden Age Holland

Christine Kooi

To be a practising Roman Catholic in the city of Gouda during the seventeenth century was sometimes an expensive proposition. In the early 1600s, Catholics paid 400 guilders per year in recognition money to the city's bailiff (*baljuw*) to allow their priests to celebrate the sacraments in peace.[1] This arrangement, however, did not prevent the bailiff from routinely disrupting services through the 1620s, collecting fines to free incarcerated priests, and demanding even higher payments from the Catholic community. In 1625 the bailiff Anthony Cloots insisted that the priest Petrus Purmerent provide still more cash, but the cleric refused until the law officer in turn accommodated more Catholic worship.[2] By 1631 a new bargain was struck that afforded Catholics some breathing-space, but later that same year the town government appointed a new bailiff, Anthoni van der Wolff, and the persecutions began anew. Unlike his predecessor, Van der Wolff initially had no interest, pecuniary or otherwise, in religious toleration, and he pursued Gouda's Catholics with sectarian zeal.[3] Even his wife (described by the Catholic chronicler Ignatius Walvis as the 'she-wolf') disguised herself as a *klopje* (an unmarried Catholic lay sister), in order to infiltrate clandestine Catholic worship services.[4]

Until the early 1640s Gouda's Catholic community suffered persistent harassment and persecution under Van der Wolff's judicial regime. In 1644, however, the bailiff and the Catholic clergy unexpectedly reached a truce and together negotiated an arrangement. Petrus Purmerent and three other priests agreed to pay Van der Wolff 700 guilders per year in exchange for toleration, and for the time being the disruptions of Catholic worship in Gouda came to an end.[5]

How Van der Wolff came to change his mind was not clear. Perhaps it was simple greed. Perhaps it was out of mortification at an error he had made the previous autumn, when he mistook a visiting Amsterdammer

[1] [Ignatius Walvis], 'Goudsche en andere daartoe dienende katolijke kerk-zaken door I.W. pastoor van der Goude anno 1709', Archief van de oud-katholieke parochie van de H. Johannes de Doper, inv. no. 597, fo. 10, Streekarchiefdienst Hollands Midden, Gouda.
[2] *Ibid.*, fo. 28v.   [3] *Ibid.*, fo. 39r, fo. 42r.   [4] *Ibid.*, fo. 64v.   [5] *Ibid.*, fo. 68r.

strolling along the river Gouwe with a local Catholic for a priest and arrested him, only to learn later that his prisoner was in fact a deacon in the Reformed Church.[6] The chronicler Ignatius Walvis suggested that fear or superstition drove Van der Wolff to toleration: not long before, the bailiff had broken up a celebration of the Mass. At a dinner party the next day he mockingly drank wine out of the confiscated Eucharistic chalice, only to discover later that night blood in his urine, 'a condition that plagued him the rest of his life'.[7]

Whether it arose from greed, embarrassment or fear, for Gouda's Catholics this respite from harassment proved to be temporary. By the end of the decade greed had reasserted itself, and Anthoni van der Wolff was insisting on more money. In 1649 matters came to a head, with the bailiff demanding an extra 100 *rijksdaalders* fine from the priest Willem de Swaan for hosting a 'conventicle' in his home. At this point Gouda's burgomasters intervened and ordered the priests and the bailiff to adhere to their agreement of 1644. Evidently the city fathers feared the conflict's effects on civic tranquility, or perhaps they wearied of Van der Wolff's in-conclusive efforts to enforce the anti-Catholic placards. Even arbitration by the town government, however, proved to be of limited effectiveness. Sporadic attacks on Catholics would continue for the next two decades.[8]

The back-and-forth between Gouda's Catholics and its law officers in the seventeenth century points to a key feature of early modern Dutch religious toleration of Roman Catholics: it was a process rather than a condition. The accommodation of Catholic worship in the Protestant Republic was a delicate and fluid set of circumstances that was sensitive to the ebb and flow of local and national politics, contingent upon the good will (or lack of it) of local authorities, Reformed consistories, and neighbours, and was even vulnerable to the aggressiveness of Catholics themselves in their pursuit of religious liberty. As a process this accom-modation was continually subject to disruption, change, or evolution. To call it 'toleration', with that word's modern connotations of inclusion and approval, does not really do justice to the muddled and protean char-acter of the Catholic confessional relationship to public authority, both temporal and ecclesiastical. We may well agree with Willem Frijhoff that 'toleration' is too value-laden a word to describe this state of affairs, which might better be served with a more neutral and less formal label such as 'coexistence'.[9] Sometimes, as this term implied, Dutch Protestants and Catholics simply lived with each other in unremarkable daily life, while at

[6] *Ibid.*, fols. 66r–v.   [7] *Ibid.*, fols. 66v–67r.   [8] *Ibid.*, fols. 70r–v.

[9] Willem Frijhoff, 'Dimensions de la coexistence confessionnelle', in C. Berkvens-Stevelinck, J. Israel, and G.H.M. Posthumus Meyjes (eds.), *The Emergence of Tolerance in the Dutch Republic* (Leiden/New York/Cologne, 1997), pp. 213–37: p. 217.

other times confessional conflict seemed to permeate the entire culture of the Republic. Whatever degree of sufferance Catholics experienced in this society was subject to constant renegotiation and readjustment: it could not be counted upon.

In theory the Dutch Republic's placards had outlawed Catholic worship since 1581, with threatened punishments of fines, imprisonment, and banishment, but this law was not uniformly enforced. There was no predictable or particular pattern or consistency to the social, political, and religious climate in which Catholics found themselves worshipping. As the nineteenth-century Dutch historian Robert Fruin noted, the relative laxity with which authorities applied the placards created for Catholics a situation of general impunity, but also one of uncertainty.[10] Sometimes different confessional groups enjoyed a degree of liberty in the Dutch Republic that astonished contemporary observers (the secretaries of a visiting Italian prince reported that on a single Christmas Day in 1667 their lord attended the services of six different confessions in Amsterdam),[11] and conversely sometimes legal persecution of religious minorities virtually matched the harshness of other, more sectarian European regimes. More often than not the situation settled down somewhere in the grey middle ground. P.W.F.M. Hamans has recently noted that the Dutch Republic was too tolerant to force Roman Catholics to become Protestants, but not tolerant enough to allow Catholics free exercise of their faith.[12] Between these two poles lay considerable room for manoeuvre; a fact which early modern Dutch Catholics recognised and thus acted accordingly, employing a variety of strategies to win or take for themselves such religious accommodation as they could. They hoped that such stratagems, devices, and defences would permit them either some confessional breathing space or at least shield them from excessive persecution. The unsettled nature of confessional co-existence in the Republic ensured that the mechanics of toleration were very complex indeed.

Such accommodation was of course nothing like the religious toleration of the sort imagined by the humanist Dirck Coornhert, who dreamed of an open, harmonious Christian pluralism, or by the Leiden preacher Caspar Coolhaes, who envisioned a society based on Christian charity where sectarian division did not exist, or by countless civic magistrates in Holland, who had hoped vainly in the late sixteenth century that with

[10] R. Fruin (ed.), *Uittreksel uit Francisci Dusseldorpii Annales 1566–1616* (The Hague, 1893), p. cxiv.
[11] G.J. Hogewerff (ed.), 'De twee reizen van Cosimo de' Medici Prins van Toscana door de Nederlanden (1667–1669). Journalen en documenten', *Werken van het Historisch Genootschap* 41 (1919), 56–9.
[12] P.W.F.M. Hamans, *Geschiedenis van de katholieke kerk in Nederland*, vol. I: *Van missionering to herstel van de hierarchie in 1853* (Bruges, 1992), p. 269.

the formal transition to Reformed Protestantism the new public Church would be a non-confessional community open to all citizens.[13] Nor was it like the legitimacy and inclusion demanded by Hugo Grotius and the Arminian minority, or the Christian Irenicism longed for by some academic humanists. Seventeenth-century intellectuals certainly expended a lot of energy and ink on the subject, but the wide-ranging theoretical and literary discussion of religious toleration engaged in by Dutch scholars, theologians, jurists, and philosophers during the Golden Age never quite found its counterpart in actual practice.[14] The principle of freedom of conscience, so often trumpeted by public authorities and enshrined in the nation's political culture since the Revolt against Spain, did not necessarily guarantee freedom of worship. In the sixteenth century, as Andrew Pettegree has pointed out, toleration had been a 'loser's creed', a plea by dispossessed religious minorities for protection.[15] As the losers of the Dutch Revolt and Reformation, Catholics experienced toleration at best negatively as the absence of persecution; it was that occasional absence that gave them some flexibility. The accommodation, the opportunity to worship that they constantly strove for, was a hard-bitten negotiation with political, legal, and religious authority, and was always in danger of being lost or taken away. Because the possibility of toleration was always in flux, Catholics were forced to demonstrate considerable flexibility in their efforts to worship relatively freely. Experience taught them that toleration, such as they found it, often demanded strategy.

The most important resource that seventeenth-century Dutch Catholics could rely upon in their search for religious accommodation was of course the Holland Mission. Under the leadership of the apostolic vicars, the Mission employed the full authority of the post-Tridentine Church to minister to the faithful in the Protestant Dutch Republic. By the second quarter of the seventeenth century the apostolic vicars had successfully established a functioning, semi-secret mission of ambulant priests based in 'stations'– usually a major town – where they travelled round to offer sacraments and pastoral care to Roman Catholics inside

---

[13] James D. Tracy, 'Public Church, Gemeente Christi, or Volkskerk: Holland's Reformed Church in Civil and Ecclesiastical Perspective, 1572–1592', in Hans R. Guggisberg and Gottfried G. Krodel (eds.), *Die Reformation in Deutschland und Europa: Interpretationen und Debatten* (Gütersloh, 1993), pp. 487–510.

[14] Jonathan Israel, 'The Intellectual Debate about Toleration in the Dutch Republic', in C. Berkvens-Stevelinck, J. Israel, and G.H.M. Posthumus Meyjes (eds.), *The Emergence of Tolerance in the Dutch Republic* (Leiden/New York/Cologne, 1997), pp. 3–36.

[15] Andrew Pettegree, 'The Politics of Toleration in the Free Netherlands, 1572–1620', in Ole P. Grell and Bob Scribner (eds.), *Tolerance and Intolerance in the European Reformation* (Cambridge, 1996), pp. 182–98: p. 198.

private homes and dwellings.[16] Although the synods and classes of the Reformed Church complained vociferously about the spread of 'popery', provincial and local authorities tended to turn a blind eye to the Mission's activities as long as they did not disrupt public order. It was these travelling priests of the Holland Mission who dealt most frequently and most directly with problems of religious toleration and accommodation, since they were usually the ones negotiating arrangements and compromises with local law officers, or, alternatively, seeking to evade the persecuting power of those same officers.

As we have seen in Gouda, one of the ways to win some measure of religious accommodation was to buy it. Some of the monies involved were the legal fines imposed on those who broke the placards, but often there was an added dimension of bribery. So-called 'recognition money' changed hands in most localities, and more than one law officer lined his pockets by extorting substantial sums from Catholic priests or congregations. The missionary priest Godefridus Loeff described to the Sacred Congregation for the Propagation of the Faith in Rome how this worked in 1652: the Catholic community would negotiate an arrangement with the local sheriff to celebrate the sacraments undisturbed in a private home. Once, twice, or even four times a year the sheriff received a payment from the community; he would then 'shut his eyes' to any Catholic meetings.[17] In effect, through its priests the Catholic community bought from the town authorities the privilege of worship as a corporation. In general this became an established, not to say mundane, practice throughout Holland's cities, whose law officers were notorious for their corruption.[18] Calvinists were well aware of the practice, and they complained bitterly that the avarice of officers made a mockery of the placards and only encouraged the spread of 'Papist insolence'.[19] Even in Dordrecht, a city with a strict Calvinist reputation, local Catholics rather airily dismissed calls by the Reformed consistory for the sheriff to suppress their worship by brazenly displaying to the elders the money they used to 'make things good'.[20] The Jesuit priest Ludovicus Makeblijde of Delft even complained once that

[16] Mathieu G. Spiertz, 'Priest and Layman in a Minority Church: The Roman Catholic Church in the Northern Netherlands 1592–1686', in W.J. Shields and Diana Blackwood (eds.), *The Ministry: Clerical and Lay* (Oxford, 1989), pp. 287–301.

[17] G. Brom (ed.), 'Godfried Loeff in en over de Hollandsche Missie ten jare 1652', *Archief voor de Geschiedenis van het Aartsbisdom Utrecht* 24 (1897), 329.

[18] L.J. Rogier, *Geschiedenis van het katholicisme in Noord-Nederland in de zestiende en zeventiende eeuw*, 3 vols. (Amsterdam, 1945–1947), vol. II, p. 465.

[19] *Anatomie ofte ontledinghe van 't verderffelijck deseyn der hedendaechsche paepsghesinde, teghen kercke en politie, en alle goede inghesetene der Geunieerde Provintien* [Knuttel no. 5136] (Groningen, 1664), fo. B3r.

[20] Notulen Kerkenraad 1634–44, 20 Jan. 1636, Archief van de Kerkenraad, inv. no. 5, Gemeentearchief Dordrecht.

the sheriff Dirck van der Dussen used Catholic recognition money to finance renovations to his house and brewery.[21] In rare instances Catholics
manipulated the greed of officers to their advantage: after surprising a
Catholic meeting in 1609, the sheriff of Hoorn began noting down the
names of those present. One well-to-do Catholic, Jan Jeroensz, offered
to pay a security if the sheriff stopped taking names. The officer agreed,
but in the subsequent court case Jan Jeroensz denied he ever made the
offer, and the sheriff was left with neither money nor names.[22] In effect,
Catholic leaders paid sheriffs and bailiffs not to enforce the Republic's
placards against them. Exploiting the corruption of such civil servants
permitted Catholics access to the sacraments.

Such annual tributes could run, as we have seen, into hundreds of
guilders. Recognition money to 'make things good' often presented a
substantial financial burden to Catholic communities. Delft's Catholics,
for example, were forced to come up with a total of 1,000 guilders for
the town sheriff within one nine-month period in 1612.[23] The monies
usually came from both the wealthier members of local congregations
and from the treasuries of the apostolic vicars. In addition to housing a
priest, maintaining a consecrated space, and all the other expenses that
taxed this clandestine, quasi-parochial life came the hardship of buying
a little security from the authorities. Many of Holland's priests reported
to the Mission their laborious efforts at negotiating what they called a
compact (*foedus*) with local law officers, one of the many tasks they had
to perform, aside from the more typical challenges of administering the
sacraments and offering pastoral care.[24] Not only did officials demand
recognition money; they also freely imposed fines of up to 200 guilders
as demanded by the placards on homeowners who secretly hosted the
sacraments and often fined each individual attending such gatherings.[25]
In addition, in some cities missionary priests had to pay fees just to get
inside the town gates.

The mercenary character of this kind of religious toleration was not lost
on its objects. 'I would gladly shed my blood for the faith of Christ, though
the rabble [*canaglia*] here does not want blood but coins', Godefridus

---

[21] P.H.A.M. Abels, *Nieuw en ongezien. Kerk en samenleving in de classis Delft en Delfland
1572–1621*, 2 vols. (Delft, 1994), vol. II, p. 135.
[22] Henk van Nierop, *Het verraad van het Noorderkwartier. Oorlog, terreur en recht in de
Nederlandse Opstand* (Amsterdam, 1999), p. 249.
[23] Abels, *Nieuw en ongezien*, vol. II, p. 133.
[24] Rombout van Medenblik [a Leiden priest] to [apostolic vicar] Sasbout Vosmeer,
14 September 1610, Oud-Bisschoppelijke Clerezij [hereafter OBC], inv. no. 10, Het
Utrechts Archief [hereafter UA].
[25] Wim Tepe, *XXIV Paepsche vergaderplaetsen. Schuilkerken in Amsterdam* (Amstelveen,
1984), pp. 22–3.

Loeff noted disgustedly.[26] The opportunities for martyrdom that priests like Loeff may have longed for were not likely to be found in an environment where religious accommodation could be bought and sold. Money was at best a shaky foundation for toleration, however; as we saw in Gouda, payment was no guarantee that the bailiff would not persecute Catholics anyway. And some sheriffs and bailiffs were zealous Calvinists who were immune to monetary inducements and assiduously prosecuted all manifestations of popery. Indeed, payoffs had at best a temporary effect. Personnel changes, shifting political winds, and simple greed forced frequent renegotiations of financial deals between Catholic communities and law officers in Holland during the seventeenth century. Nevertheless, recognition money was the most common and, on the whole, the most effective means by which Dutch Catholics could win some toleration in Holland's complicated multiconfessional landscape.

Another strategy Catholics might employ to obtain some accommodation was to secure the favour, patronage, or simply the neutrality of political authorities. In the decentralised, confederate Dutch Republic this usually meant relying on the forbearance, indulgence, or even indifference of powerful civic magistracies, especially those of Holland, the richest and largest province. In all of the major towns of Holland, from liberal Gouda to orthodox Dordrecht, Catholic communities were able to live and worship in part because of the reluctance or disinterest of town councils in implementing the States' placards fully. The willingness of priests to co-operate with the authorities and to keep Catholic worship out of the public sphere usually increased this latitudinarian tendency. The magistrates of Haarlem, for example, allowed the Mission priests to work privately in their city as long as they reported to the civic authorities beforehand and swore an oath of loyalty to the States of Holland.[27] Likewise, in Leiden the *Gerecht* of burgomasters and aldermen tended to look the other way when reports of Catholic activities in the city's many *hofjes*, or almshouses, reached its ears. When in 1597 one scandalised inhabitant complained of Masses being celebrated by her neighbours in one of the *hofje* dwellings, the magistrates assured her they would look into it and then promptly dropped the matter.[28] Gouda's magistrates, as we saw, were willing to intervene when disputes between Catholic priests and the city's bailiff got out of hand. The town government

---

[26] Brom (ed.), 'Godfried Loeff', 317.

[27] Joke Spaans, *Haarlem na de Reformatie: Stedelijke cultuur en kerkelijk leven, 1578–1620* (The Hague, 1989), p. 97.

[28] Inv. no. 3419a, 22 Augustus 1597, and Gerechtsdagboek D, inv. no. 48, 16 October 1597, fo. 234v, Gemeentearchief Leiden, Stadsarchief na 1574 [quoted hereafter as: GAL SA II].

of Amsterdam, the largest and by far the most cosmopolitan of
Holland's cities, went so far as to temper the enforcement of placards
by its more zealous law officers. The city council once condemned sheriff Jan Grootenhuys for disrupting a funeral conducted by the respected
pastor Leonard Marius; citing the smallness of the gathering and respect
for the widow, the council excused the priest, who they knew normally
observed the placards, from paying the usual fines.[29] The apostolic vicar
Johannes van Neercassel, the head of the Holland Mission in the later
seventeenth century, enjoyed rights of citizenship in Amsterdam and was
friendly with many of that city's regents.[30] In the same city in 1663 the
Jesuit Henricus van Alkemade moved to a station on the Keizersgracht;
the seven Reformed ministers who lived on the same street complained
to the magistracy without success.[31] Many more such instances can be
found in the archives, and the preponderance of evidence suggests that
most town regents were inclined to laxity in implementing the placards
against Catholic communities. Even as fierce an anti-Protestant as the
Catholic chronicler Franciscus Dusseldorpius had to admit that this was
true and suspected that the States of Holland issued the sternly worded
placards primarily in the hopes of intimidating his co-religionists into
good behaviour.[32] Holland's anti-Catholic statutes, it seemed, had more
bark than bite. Catholics benefited directly from this forbearance by cap-
italising on the opportunity it gave them to worship relatively freely in
private spaces.

Where the regents' tolerant attitude stemmed from is a question with
any number of answers. In general it does not seem to have derived from
any principled, Erasmian standpoint, though the Leiden magistracy was
particularly vocal in its expressions of belief in its citizens' freedom of
conscience (this did not, however, stop it from instigating occasional
roundups of Catholic priests in the seventeenth century).[33] There was
a long spiritualist tradition in Dutch Christianity that emphasised inner
devotion rather than external ritual and dogma, though to what extent
this translated into the political and social spheres remains uncertain.[34]
Indeed, there is not much evidence that civic rulers considered the issue of

---

[29] Tepe, *XXIV Paepsche vergaderplaetsen*, pp. 23–4.
[30] H.A. Enno van Gelder, *Getemperde vrijheid* (Groningen, 1972), p. 132.
[31] F. van Hoeck, *Schets van de geschiedenis der Jezuieten in Nederland* (Nijmegen, 1940),
   p. 42.
[32] Fruin (ed.), *Uittreksel uit Francisci Dusseldorpii Annales*, pp. 254–5.
[33] Inv. no. 3458, GAL SA II. See also Gerechtsdagboek C, 26 May 1595, inv. no. 47, ff.
   181v–183r, GAL SA II, where the Leiden burgomasters invoked the notion of freedom
   of conscience while dealing with the city's small Lutheran confession.
[34] M.E.H.N. Mout, 'Spiritualisten in de Nederlandse Reformatie van de zestiende eeuw',
   Bijdragen en Mededelingen betreffende de Geschiedenis der Nederlanden 111 (1996), 297–313.

religious toleration in any organised or concentrated fashion, though they perhaps recognised the deleterious effect of prejudice on an economy so dependent on foreign trade. It is more likely that practical considerations prevailed; in crowded towns with large Catholic minorities, systematic or consistent religious persecution would have threatened public order. And those minorities existed in part because the prevailing public Reformed Church, which had a sharp sense of confessional boundaries, refused either to missionise extensively or to allow easy access to membership in its congregations. All were free to hear the preaching of God's word, asserted Reformed divines, but entrance into the communion of the Saints demanded a rigorous and daunting examination of life and belief.[35] Furthermore, in many cities (such as Rotterdam, Delft, and Dordrecht, for example) lay Catholics and even a few priests had direct kinship ties to the regent patriciate, and in some cases the bonds of family may have proved stronger than the dictates of sectarianism in extending security or patronage to professing Catholics.[36]

Related to the tactic of taking advantage of the latitudinarian stance of civic magistracies was the less common strategy of individual patronage. We know of more than one instance of members of the Republic's political and social elites using their influence or privileges to grant some protection or favour to individual Catholics, especially to clergymen. The Catholic widow Maria de Vianen, for example, felt comfortable enough to ask the Grand Pensionary Johan de Witt, whom Calvinists suspected of being soft on Popery, not to enforce the placards in the case of a priest who had baptised a child in the village of Putten, where De Witt's brother Cornelis was steward.[37] The Stadholder Frederick Henry enjoyed a certain amount of popularity among his Catholic subjects, perhaps in part because of his efforts to preserve Catholic religious freedom in the city of 's-Hertogenbosch after he captured it in 1629.[38] Of all the seventeenth-century apostolic vicars, Johannes van Neercassel enjoyed the most personal freedom (at least until his support of Louis XIV's invasion in 1672); he travelled in circles that included the patrician Hooft family of Amsterdam and Amalia van Solms, widow of Frederick Henry.[39] Another source of patronage and protection lay in the nobility, especially

[35] J.J. Woltjer, 'De plaats van de calvinisten in de Nederlandse samenleving', *De Zeventiende Eeuw* 10 (1994), 3–23.
[36] Abels, *Nieuw en ongezien*, vol. II, p. 138.
[37] R. Fruin and N. Japikse (eds.), *Brieven aan Johan de Witt*, vol. II: *1660–1672* (Amsterdam, 1922), pp. 188–9.
[38] J.J. Poelhekke, *Frederik Hendrik, Prins van Oranje. Een biografisch drieluik* (Zutphen, 1978), pp. 290–5, 510.
[39] C.P. Voorvelt, 'Enkele minder bekende facetten van het leven van de apostolisch vicaris Johannes van Neercassel (1663–1686)', *Trajecta* 5 (1996), 45–6.

outside Holland. Local nobles in Zeeland offered protection to that province's sparse population of Catholics in the late 1500s.[40] In the latter part of the seventeenth century the court of the Marchioness of Bergen op Zoom functioned as a secure enclave for Catholic worship, despite the vocal disapproval and resistance of that Brabançon town's Reformed ecclesiastics.[41] Another possibility for some was to worship inside the homes of ambassadors from Catholic states in the Hague. Dutch Catholics proved to be adept at exploiting the complex, intricate social and political networks that characterised life in the early modern world in order to win for themselves if not positive toleration, then at least some security against persecution.

If bribing the law, official forbearance, or individual patronage failed, however, another strategy to gain accommodation for Dutch Catholics was to steal it or disguise it. This was especially necessary as they traversed the boundaries between public life and private space. Lay Catholics, especially *klopjes*, maintained altars and Eucharistic paraphernalia in hidden spaces, such as attics or concealed rooms, in private dwellings.[42] The Reformed Church, aware of these secret spaces, even lobbied the States of Holland to forbid priests to build special entries into their homes and to demolish any unusual walls, fences, or shelters found around them.[43] If the local sheriff could not be bought, then worship services sometimes took place under cover of night.[44] Catholic printers sometimes placed fictitious addresses in Antwerp or Cologne on the title pages of devotional literature they sold so as not to get into trouble with the authorities.[45]

Subterfuge was also a way to insulate oneself against the worst excesses of anti-Catholic onslaughts, especially for the clergy of the Holland Mission, who had learned from the beginning that wiliness was their most effective defence. In 1613 one cleric wrote admiringly of the first generation of Mission priests: 'they have taught us, their successors, in the midst of wolves to keep the cunning of snakes while never losing the

---

[40] J.M. Roof, 'De rooms-katholieke Zeeuwen in het laatste kwart van de zestiende eeuw: van zelfredzaamheid tot late wederopluiking', in J.P. van Dooren (ed.), *De Nationale Synode te Middelburg in 1581* (Middelburg, 1981), pp. 208–9.

[41] Charles de Mooij, *Geloof kan Bergen verzetten. Reformatie en katholieke herleving te Bergen op Zoom 1577–1795* (Hilversum, 1998), pp. 412–17.

[42] See, for example, A.J.J. Hoogland (ed.), 'Drie klopjes voor het Gerecht te Leiden', *Bijdragen Bisdom Haarlem* 6 (1878), 69–76.

[43] W.P.C. Knuttel (ed.), *Acta der particuliere synoden van Zuid-Holland 1621–1700* (The Hague, 1910), vol. III, p. 436.

[44] Brom (ed.), 'Godfried Loeff', 330.

[45] Lienke Paulina Leuven, *De boekhandel te Amsterdam door katholieken gedreven tijdens de Republiek* (Epe, 1951), p. 23.

innocence of doves'.[46] The history of the Mission is replete with tales of priests travelling in disguise to minister to the Catholic faithful. The priest Nicolaas Wiggers van Cousebrant of the Haarlem chapter routinely criss-crossed the North Holland countryside dressed as a merchant, fisherman, farmer, or even a noble. His colleague Willem Coopal once even disguised himself as a woman to escape the sheriff of a village outside Schiedam.[47] Masquerading as soldiers, however, did not shield the Vicar-Coadjutor Jacobus de la Torre and a dozen fellow priests from detection and attack by law officers at a large gathering of Catholics outside the North Holland hamlet of Zijdewind in 1649.[48]

Clergymen went to great lengths to preserve the clandestine character of the Mission. In their correspondence the apostolic vicars usually used pseudonyms and often wrote in a kind of linguistic camouflage: when writing to his brother Tilman, a priest in the Mission, Sasbout Vosmeer would refer to a bishop as 'father' and the Pope as 'grandfather'.[49] In a disguised report to Vosmeer of 1602, the Amsterdam priest Anthonius van Oirschot related the recent capture and imprisonment of the Haarlem vicar Adalbert Eggius in language disguised to make the writer sound like a Protestant. On the pretext of describing a particularly bad outbreak of plague in Amsterdam, Van Oirschot wrote:

There are many Papists, citizens and inhabitants here who say that this great scourge and plague have come over this city because about four months ago there was caught and imprisoned in the Hague a Papist priest named Elbert, whom I assume is not known to you; if this is true, I hope that the same Papist will be freed and we will be rid of this plague, . . . and furthermore I hear that in jail he leads a life, with daily prayer and fasting, that makes such an impression on the common folk that everyone talks about it in carriages and barges; those who had gone to see him to mock him come away impressed, admitting that he is a wise and good man and that they don't have such a one among their own preachers.[50]

---

[46] Quoted in Richard Reisberman, *Bijdragen voor de geschiedenis van de roomsch-katholieke kerk in Nederland* (Rotterdam, 1888), p. 72.

[47] Dalmatius van Heel, *Nicolaas Wiggers van Cousebrant als seculiere priester 1555–1603 en als minderbroeder 1602–1628* (Haarlem, 1928), p. 35; J.C. van der Loos, 'De kleeding der priesters in het Hollandse kerkdistrict', *Bijdragen Bisdom Haarlem* 58 (1940), 417.

[48] J.J. Poelhekke, 'Het geval Zijdewind', in J.J. Poelhekke, *Geen blijder maer in tachtigh jaer. Verspreide studiën over de Crisisperiode 1648–1651* (Zutphen, 1973), pp. 108–10.

[49] Sasbout Vosmeer to Tilman Vosmeer, 30 Sept. 1589, OBC, inv. no. 440, UA.

[50] 'Hier zyn veel papisten ende andere borgers ende ander inwoenders die seggen, dat de groot geessel ende plage daer op over deese stadt is overmidts dat over een maent oft vier geleden, daer gevangen is ende inden Hage gebracht een priester oft paep, genaempt Elbert, die ick vermoede U.E. onbekent te syn, voer waer soude dat waer syn, so woude ick wel dat den selve paep eerst dacht vry gelaten weerde ende dat wy die pest quijt waren, . . . ende boven dien soe hoere ick dat hy in de gevanckenisse sulcken leven leyt, met bidden ende vasten dagelix, dattet wonder roep maeckt onder de gemeene luyden sulckx datmen daer in wagens ende schuyten genoch oft weet te praten, oock sommige

Under the cover of sectarian vocabulary this Catholic priest was able to convey to the apostolic vicar both Eggius' condition in prison and the effect his capture was having on public opinion, without putting himself at risk of harassment by the authorities. The language of intolerance, then, became a source of protection. The use of these codes extended to lay Catholics as well. In 1605 a Dordrecht Catholic complained to Vosmeer about the planned removal of the popular priest Lambertus Feyt from that city; in the argot of Holland's business world he expressed the disappointment of the 'whole company' at the prospective departure of their 'factor' (that is, Lambertus Feyt) and feared that his successor would not enjoy the same degree of 'credit' that Feyt had.[51] Such subterfuge carried risks, of course, in that as a strategy excessive amounts of secrecy might in fact alert authorities nervous about law and order. Nor of course was secrecy always necessary; in certain times and places some priests and *klopjes* could walk through their town streets in their normal religious garb. But it could serve a useful purpose during periods of heightened confessional tension both to shield laymen and clergy from the worst excesses of persecution and to allow some basic functioning and communication within the Catholic community. It permitted them some safety within the public sphere, where technically they were not acknowledged. To safeguard what accommodation did exist in Holland's multiconfessional society, artifice and guile were valuable tools.

Perhaps the most singular armour against intolerance that Dutch Catholics felt they could rely upon was the supernatural. Willem Frijhoff has underscored the importance of miracles within the Catholic subculture in buttressing a sense of identity, security, and vindication in an unfriendly Protestant environment. Divine occurrences, apparitions, and interventions, ranging from monsters in the sky to thaumaturgical priests to Protestant preachers struck dumb, served to comfort the faithful, confound the heretics, and persuade the uncertain.[52] The appearance of blood in the urine of Gouda's bailiff Anthoni van der Wolff after he violated a Catholic altar and mocked the Eucharist certainly fell under this category; the Catholic chronicler of this incident clearly believed it to be a case of divine retribution for persecution. Sometimes wondrous signs were intended to bolster Catholic loyalty and steadfastness. In 1588 a priest reported to the hierarchy his efforts to help three young

van de genen die hem seer plegen te lasteren, doer het dick by comen by deesen gevangen paep, schynen hem seer te prysen, hem naegevende, dat hy een wijs goet man is ende dat sy onder haer predicanten sulckx geen en hebben . . . ': Anthonius Adriansz van Oirschot to Sasbout Vosmeer, 15 Sept. 1602, OBC, inv. no. 274, UA.

[51] F.F. to Sasbout Vosmeer, 17 May 1605, OBC, inv. no. 275, UA.

[52] Willem Frijhoff, 'La fonction du miracle dans une minorité catholique: Les Provinces-Unies au XVIIe siècle', *Revue d'Histoire de la Spiritualité* 48 (1972), 160–1.

girls from the village of Laren who were apparently possessed by spirits. Interrogating the girls in the local church he discovered they were in fact possessed by the angel Gabriel, who warned that all must convert, for the Last Judgement would soon be at hand. The 'old Catholic faith' was the only true faith, the angel's voice confirmed, and those who did not return to it would be 'forever lost'. As if to demonstrate the divine authenticity of the event, a hitherto mute child in the company of on-lookers suddenly and miraculously began to laugh.[53] Such supernatural affirmations reinforced Catholic self-awareness and self-confidence in a sectarian society and reminded the faithful that God was on their side. It was equally important to remember on whose side the heretics were on. In his annals Franciscus Dusseldorpius recounted the story of a priest's servant girl from Gouda who had been possessed by the devil; after re-covering from her possession she was walking in the city market one day when she encountered him again, complete with long beard and fur-lined gown. He explained that he had left her in order to teach the heretical ministers and to stand in their pulpit. The maid fled in fear but sure enough, a few days later she passed by the Reformed Church and saw the devil occupying the pulpit behind the preacher.[54] A contemporary biography of the Delft priest Jan Stalpart van der Wiele claimed that after he converted a woman who had given birth only to stillborn children, she was blessed with a healthy baby.[55] Such supernatural tales, which circu-lated throughout the Catholic community, dramatised in unsubtle fash-ion the sharp moral contrast that the clergy drew between true faith and heresy, as well as the dangers inherent in the mechanisms of confessional co-existence.

Catholic propagandists were quick to publicise instances of miracles that seemed to favour their co-religionists and to condemn Protestant intolerance. A good example of this can be found in a pamphlet printed in Antwerp in 1602, titled 'A Very Strange, Miraculous, Awful and True Story', which described an episode in the North Holland town of Edam in which divine wrath was visited upon a group of anti-Catholic hooligans.[56] On Shrove Tuesday (that is, the last day of Carnival) a carousing group of thirty soldiers, recently arrived from Ostend, dressed up in vestments as if they were Catholic clerics and danced their way down the street

<hr />

[53] Quoted in Martien Parmentier, *Vitale kerk*, vol. I: *Geschiedenis van (oud-)katholiek Hil-versum 1589–1889* (Hilversum, 1989), p. 203.

[54] Fruin (ed.), *Uittreksel uit Francisci Dusseldorpii Annales*, p. 124.

[55] B.A. Mensink, *Jan Baptist Stalpart van der Wiele. Advocaat, priester en zielzorger 1579–1630* (Bussum, n.d.), p. 211.

[56] *Een seer vreemde, miraculeuse, vreeselijcke/ ende waerachtighe historie/ gheschiedt binnen de stadt van Edam/ gheleghen in Noort-Hollant/ den eersten sondach van den Vasten des teghen-woordighen jaers 1602* (Antwerp, 1602).

singing and shouting *Dominus vobiscum* to passers-by. They gave one of their number a mock burial, and then entered the town church to drink four barrels of beer, accompanied by the town burgomasters. The next day, Ash Wednesday, they dressed up one of their company as a bishop, complete with a mitre and candle, and drove him around in a cart while continuing to insult and mock the Catholic Church. This burlesque would have continued for a third day but for divine intervention: that evening a bolt of lightning struck the church, releasing an evil spirit in the form of a fire-breathing serpent that roared *Dominus vobiscum*. The fire from the beast's mouth burned down the church tower and sixty houses in its vicinity, except for one, which had been the pastor's home in Catholic times and in which several Catholics still lived. The moral of the story was clear: God would not suffer the ridiculing of the true Church by drunken, malicious heretics. What in an earlier era would have been seen as the normal, if obstreperous, excesses of the Carnival season were now in this confessional age pictured as dire threats to true religion. The upside-down world of Fat Tuesday was violently and decisively reduced to the severe penances of Ash Wednesday. The vividness of such a tale, complete with fire and serpent, emphasised both the hostility Catholics faced in this Protestant society and their faith in ultimate vindication. God was on the side of the persecuted and occasionally, miraculously, He intervened to protect the faithful in their efforts to exercise their beliefs. The supernatural was a powerful, if unpredictable, support to Dutch Catholics in the process of religious accommodation, more of a comfort, perhaps, than an instrument.

All these strategies, corruption, forbearance, patronage, subterfuge, and miracles, were but a few of the means by which early modern Dutch Catholics attempted to secure a place for themselves in the officially Protestant Dutch Republic. These devices were not always necessary, for on an informal and quotidian level in Holland's crowded towns and cities Catholics could and often did enjoy harmonious relations with their political leaders and confessional neighbours. Catholics and Protestants lived and worked together and even married each other; the efforts of the Holland Mission were common knowledge, and everyone knew where the priest or *klopjes* lived in his or her town.[57] Yet at the same time the status of Catholics remained complicated and therefore precarious. In a society where religious persecution was haphazard, sporadic, inconsistent, and unpredictable, always possible but often ineffectual, the means to cope with it tended to be equally fluid, contingent, adaptable,

---

[57] A recent interpretation of the Dutch Golden Age refers to this as 'everyday ecumenism' (*omgangsoecumene*): Willem Frijhoff and Marijke Spies, *1650: Bevochten eendracht* (The Hague, 1999), p. 50.

provisional, and incidental. Dutch Catholics in the Golden Age did not regard themselves as the beneficiaries of toleration, but they were canny enough to recognise that occasional opportunities to protect themselves against the confessional antagonism that characterised their world did exist and could be exploited. Toleration to them represented at best a fluid, mutable set of conditions. For them any strategy, from the mercenary to the miraculous, from official goodwill to aristocratic shelter, from disguised priests to corrupt sheriffs, presented an occasion to pry open a bit wider the window of accommodation. They used these strategies without consistency and sometimes without success, but always acted in direct response to the exigencies of the volatile, inconstant, and capricious circumstances in which they lived. As Gouda's Roman Catholics discovered, 'toleration', which they experienced and understood as freedom from persecution, was an ongoing, messy process.

Dutch religious toleration presented, paradoxically, both limitation and opportunity. It confined Catholic worship to a largely private sphere where its security was not always assured, yet it also allowed Catholics various avenues, means, and devices to create a functioning sacramental system for themselves. What Catholics did with those opportunities determined to a great extent the contours of their co-existence with Reformed Protestantism. Paying off the sheriff, hoping for a miracle, trusting in magisterial benevolence, and participating in occasional chicanery were all integral steps in the complicated confessional choreography of post-Reformation Holland.

7 Sewing the bailiff in a blanket: Catholics and the law in Holland

Henk van Nierop

In the summer of 1616 Baernt van Neck, bailiff (*baljuw*) of Texel, decided to crack down on the growing number of Papists on the island. For a long time the Catholics had organised clandestine meetings, in full daylight and in defiance of placards. But the bailiff's pursuit was unfortunate. When he tried to disrupt one of their gatherings, the Papists beat up his substitute – who was incidentally his brother-in-law – until he was 'bloody and blue' and kicked him unceremoniously out of their meeting. Nor was this all. They threatened the bailiff himself (despite his advanced age) with rakes, and 'the women ... tried to sew [him] in a blanket'.[1]

Such a monstrous crime could not go unpunished. Yet instead of simply summoning the malefactors before his own court, the bailiff cited them before the *Gecommitteerde raden van het Noorderkwartier*, a body charged with the day-to-day administration of the northern part of the province of Holland, residing in Hoorn and consisting of representatives of the seven major cities of North Holland.[2] The defendants contested the legality of this summons and appealed to the ancient privileges of the island, granting them the right to appear before a local court. On their behalf the magistrates of Texel sent a petition to the highest court of law of the province, the *Hof van Holland* in The Hague, to protest against this glaring and unprecedented infringement of Texel's privileges. The *Hof* duly dispatched a letter to the bailiff, enquiring as to why he had not been content to summon the offenders before their 'daily and competent judges'.

The bailiff's reply was a curious piece of reasoning. Summoning the evildoers before the *Gecommitteerde raden*, according to the bailiff, was fully in compliance with 'ancient customs', since this body was eminently

---

[1] A. van Lommel (ed.), 'Bouwstoffen voor de kerkelijke geschiedenis van de verschillende parochiën thans behoorende tot het Bisdom Haarlem', *Bijdragen tot de Geschiedenis van het Bisdom Haarlem* 6 (1878), 156–61.

[2] On the Gecommitteerde raden van het Noorderkwartier, see J. R. Persman, 'De bestuursorganisatie in West-Friesland en het Noorderkwartier vanaf de eerste vergadering van de Staten van Noord-Holland in 1573 tot en met 1795', *West-Frieslands Oud en Nieuw* 40 (1973), 136–60.

competent in the adjudication of 'spiritual matters' (*geestelycke saecken*). As to the privilege *de non evocando* to which the inhabitants of Texel had so rashly appealed, this was only valid in the realm of 'political' law. Canonical law (*geestelijk recht*) was surely beyond the understanding of the simple islanders. And finally a trial before the local bench of magistrates would be useless. The majority of Texel's magistrates were *ejusdem formae homines*, men of the same sort, who for the most part had themselves attended the Popish meetings in question.

The bare facts underlying this legal squabble are anything but remarkable. All over the United Provinces – but perhaps particularly in Holland's Noorderkwartier, roughly the area north of Amsterdam – the authorities were confronted with huge assemblies of Roman Catholics celebrating Mass, partaking in processions and pilgrimages and performing all manner of Catholic rituals. Their meetings were illegal, but in view of their massive scale the magistrates were powerless to act. Yet the bailiff's reaction is interesting for at least two reasons. First, it draws our attention to the little-known fact that the *Gecommitteerde raden* did in certain cases act as a court of justice. An instruction dating from 1 November 1595 authorised this body to adjudicate not only in fiscal affairs, but also against 'those common enemies who have been captured and who are suspected of treason, mutiny, sedition, uprising, coining counterfeit money, and mistreatment of the provisions, ammunition and other goods of the country'.[3] Instructions drawn up in 1622 for the *landdrost* (an official whose main task consisted of rounding up vagabonds in North Holland) stipulated that he see to the strict observance of the statute against 'Popish conventicles, ceremonies and superstitions'. If such crimes had taken place in one of North Holland's seven walled towns, the *landdrost* must contact the local legal officer, who then had to bring the case before his local court. In all other cases the *landdrost* himself was expected to institute legal proceedings before the *Gecommitteerde raden*, who would then hear the case 'according to ancient usage'.[4] Apparently, participation in Catholic gatherings was regarded as high treason.

Secondly, the bailiff's appeal to canonical law underscores the utter bewilderment the authorities experienced when they were faced with the novel political and religious realities of toleration in the Dutch Republic. The bailiff's claim that the *Gecommitteerde raden* were competent in religious matters was nothing short of outrageous. Canonical law was never

[3] Archief van de Gecommitteerde Raden van West-Friesland en het Noorderkwartier, inv. no. 244, fo. 53 *et seq.*, articles vii and viii, Rijksarchief in Noord-Holland [quoted hereafter as RNH]. A printed version in the same Archief, inv. no. 329, RNH.
[4] A. de Goede, 'De landdrost van Westfriesland', *Rechtsgeleerd Magazijn Themis: Tijdschrift voor Publiek- en Privaatrecht* (1948), 546–8.

officially abolished in the United Provinces, but it became obsolete after the exercise of the Catholic religion had been forbidden and clerics had ceased to exist as an officially recognised separate order. It was replaced in part by secular legislation, such as the so-called Political Ordinance of 1580, which regulated marriage affairs.[5] In addition a number of statutes – issued by the States-General, the various provincial states assemblies, and the individual towns – forbade the celebration of Mass and the performance of other Catholic rituals. Such laws were supposed to be enforced by ordinary secular law courts, such as the *schepen* benches in the towns and villages and by the provincial courts of law, not by special tribunals.

What exactly was the situation of the Catholics in the early Dutch Republic? Historians have often applauded seventeenth-century religious toleration in the United Provinces as a policy foreshadowing the modern separation between Church and state. More recently, though, there is a tendency to temper this Whiggish enthusiasm.[6] In the first place, scholars stress that few contemporaries went so far as to advocate religious toleration as an end in itself. Such diverse champions of tolerance as Erasmus, Cornelis Pietersz Hooft, and even the maverick Dirck Volckertsz Coornhert ultimately strove for religious concord, not diversity.[7] If tolerance of the unorthodox was acceptable as a temporary expedient under certain conditions, it was not a goal to be striven for. Secondly, recent scholarship strongly underscores the limits of toleration. Erasmus had no patience for the Jews, nor did John Locke propose toleration for atheists and Catholics. The Spinozist and anti-Trinitarian writer Adriaen Koerbagh was convicted for publishing his blasphemous opinions and died in gaol.[8] Cornelis Pietersz Hooft, the humanist merchant and twelve times burgomaster of Amsterdam, spoke out against persecuting

---

5 J.Ph. de Monté Ver Loren, *Hoofdlijnen uit de ontwikkeling der rechtelijke organisatie in de Noordelijke Nederlanden tot de Bataafse omwenteling*, ed. J.E. Spruit (Deventer, 1982), pp. 227–8.
6 Recent studies include C. Berkvens-Stevelinck, J. Israel, and G.H.M. Posthumus Meyes (eds.), *The Emergence of Tolerance in the Dutch Republic* (Leiden/New York/Cologne, 1997); Andrew Pettegree, 'The Politics of Toleration in the Free Netherlands, 1572–1620', in Ole Peter Grell and Bob Scribner (eds.), *Tolerance and Intolerance in the European Reformation* (Cambridge, 1996), pp. 182–98; Heiko A. Oberman, 'The Travail of Tolerance: Containing Chaos in Early Modern Europe', *ibid.*, pp. 13–31; and Jonathan Israel, *The Dutch Republic: Its Rise, Greatness and Fall, 1477–1806* (Oxford, 1995), pp. 372–7. See also Hans R. Guggisberg, 'Veranderingen in de argumenten voor religieuze tolerantie en godsdienstvrijheid in de zestiende en zeventiende eeuw', *Bijdragen en Mededelingen betreffende de Geschiedenis der Nederlanden* 91 (1976), 177–95; and Gerhard Güldner, *Das Toleranzproblem in den Niederlanden im Ausgang des 16. Jahrhunderts* (Lübeck, 1968).
7 Coornhert is usually regarded as a proponent on principle of religious toleration. For a different view see the forthcoming PhD thesis by Marianne Roobol (University of Amsterdam).
8 Israel, *The Dutch Republic*, pp. 787–9, 919–20.

Catholics; but he was by no means disposed to permit them free exercise of their religion since they imperilled the security of the state.[9] Toleration, as Andrew Pettegree put it, was 'a loser's creed ... the party cry of the disappointed, the dispossessed, or the seriously confused'.[10] Roman Catholics were the principal victims of a policy that was explicitly and consciously intolerant. In 1579 the Union of Utrecht guaranteed freedom of conscience for all, including Catholics; yet it did not grant them the freedom to practise their religion actively.

There is broad agreement as to the factors underlying the ban on Catholic activities. The Reformed ministers, forever prompting the authorities to prosecute, regarded Catholicism not just as a problem of blasphemy. Catholics were their rivals in the interconfessional struggle for souls. Many town magistrates, all of them members or at least supporters (liefhebbers) of the Reformed Church, shared these feelings. But in the last analysis the magistrates were motivated by political rather than religious considerations.

William of Orange, when he planned his invasion of Holland and Zeeland in 1572, had envisaged a regime based on the peaceful co-existence of the Catholic majority and the Calvinist rebels. The Dordrecht convocation of the States of Holland, held in the same year, endorsed this principle. But Orange's policy of toleration floundered in the face of his own Beggar troops, sacking churches and harassing priests and monks, while at the same time the relentless advance of the Spanish army marked outspoken Catholics as potential traitors.

By the spring of 1573 Orange and the States abandoned the policy of peaceful co-existence. The States of Holland proscribed the celebration of the Mass, forcing most priests and clerics (if they did not convert to the new religion) to flee to areas controlled by the Spanish army. Catholic life ground to a complete standstill in the rebellious provinces, even though the majority of the population remained aloof from the new Reformed Church. In 1576 the Pacification of Ghent, while ending the war in Holland and Zeeland, froze the existing religious situation. Orange's programme for religious peace (Religionsfried, religievrede), granting religious freedom for Catholics in Holland and Zeeland and for Protestants in the other provinces, proved unworkable.

Both religions strove for monopoly, confident of their legitimacy as defenders of the true faith; partisans on both sides of the breach became embedded in deep mutual distrust. For Calvinists, the defection in 1580 of Rennenberg, the governor of Friesland and Groningen, offered

[9] H.A. Enno van Gelder, De levensbeschouwing van Cornelis Pieterszoon Hooft, burgemeester van Amsterdam 1547–1626 (reprint Utrecht, 1982), pp. 113, 131–2.
[10] Pettegree, 'The Politics of Toleration', p. 198.

undeniable proof that Catholics were not to be trusted. A constant flow of legislation outlawing Catholic practices ensued: five edicts in 1580, six in 1581, four in 1582. While previously only the public exercise of the Mass had been forbidden, a 1581 edict issued in Holland (and re-issued in 1622, 1629, 1641, and 1649) made all Catholic assemblies illegal. The edict asserted that while the States of Holland did not wish to burden the mind or conscience of anyone, assemblies of Catholics 'might easily give rise to unrest and sedition, and cause deceitful assaults'.[11] A committee of the States of Holland, charged with mapping out a new religious policy, had already declared in 1575 that 'one ought, in fact, to tolerate the exercise of the Popish religion, if it were not for the priests and monks, our sworn enemies, who had tried to use the same for [fomenting] sedition'.[12] Subsequent edicts were similarly legitimised by appealing to state security.

These suspicions of treason were not entirely unfounded. In all the towns of Holland and Zeeland that joined Orange's revolt in 1572, large sections of the magistracy and the population had fled. They waited in Amsterdam and other royalist towns for a victory of the Spanish army that would enable them to return to their homes, and some of them indeed actively supported the Spanish war effort. But many of those who had remained behind in the rebellious areas were also deeply unhappy with the new regime. There were counter-revolutionary plots in Haarlem, Delft, Gouda, and Dordrecht, where wealthy and well-connected citizens intrigued to open the town gates for the Spanish army. In 1575 persistent rumours circulated that the rural population of the Noorderkwartier was conspiring to let in the Spanish troops. These rumours turned out to be unfounded, but it is significant that many people believed them, including Orange himself, the military commander of North Holland, Sonoy, and the magistrates of nearly all the North Holland towns.[13]

While war in Holland and Zeeland prevented the authorities from granting full religious rights to the Catholics, the termination of warfare in 1576 did not alter the situation. A number of incidents convinced the authorities that Catholics were potential traitors: the untrustworthy behaviour of Philip II's governor-general Don Juan (who broke his treaty with the States-General by seizing Namur), the reconciliation with the

---

[11] H.A. Enno van Gelder, *Revolutionnaire Reformatie. De vestiging van de Gereformeerde Kerk in de Nederlandse gewesten, gedurende de eerste jaren van de Opstand tegen Filips II, 1575–1585* (Amsterdam, 1943), p. 114.

[12] *Oude kerkordeningen der Nederlandsche Hervormde Gemeenten (1563–1638) en het concept-reglement op de organisatie van het Hervormd Kerkgenootschap in het Koninkrijk Holland*, ed. C. Hooijer (Zaltbommel, 1865), pp. 117, 129.

[13] Henk van Nierop, *Het verraad van het Noorderkwartier. Oorlog, terreur en recht in de Nederlandse Opstand* (Amsterdam, 1999), reference to treason plots in the towns of South Holland on pp. 113–14.

king of Spain of the Walloon provinces united in the Union of Arras in
1579, the 'betrayal' of turncoat Rennenberg, and several attempts to assassinate William of Orange, first in 1582 and then – successfully – in
1584. In 1592 the authorities tried and executed a priest who had cons-
pired to assassinate Stadholder Maurice, and in 1599 a Catholic zealot
stabbed and killed the minister of Deventer.[14] These atrocities confirmed
the worst suspicions of the Calvinists, and the authorities duly responded
with stern repressive measures.

More astonishing than the fears of the rebels was that the majority
of the Catholic population remained, in fact, stubbornly loyal to a state
that was bent on the destruction of their religion. In this respect the
Dutch Catholics resembled the English Recusants, although it should
be pointed out that the Dutch Catholics were far more numerous than
their English co-religionists. Paradoxically, the same war that was responsible for the disparagement of the Catholics also brought about their
loyalty to the Orangist cause. Philip II had declared himself the champion
of the restoration of Catholicism, but his main instrument for reaching
this goal, the army, had made itself tremendously unpopular. The sacking of Mechelen, Zutphen, and Naarden (1572), Oudewater (1575), and
Antwerp (1576) made it abundantly clear that Catholics – even priests and
monks – had nothing to expect from the Spanish military. The soldiers
looted monasteries, shrines, and churches and massacred Catholics along
with the rest of the population. Since Spanish atrocities made it easy for
the authorities to discredit Catholics, it became imperative for the latter
to distance themselves from suspicions of disloyalty and treason.

A further incentive for Catholics to remain loyal to the new state
must have been the connivance of the authorities. Notwithstanding the
avalanche of anti-Popish edicts, Catholics were remarkably free to practise
their religion – especially in the countryside and in areas with a Catholic
majority, such as Holland's Noorderkwartier.

Life is messier than legislation (or historiography) suggests. It has been
well established that a broad chasm existed between everyday reality
and the rigid edicts banning Catholic activity. There are many excellent studies treating the legal, social, and political situation of Catholics
in the United Provinces, and these testify to the tension between theory
and practice, between the law and its enforcement. From 1580 onwards,

---

[14] Pieter Christiaensz Bor, *Oorsprongk, begin en vervolgh der Nederlandscher oorlogen*, 4 vols.
(Amsterdam, 1679–1684), vol. III, p. 815, and vol. IV, p. 528. A probably exhaustive list of
Catholic treason attempts in [A. van den Berg], *Verdediging van de zaak der Hervormden,
tegen zeker advys en consideratiën, welke die van Overbetuwe, door den burger J. Glover, op
den Gelderschen landdag, hebben doen voorlezen, betrekkelijk de kerkelijke en armengoederen*
(Amsterdam, 1797), p. 63.

hardly a year passed without a fresh batch of anti-Catholic edicts. Only after 1688 did the pace of legislation slacken. The very fact that anti-Catholic edicts were so frequently re-issued testifies that the authorities were unable – and often unwilling – to enforce them.[15]

Historians have offered a number of explanations for the apparent paradox of official repression combined with actual connivance. H.A. Enno van Gelder has underscored the tolerant mentality of the regent class (with the spirit of Erasmus always lurking around the corner), but J.L. Price has pointed out that in education and general outlook the Dutch political classes were not different from other rulers in Europe.[16] It is possible that an older tradition did play a role. During the reign of Charles V and Philip II there had been a similarly blatant discrepancy between the government's harsh anti-Protestant edicts and the tolerant attitude of local authorities. There was, moreover, a strong Erastian tradition in the Low Countries, with the town regents, even when they were members of the Reformed Church, unwilling to accept the leadership of the consistories.

The overwhelming numbers of Catholics in the United Provinces made effective prosecution a practical impossibility. Catholics comprised nearly one-third of the population of the towns in Holland and almost half the population of the Dutch Republic as a whole, and during the seventeenth century their numbers were growing. Locally, in the Generality Lands and in most areas outside the cities, they formed the majority of the population. Effective action was unthinkable, short of inciting rebellion or driving the local population into the arms of the Spanish. The judicial authorities had no police force at their disposal capable of acting on such a scale, and they were unwilling to call up the army. The town militias (*schutterijen*) were not at all prepared to act against their fellow citizens, Catholic or otherwise. Since Catholic citizens made up a large segment of the militias, these bodies were clearly unfit for such a task. And although the sources never explicitly mention this, the burgomasters probably considered effective anti-Catholic action suicidal from an economic point of view. Demographically and economically, the towns were heavily dependent on the influx of immigrant labour from the surrounding countryside and from Catholic areas in the Empire.

[15] W.P.C. Knuttel, *De toestand der Nederlandsche katholieken ten tijde der Republiek* (The Hague, 1892); H.A. Enno van Gelder, *Getemperde vrijheid. Een verhandeling over de verhouding van kerk en staat in de Republiek der Verenigde Nederlanden en de vrijheid van meningsuiting in zake godsdienst, drukpers en onderwijs, gedurende de 17e eeuw* (Groningen, 1972), pp. 111–50; A.Th. van Deursen, *Plain Lives in a Golden Age: Popular Culture, Religion and Society in Seventeenth-Century Holland* (Cambridge, 1981), pp. 290–7.
[16] Van Gelder, *Getemperde vrijheid*, pp. 123–7; J.L. Price, *Holland and the Dutch Republic in the Seventeenth Century: The Politics of Particularism* (Oxford, 1994), pp. 85–9, 201.

While the magistracies of towns represented in the provincial states assemblies were Protestantised during the Revolt, in the smaller towns many Catholic regents remained in place. In the villages, too, many magistrates were Catholics.[17] Even if the sheriff (*schout*) or bailiff – often an outsider – managed to bring a culprit to trial, he could expect the local *schepenen*, as often Catholics as not, to acquit the defendant. As we have seen, this was precisely the reason the bailiff of Texel referred his case to the *Gecommitteerde raden*. Many local seigniors (*ambachtsheren*) were also Catholics, who appointed Catholic sheriffs, and these were not at all disposed to prosecute their co-religionists.

Another factor contributing to transforming the anti-Catholic edicts into a dead letter was the practice of *compositie* (recognition money). This was a system whereby Catholics avoided legal action by paying the judicial authorities, in effect buying religious freedom for themselves. Many law officers lined their pockets with a regular flow of bribes, paid without demur by the local Catholic community.

As food for thought I would like to suggest an additional explanation for the reluctance of the authorities to implement anti-Catholic legislation. Christine Kooi in her contribution to this volume describes the manifold and flexible strategies employed by Holland's Catholic community to accommodate to a hostile environment. All these strategies were played out against the backdrop of a civic culture in which the law and respect for the law played a significant role. It is revealing that unlike their co-religionists in Ireland and England or in the eastern provinces of the Dutch Republic (as Maarten Prak explains elsewhere in this volume), Catholics in Holland were never limited in their civic rights. Although they were denied the right to practise their religion, they enjoyed the full protection of civic privileges. Elsewhere I have called attention to the extraordinary degree to which the Dutch placed their trust in the law, insisting that the authorities also be subject to the rule of law, even under conditions of warfare.[18] In their reverence for the law and for due legal process, the Dutch were perhaps different from other Europeans in this period, but further research would be needed to bear this out. It is also worth mentioning that although the law was unequivocal in its absolute ban on Catholic activities, resourceful citizens still had an impressive array of legal devices at their disposal to avoid conviction.

The case of the bailiff of Texel, cited at the beginning of this chapter, reveals a good deal about the resourcefulness of the Catholics. In spite of the bellicose stance of the bailiff, this case too was probably settled

---

[17] Knuttel, *Toestand der Nederlandsche katholieken*, pp. 347–54 (Appendix A) provides a list of Catholic officials in the countryside of Holland in 1658.

[18] Van Nierop, *Het verraad van het Noorderkwartier*, pp. 231–336.

through the payment of recognition money. The magistrates of Texel privately approached the *Gecommitteerde raden* in an attempt to have them drop the case. The latter answered that they could not avoid hearing the case, but urged the magistrates to appear before their court and settle the case 'by friendly agreement' with the bailiff.[19]

A comparable case occurred in Nibbixwoud (a village near Hoorn in North Holland) in 1624, where 'Popish superstition' was so common that large groups took part in processions and religious services in broad daylight. The *drossaart* of West-Friesland complained that the villagers refused to appear before the *Gecommitteerde raden* since they claimed to fall under the jurisdiction of the town of Hoorn.[20] The defiant attitude of Catholic peasants suggests that citizens were steeped in a way of thinking more legalistic than republican.

In 1594 the sheriff of Enkhuizen attempted to prosecute a group of Catholics who had organised a religious gathering in the nearby countryside. The citizens pleaded not guilty, pointing out that the edicts forbade only the administration of the sacraments. In this case, they asserted, no priest had been involved. A layman, a simple peasant, had merely read an elucidation of the Gospels. A committee of twelve lawyers advised that this was not forbidden by the edicts, but the *Hof van Holland* took a different position. Baffled by the contrary opinions, the *schepenen* of Enkhuizen turned to the States of Holland for advice in this arcane affair.[21]

The small town of Purmerend, finally, harboured a *huiskerk* or hidden church, a spacious building specially erected for conducting Catholic services, situated behind an ordinary townhouse but towering above all other buildings in the neighbourhood. On Sundays large crowds of believers from Purmerend and the surrounding countryside flocked to the *huiskerk* to hear Mass, unabashedly and openly, summoned by the very bells of the main Reformed Church of Purmerend. The *Hof van Holland* suspected the bailiff of Purmerend of making huge profits from recognition moneys and spurred him into action. In 1624 the bailiff finally summoned the owner of the clandestine church before the local magistrates' court. It was to no avail. The bailiff notified the *Hof* that he believed the pertinent legislation was not applicable (although the edict in question unequivocally prescribed a stiff fine of 200 guilders for the offence). He had therefore resorted to Roman Law (the so-called *Titulum Codicis de Haereticis et Manichaeis*). The perplexed *schepenen*, simple citizens without academic legal training, had no experience with such abstruse legal

[19] Archief van de Gecommitteerde Raden van West-Friesland en het Noorderkwartier, inv. no. 247, fo. 384 *et seq.*, RNH.
[20] Van Lommel (ed.), 'Bouwstoffen voor de kerkelijke geschiedenis', 167–70.
[21] Van Nierop, *Het verraad van het Noorderkwartier*, p. 247.

proceedings. They were afraid 'to condemn or absolve rashly' and re-ferred the case to a committee of learned lawyers steeped in Roman Law. In the end, of course, nothing at all happened. The Catholics quietly continued to attend their clandestine religious services, while the bailiff (one must assume) continued to live well from the proceedings.[22]

These cases, and scores of similar ones, testify to the significant role played by the law in the lives of ordinary citizens of the United Provinces. They also illustrate the very substantial degree of toleration that religious dissenters enjoyed in practice – in spite of abundant legislation which was every bit as intolerant as in the rest of Europe.

---

[22] Van Lommel (ed.), 'Bouwstoffen voor de kerkelijke geschiedenis', 163–4.

8 Anabaptism and tolerance: possibilities and limitations

Samme Zijlstra †

One of the main victims of the religious clashes in sixteenth-century Europe was the group of Anabaptists. The great majority of the approximately 2,000 death sentences pronounced on the charge of heresy in the Netherlands during that century are related to Anabaptists. By rejecting infant baptism, refusing to take an oath, and their separation from the 'world' they had moved far away from mainstream Christianity. The shortlived kingdom of Munster (1534–5) had tainted the Anabaptist movement with the odium of violence and rebellion. Notwithstanding this, in the course of the century the following of Menno Simons had increased and had become an important movement which, at the end of the sixteenth century, in some regions like Friesland comprised about one-quarter of the population.

After the successful Revolt of the Netherlands against the Spanish king, the Dutch authorities had to cope with the presence of the Mennonites in society. Because of their large numbers the Mennonites could not be simply outlawed, while physical extinction was no option either. The authorities soon began following a policy of connivance, of grudgingly tolerating the Mennonites, to the regret of the ministers of the Reformed Church who demanded strict measures against Anabaptism. But although the Reformed Church had been given the status of a privileged Church in the Dutch Republic, it never became the State Church. Mennonites and other denominations like Jews and Lutherans were tacitly allowed – albeit with some restrictions – to profess their faith. The Dutch authorities had accepted that there was more than one religion in their territories.

Internally, the Anabaptist movement was deeply divided. Around 1545 a strong spiritualist current dominated the movement. Disagreement concerning the practice of banning and shunning caused a rift in 1557, which was followed by several others, so that at the end of the sixteenth century at least six major denominations were to be found among the Mennonites, and all of them utterly disliked each other.

During the first decades of the seventeenth century the idea gained ground that the differences between the various Mennonite denominations were not profound enough to justify the existence of different groups. All denominations agreed on the essential points, while the points of difference were not essential to faith and had to be tolerated. The question, however, was what were the essentials and non-essentials, and how far could tolerance be stretched?

Mennonites in the Republic: a tolerated minority

The year 1579 thus marks the beginning of a period of uneasy cohabitation of a Reformed Church which was favoured by the state with various other denominations, most important of which were the Catholics and Mennonites. The crucial difference was the interpretation of freedom of conscience, laid down in the Union of Utrecht. Should the interpretation be very restrictive, and thus imply that a person was allowed to profess his religion only secretly behind closed doors, as the Reformed ministers thought, or had the clause to be read in a broader sense, namely as freedom of religion, as was the view of the Mennonites?[1] Around 1600 the government came to a solution. The authorities tacitly declared the Mennonites to be a connived (tolerated) religion, an expression that did not mean freedom of religion, but otherwise interpreted freedom of conscience more broadly than the Reformed thought to be wise. With this interpretation, the authorities abandoned the idea of one country, one religion. The term 'connived' already indicates that the Dutch authorities were no supporters of religious pluralism on principle, but they tolerated the situation for want of anything better. Although the Reformed ministers urged for measures against the Mennonites, the authorities rarely took action; on the contrary, they met the Mennonites' objections to the use of arms, to swearing, and to marrying in the Reformed Church. Mennonites could buy off their military obligations; instead of taking an oath, their word of honour was sufficient, and their marriages could be performed before the magistrates. The authorities turned a blind eye to the building of churches by the Mennonites.[2]

[1] The restrictive approach was still defended in 1629 by the minister Henricus Arnoldi from Delft in his *Van de conscientiedwangh*: J.I. Israel, 'Toleration in Seventeenth-Century Dutch and English Thought', in S. Groenveld and M. Wintle (eds.), *Religion, Scholarship and Art in Anglo-Dutch Relations in the 17th Century* (Zutphen, 1991), pp. 13–30, especially p. 19. For a long time, this approach prevailed: we shall see that the Frisian minister Nicolaus Schuyring used the same arguments in a treatise against the Mennonites published in 1662.

[2] This process of accommodation did not occur at the same time in the different provinces of the Republic. The Mennonites in Holland were the first to enjoy these privileges. Later on the other provinces gradually followed the example of Holland. This process was completed around 1650. Israel paints too negative an image of the situation of the Mennonites around 1600: J. Israel, 'The Intellectual Debate about Toleration in the

In their turn, the Mennonites went along with the wishes of the government. They bought off their military obligations or fulfilled them by doing guard duty or digging trenches. They also paid their taxes, although they knew that the major part of these was used to finance war efforts. During their services they prayed for the authorities.[3] The Mennonites soon proved to be loyal citizens who, with their activities in trade and industry, contributed significantly to the treasury. This was one of the reasons for the Dutch authorities to protect them against attacks from the side of the Reformed Church. In addition, the authorities were certainly not inclined to replace the recently abolished Spanish Inquisition with one based on the Genevan model, and were determined to follow a policy of connivance. Of course, this policy had its limitations: the Mennonites were not allowed to build churches in main streets, and they were also excluded from holding public office. The latter limitation, however, did not much harm them, for they did not covet office, but kept aloof from it as much as possible.

The Mennonites were in fact very pleased with their position as a tolerated minority. Like other dissenting groups, such as Jews and Lutherans, they accepted the restrictions with regard to their residence in the Republic and never asked to be granted equal rights. Full state recognition would not have been as attractive as it might seem at first sight, for it would have put the Mennonites in an awkward position. For example, they would have to allow that they were monitored by the government (a practice they deeply disliked) like the Reformed Church, whose synods were carefully monitored by representatives of the provincial governments. Sometimes the lack of state control aroused the jealousy even of some Reformed ministers. The Mennonites realised quite well that nowhere in Europe did they fare better than in the Netherlands, for here they were left alone, while in other parts of the continent they were – even at the end of the seventeenth century – persecuted and driven from their homelands.

Dutch Republic', in C. Berkvens-Stevelinck, J. Israel, and G.H.M. Posthumus Meyjes (eds.), *The Emergence of Tolerance in the Dutch Republic* (Leiden/New York/Cologne, 1997), pp. 3–36, especially p. 5.

[3] Around 1618 the Flemish elder Fr. de Knuyt wrote a short confession of faith, entitled *Onder verbeteringe, een corte bekentenisse onses geloofs, van Vader, Sone ende heyligen geest, den heylighen doop, het ampt der overheyt ende het eedt-sweren* (n.p., n.d.). The confession ends with a prayer for the authorities (p. 208): 'O Lord, prevent them from becoming persecutors of thine holy congregation, but make them members and supporters of it, so that we may do our jobs and trade in peace, and we may live in peace and lead a holy life' ('Bewaertse o Heere datse gheen vervolghers van uwe H. Ghemeente, maer liever belijders ende voorstanders der selve moghen worden, dat wy alsoo in goede ruste ende vrede by onsen neeringe gerust ende stille in uwe vreese salighlyck ende heylighlijck moghen leven').

We may conclude that the position of the Mennonites in the Republic was that of a community with restricted freedom. In their turn, they were loyal to the authorities. Their view of the authorities is strikingly characterised by Pieter Jansz Twisck, elder of the Old Frisians, one of the many denominations among the Dutch Mennonites. In his *Religions Vryheyt* (Freedom of Religion), published in 1609,[4] he starts with a rhetorical question: 'What is the use of this description in the manner of a chronicle of religious liberty? Are you or is anyone molested or is your freedom of conscience under attack? One has to confess (thankfully) no.' The treatise therefore was meant to praise the government of the Netherlands. Its benevolence had to be rewarded with gratitude and respect, as well as with the paying of taxes and civil obedience.[5]

The subtitle of *Religions Vryheyt* shows what Twisck meant by religious freedom:

A short description in the manner of a chronicle of freedom of religion against the coercion of conscience, collected from many books written from the times of Christ to the year 1609, in which one can see as clearly as in a mirror how many emperors, kings, lords, rulers, counts, noblemen, old and new teachers and scholars as well as common and experienced men (from different denominations) advise, learn, and practice how to deal with heretics. That the sword of steel of the secular authorities should not be used to exert coercion in matters of faith, that the heretics and nonbelievers should not be won over with violence, but with the word of God. That differences in religion do not bring destruction or endanger the peace in a country or town. That the realm of Christ is not of this world and that the Gospel ought not be defended with the sword.[6]

In two volumes Twisck quotes more than a thousand different authors and documents in order to prove his thesis. The greater number of the quotations are derived from writings dating from the first decades of the Dutch Revolt; pamphlets written on behalf of William of Orange

---

[4] P.J. Twisck, *Na beter. Religions Vryheyt. Een korte cronijcsche beschryvinghe van die vryheyt der Religien* (Hoorn, 1609).

[5] Twisck, *Religions Vryheyt*, voorreden: 'Waertoe toch dese chronycksche beschrijvinghe van religions vryheyt? Geschiet u ofte iemant anders alhier nu eenige overlast ofte perssinge in de conscientien? Men moet goetwillich (met danck) bekennen: neen.'

[6] 'Een corte cronijcsche beschryvinghe van die vryheyt der religien tegen die dwang der conscientien ghevoelen, wt veel verscheyden boecken van Christus tijt af tot den jaer 1609 toe, waer wt dat men als in een spiegel claerlijck sien mach veel keyzeren, coninghen, Heeren, vorsten, graven, edel-luyden, ouden ende nieuwe leeraers, geleerden, oock gemene en wel eervaren mannen (van verscheyden ghesintheden) haer raet, leer, werck ende insien hoe men met ketters handelen sal. Dat het staelen sweert van die wereltlycke overheyt tot geloofsdwang over die conscientie niet en streckt, dat die ketters ende misgeloovigen niet met haer gewelt, maer met Gods woort moeten overwonnen worden. Dat verscheyden religien geen verderf of onvrede in een lant ofte stadt brengen. Dat het rijck Christi van deser werelt niet en is en dat het evangelium met den sweerde niet behoeft verdedicht te worden.'

and the statutes of the States-General are often quoted, but the opinion of Lutheran and Calvinist theologians are also brought to readers' attention. We also find references to the works of Caspar Coolhaes and Herman Herberts, two Reformed ministers who in the last decades of the sixteenth century cherished Libertine views and who were opposed to the Reformed oppression of the Mennonites, as well as quotations from the polemic that was aroused by the so-called 'Severe Edict' proclaimed by the town of Groningen in 1601.[7]

Practically all celebrities who had written in favour of religious tolerance are quoted, for example, Desiderius Erasmus (II, 30–3), Sebastian Franck (II, 69–70), the Italian refugee Jacobus Acontius (II, 194–5), Dirk Volkertz Coornhert (II, 191, 202–17), the editor of the Acts of the peace negotiations of Cologne of 1579 (Agge van Albada) (II, 85–92), and above all Sebastian Castellio. To the latter author Twisck devotes no less then twenty-three pages (II, 93–116). He also quotes, via the aliases Georgius Kleinbergius, Augustinus Eleutherius, Basilius Montfortius, and Martinus Bellius, almost the whole *De haereticis an sint persequendi*, written by Castellio (I, 93–4, II, 51, II, 88–92, II, 155). Twisck even quoted the Socinian author Ostorodt (II, 243–6), and – albeit without mentioning the author's name – the archheretic David Joris' *Dialogue between Philip and Jacob* (II, 93).[8]

Twisck confronted other countries with the example of the Republic. After the expiration of the Twelve Years' Truce in the war with Spain (1621), Twisch wrote in his *Comeet boecxken* (Booklet on Comets) that kings and rulers in countries near and far should not make war because of differences in religion, 'but let their subjects live freely according to their religion'.[9]

The *Grote Vergadering* of the States-General of 1651 once more confirmed the position of the Mennonites. They belonged to the denominations tolerated by the Dutch authorities who, with certain restrictions, were allowed to profess their religion freely. After having paid enormous amounts of money to finance the wars against England and France in 1665 and 1672 – in Friesland alone the Mennonites yielded more than a million guilders – they obtained *de facto* freedom of religion.

---

[7] In 1601 the town of Groningen proclaimed a 'Severe Edict' against the Mennonites that practically outlawed them and prohibited the practice of their religion. It caused a fierce polemic between supporters and adversaries of the edict. See: S. Zijlstra, 'Het "scherpe plakkaat" van Groningen uit 1601', *Doopsgezinde Bijdragen* 15 (1989), 65–78.

[8] David Joris, *Een tweespraeck tusschen twee religiose personen, Philips unde Jacob genaemt, tracterende teghen 't vervolch* (n.p., 1551).

[9] P.J. Twisck, *Comeet boecxken midsgaders eenige teyckenen die verschenen zijn tsedert de geboorte onses Salichmakers Jesu Christi met hare werckingen ofte volgende veranderingen, beroerten, ellende ende plagen* (Hoorn, 1624), p. 142.

But earlier, the Mennonites had had to face stiff opposition from the Reformed ministers. During the first half of the seventeenth century the ministers wrote bitter polemics against the Mennonites, but around the middle of the century the polemics abated. One of the last contributions was made in Friesland. In a booklet written by C. de Vries, a medical doctor in the town of Harlingen in 1662, the Mennonite stand is discussed in more detail. De Vries had composed his treatise against a book entitled *Doolhof der Mennisten* (The Maze of the Mennonites) written by a Frisian minister, the Reverend Nicolaus Schuyring.[10] Schuyring had exhorted the States of Friesland to take action against the Mennonites by forbidding them to build churches. Their elders should also be banned from preaching in places other than their residences. He wanted the Mennonites to be removed from public view. Schuyring argued that the Mennonites had received only freedom of conscience, which meant that they were allowed to practise their religion only behind closed doors, instead of publically. All other so-called rights the Mennonites pretended to were not given to them by law or statute, but were based only on connivance. To prove his point, Schuyring had consulted the resolutions of the States-General as well as several books by renowned historians such as Pieter Bor and Everard van Reydt.[11] Strictly speaking, Schuyring was right, but we have seen that the authorities actually steered a different course, for they conceived freedom of conscience in a much broader sense than Schuyring wished to admit.

According to De Vries, the reverend tried to discredit the Mennonites with the authorities. As Twisck had done before him, De Vries (who probably borrowed many of his arguments from the pamphlet *Hollandsche Zeep* (Dutch Soap), published in 1643)[12] thanked the Dutch authorities elaborately for granting the Mennonites freedom to profess their religion. He especially referred to the recent past to show that this was more than mere freedom of conscience. As we have seen, this line of defence was a

---

[10] C. de Vries, *An den Eerwaerden en gheleerden Heer N. Ioannis Schuyring, predicant op Bexterzwaegh, ziende op zijn uit-ghegheven boexken, ghenaemt Doolhof der Mennisten* (n.p., 1662). This polemic is discussed in: S. Zijlstra, 'In doalhôf fan 'e menisten. De polemyk tusken grifformearde predikant en in meniste dokter om 1660 hinne', *De Vrije Fries* 78 (1998), 57–73.

[11] Zijlstra, 'In doalhôf fan 'e menisten', 68. The Reverend Schuyring probably borrowed these views from the minister Henricus Arnoldi, who took the same stand in his *Van de conscientiedwangh* published in 1629; cf. Israel, 'The Intellectual Debate', pp. 17–18.

[12] G. van Vryburgh, *Hollandsche Zeep tegen de uytheemsche vlecken en vuyligheden daer mede P. Bontemps, Walsch predicant tot Haerlem door sijne schriften nu onlanghs uytgegeven de Mennoniten heeft soecken te bekladden* (Amsterdam, 1643; a second edition appeared in 1644). Van Vryburgh was an alias of Abraham Davidsz Volboet. He polemicised together with the Remonstrant Passchier de Fyne against Petrus Bontemps' (minister of the Walloon Church of Haarlem) *Kort Bewijs van de menighvuldige doolingen der Wederdoopers ofte Mennisten* that had been published in 1641.

common one in Mennonite polemics: for preference they referred back to a situation that existed during the early decades of the Revolt and rarely quoted from authors like Erasmus or Castellio.[13] By obtaining most of his arguments from this period De Vries was thus no exception to the rule. He concluded, for instance, that during the peace negotiations in Cologne (1579) the States-General had exhorted the king of Spain to allow 'everyone to live according to their religion and to give them the opportunity to profess the prescripts of his religion'.[14] Faith could not be enforced, but was a gift of God. The States-General had also concluded that those who professed a religion different from Catholicism should not be deemed wholly bereft of its practice, because without profession of their own faith their consciences would be severely troubled.[15]

The records of the Cologne peace talks were edited in 1580 and are often mentioned in pleas on behalf of tolerance. The Frisian lawyer Agge van Albada, who represented the States-General in Cologne as their speaker ('orateur ende taalman'), was a great supporter of tolerance. As a follower of the Silesian noblemen Caspar von Schwenckfeld he had strong Spiritualist inclinations. Especially in his annotations of the records of the peace negotiations, Albada succeeded in explaining his views concerning the need for tolerance. His name soon sank into oblivion: the annotations are usually attributed to an anonymous 'writer of the annotations'.[16]

Additionally, De Vries referred to the reproval given to the town of Middelburg in Zeeland by William of Orange in 1576, when the magistrate pressed hard against the Mennonites and, among others, forbade them to be active in business and trade. The Prince of Orange stated that the war was waged on behalf of freedom of conscience, and it would be improper to deny this freedom to the Mennonites. The magistrate had no right 'to meddle with anyone's conscience'. Thus, according to the Prince of Orange, conducting business and trade without being molested was part of freedom of conscience. Moreover, the Mennonites helped to win the war by paying taxes, and endangered their lives. De Vries further quoted the complaints made by the States-General about the Count of Leicester in 1587 in which they stated that in view of the different denominations,

---

[13] Israel, 'The Intellectual Debate', p. 3. In the pamphlet *Hollandsche Zeep*, p. 65, for example only Georgius Kleynberg, one of the authors from S. Castellio, *De haereticis an sint persequendi* (n.p., 1554), is mentioned, albeit by quoting the writer of the annotations.

[14] De Vries, *An den Eerwaerden en gheleerden Heer N. Ioannis Schuyring*, pp. 3–4: 'te laeten by haer conscientien blijven en te verleenen openbaere exercitie van religie'.

[15] De Vries, *An den Eerwaerden en gheleerden Heer N. Ioannis Schuyring*, pp. 4, 8.

[16] *Acta pacificationis quae coram Sac. Caesare Majest. commissariis inter seren. Regis Hispaniorum et Principis Matthiae archiducis Austriae gubernatoris, et Ordinumque Belgii legatos, Coloniae habita sunt* (Leiden, 1580). On Albada, see: W. Bergsma, *Aggaeus van Albada (c. 1525–1587), schwenckfeldiaan, staatsman en strijder voor verdraagzaamheid* (Meppel, 1983), especially pp. 21–9 and 95–105.

the Churches had to be left free and nobody should be forced to join a particular group. By acting otherwise, the unity of the state would be jeopardised.[17]

From a more recent past (1615) dated the reaction of the States-General towards the behaviour of the magistrate of the town of Aardenburg. They wrote that the treatment meted out to the Mennonites there had surprised them. In flagrant violation of all resolutions, the magistrates had been trying to curb the Mennonites in professing their religion. Like the Prince of Orange, the States-General interpreted freedom of conscience in a broad sense. The same freedom they enjoyed elsewhere in the Republic had to be bestowed upon the Mennonites of Aardenburg as well. It was strictly forbidden for the magistrate 'to meddle with an individual's conscience'.[18] In recent years, De Vries continued, the States-General had protested against the treatment of the Mennonites in the Swiss towns of Berne and Zurich.

Finally, De Vries presented as part of his argument the opinion of a number of unexpected persons. He referred to the Catholic Stephen Bathory who, in the second half of the sixteenth century, had been king of Poland and had concluded: 'Ego sum rex populorum, non conscientiarum.'[19] According to the records of the Council of Trent, the duke of Savoy had given freedom of religion to his subjects against the wishes of the Pope. Calvin is quoted too, for he had concluded that the Calvinists did not strive for power or want to use violence, but were satisfied with the only weapon that counted, namely the power of God's word. Coercion in matters of faith was not effective: the Count of Alzey in Germany had once declared, with reference to the Anabaptists: 'The more I kill, the more new adherents come forward. The Inquisition had failed to wipe out Anabaptism in the Low Countries, the Calvinists would also fail.'[20]

A ban on practising religion thus had no use. But De Vries was fully confident that the authorities in the Netherlands did not want to tear down freedom as it was an established fact that the Mennonites did not want to dominate the country, but only asked instead to be left alone and

---

[17] De Vries, *An den Eerwaerden en gheleerden Heer N. Ioannis Schuyring*, pp. 4–5.

[18] The same answer was given to the authorities in the province of Groningen in 1607, when the Mennonites had complained about the harassments they had undergone. Their complaint was supported by Stadholder Willem Lodewijk. The Estates-General stated that the Mennonites should not be treated otherwise than was proscribed by law and reasonableness or treated in a different way as was common use in the other parts of the Republic: Zijlstra, 'Het "scherpe plakkaat"', 69.

[19] King Stephen Bathory and the example of Poland were often quoted by Remonstrant authors too, to prove that it was possible for various Churches to live in harmony: Israel, 'Toleration in Seventeenth-Century Dutch and English Thought', p. 20.

[20] De Vries, *An den Eerwaerden en gheleerden Heer N. Ioannis Schuyring*, pp. 8–9, 11.

to live in peace according to their religion. He made only one restriction: the Mennonites would never renounce their right to express their opinions, and to sow the Godly word in this world: in other words to propagandise their views. With regard to propaganda, they were obliged to be more obedient to God than to men. But he did indeed regret the heat and ferocity which accompanied the polemics of both sides.[21]

We rarely encounter fundamental pleas like those of De Vries. They were composed mostly when the Mennonites felt themselves threatened by the Reformed attacks. They were well aware that the tolerance practised in the Republic depended on the support of the authorities. Moreover, tolerance had its limits, and those who transgressed these limits had to pay the price. In the first instance the fundamental Christian doctrines established limits, for instance the belief in the Triune God: it was explicitly forbidden to spread anti-Trinitarian ideas. In the second place the authorities were aloof from opinions that might endanger peace and order. So Schuyring tried (in vain) to depict the Mennonites as a danger to the state in order to persuade the government to take action against them. De Vries opposed him by stating that the Mennonites were not anti-Trinitarians, nor did they endanger public order.

But not every Mennonite was as orthodox as De Vries supposed. Uke Walles, the leader of the Groningen Old Flemish, a very conservative Mennonite denomination, taught that in the end all sins would be forgiven. Even Judas, who had betrayed Jesus Christ, would be saved. This opinion was not only heresy, but was also a threat to society: the limits between right and wrong would blur, for why should men live an honest life, when they were already certain of eternal bliss? The Reformed ministers of Groningen brought charges against Uke Walles, who was banished from the territory of Groningen. He settled in East Friesland and in 1645 he wrote two books in which he defended himself against the treatment meted out to him. He stated that only God, not the secular authorities, had the right to judge consciences, so God had to judge whether his opinion was right or wrong. Walles also compared the persecutions by the Reformed with the Inquisition and was amazed that they,

---

[21] De Vries, *An den Eerwaerden en gheleerden Heer N. Ioannis Schuyring*, p. 10. The same kind of argumentation as used by De Vries was mentioned by the above-named Gerard van Vryburg alias Abraham Volboet in his polemic of 1645 with the minister Bontemps, who in his writings had attacked the Mennonites. He was also opposed to the smear campaign of the Reformed against the Mennonites, who tried to incite the authorities against them. This attack on freedom of conscience would eventually lead to the killing of heretics. Vrijburg, however, did not expect that Bontemps would rally many allies, not even among his fellow ministers: G. van Vryborch [Vryburgh], *Proeve van Bontemps Logen-water, hoe langher hoe vuyler, in het welcke worden overwogen die dingen die Bontemps aldaer noopende het verschil der leer tusschen hen ende de mennisten eenighsins aenroert* (Amsterdam, 1645), pp. 4–5, 30.

who once had been compelled to flee persecution, now themselves had become persecutors.[22]

Finally, Walles stated that no one should be persecuted or put to death by reason of his faith, quoting Castellio's *De haereticis*.[23] The punishment of heretics should not be persecution or the death penalty, but excommunication. Moreover, tolerance was useful to the state: the Netherlands, for instance, where these values had been brought into practice, flourished.[24] Uke Walles' appeal was, of course, to no avail for, as we have stated, tolerance in the Netherlands had its limitations. The authorities would not and could not tolerate Walles' opinions.

De Vries and Uke Walles were exceptions to the rule. The majority of the Mennonites had nothing to fear from the authorities. So there was no need to compose elaborate and fundamental pleas for tolerance as it was enough for them to cherish and occasionally to defend the rights that were bestowed upon them. They clung to their ideological heritage – for instance the principle of non-violence – and acknowledged the authority of the state, which provided the opportunity to practise their religion.[25] The Mennonites did not see or did not want to see the contradiction between their vision of non-violence and the acceptance of a regime that had come to power after a violent war of independence.

The Waterlander view on tolerance

Tolerance, or the acceptance of the fact that deviant views did exist within one society, was a successful means to create harmony. In view of the thriving condition of the Republic, it was apparent that it worked. A number of Mennonite denominations gradually began to consider the use of tolerance as a solution to one of their main problems, discord, or to use tolerance to restore the unity of the movement.

[22] Uke Walles, *Een weemoedige klaghende supplicatie aen alle Heeren rechteren, officieren, ende aen alle menschen so hooghe als nederige standes tot ontlastinghe ende verantwoordinghe van veele onware beschuldigingen over mijn persoon* (n.p., 1645), pp. 15, 18, 27.

[23] Castellio, *De haereticis an sint persequendi*, p. 129: 'O principes et magistratus omnes, aperite oculos, aperite aures, timete Deum, et cogitate tandem de reddenda Deo ratione villicationis vestrae. Multi graves poenas dederunt propter crudelitatem, nemo propter clementiam. Munti in extremo iudicio damnabitur, quia occiderunt insontes, nemo damnabitur, quia non occiderit.'

[24] Uke Walles, *Twee brieven aen Laurens Pimperlingh gesonden tot ontschuldiginghe ende onderrichtinge van sijne ghedane lasteringe over mijn persoone* (n.p., 1645), ff. A3r, A4v–A5r, and pp. 19, 27, 47. The argument that tolerance only strengthens the state is also used by the Remonstrant Episcopius: Israel, 'Toleration in Seventeenth-Century Dutch and English Thought', p. 21.

[25] For instance Galenus Abrahamsz, elder with the United Flemings and Waterlanders in Amsterdam, in his *Verdédiging der Christenen die Doopsgezinde genaamd worden, beneffens korte grondstellingen van hun gelove en leere* (Amsterdam, 1699), pp. 30, 31.

The different denominations were afflicted with rifts and secessions. The Waterlanders had seceded after disagreements about the practice of banning and shunning; they declined to follow the rigid interpretation of Menno Simons and seceded around 1557. Another denomination, the High Germans, left Menno and his supporters shortly afterwards for the same reason. About 1565 the Mennonites who had not seceded clashed in Friesland on organisational and ideological issues. The two factions at the beginning of the conflict had consisted mainly of Frisians and Flemings who had taken refuge in Friesland, therefore the groups were named after their country of origin. Both Frisians and Flemings shunned each other; both in their turn split in 1587 and 1599 into a conservative and a more liberal branch, called Old Flemings and Young Flemings and Old and Young Frisians. About 1625, the very conservative Groningen Old Flemings seceded from the Young Flemings.

The division inside the movement was a thorn in the flesh of many Mennonites. They saw in tolerance the opportunity to hold together their denomination or even reunite the different groups, and referred to the example of the Waterlanders. The Waterlanders, who were not troubled by secessions, did not consider their congregation as the only true congregation, without blemish, the way the majority of groups did. True Christians were to be found among other denominations too. Also they did not interpret doctrines and usages very strictly, but tolerated deviating opinions to a certain extent. Like any individual, the congregation as a whole was not free from defects. Beyond that, tolerance was prescribed by Christ and Paul, and the Word of the Lord was far more important than human decisions and resolutions, which had no binding effect.

In a book written in 1638 by the Haarlemmer Jan de Witte, the author explained what was meant by tolerance in Waterlander circles. Peace and unity had to be founded on the touchstone of Jesus Christ, and the congregation had to be held together by mutual tolerance. De Witte, who aimed at reunion of the Waterlanders with other denominations, tried to minimise the importance of all doctrines as much as possible. According to him, believing that Jesus was incarnated and acknowledging that no other Saviour had to be expected was sufficient; speculations about how the incarnation had taken place were superfluous, while different views concerning this matter had to be tolerated in love.[26] Thus, differences between the groups could also be vanquished. 'At the end, true faith

---

[26] The Mennonite doctrine of incarnation read that Christ had taken no flesh from Mary, but went through her like water through a pipeline. Especially the orthodox groups among the Mennonites clung to this interpretation. See S. Voolstra, *Het woord is vlees geworden. De Melchioritisch-Menniste incarnatieleer* (Kampen, 1982).

is not like science, that lives and rests in the understanding brain, but is like a force that has its seat in the spirit.'[27] Tolerance must only be restricted if the foundations of the Christian faith were jeopardised. But De Witte also provided a solution to this problem: a number of persons, chosen by the elders of the denomination, should clear these issues. De Witte did not wish the members of the congregation to take decisions concerning these contending points, for this would lead to confusion and discord.[28]

Of course, the 'foundations of religion' formula was subjective and called for different opinions. A certain issue could be considered as essential by one man, while another would consider it a matter of secondary importance.[29] Moreover, the Waterlanders could not prevent the introduction of practices not mentioned in the Bible, such as praying aloud, chairs being reserved for important persons, and the singing of Psalms: elements they ferociously defended against dissidents.[30]

The tolerance of the Waterlanders was in fact not unlimited. For example, the confession of Hans de Ries, one of their most influential leaders, was formally not binding, but in reality it did prove to be authoritative within the majority of the Waterlander congregations. This confession provided the possibility of resisting undesirable elements like Socinianism, which denied the divine nature of Christ, as well as preserving group identity. The tolerance of the Waterlanders differed from that of the Collegiants who favoured unlimited tolerance, gave everyone who was present at their meeting the right to speak, and desisted from creating congregations.[31] The Collegiants were barred by many of the Waterlander congregations, while they also excluded the Socinians, especially because the latter were outlawed by the authorities.

---

[27] J. de Witte, *Vrede-schrift, daar inne gehandelt wort van de voornaamste verschillen in leere en verstanden onder de doopsghesinde gemeenten* (Amsterdam, 1638), pp. 24–5, 29, 61, 71: 'Int eynd, het ware geloof is niet gelijk een wetenschap, die in 't begrijpelijke breyn woont en rust, maar is als een kracht die sijn plaats heeft in 't gemoed.'

[28] De Witte, *Vrede-schrift*, pp. 84–5.

[29] P. Visser, *Broeders in de geest. De doopsgezinde bijdragen van Dierck en Jan Philipsz. Schabaelje tot de Nederlandse stichtelijke literatuur in de zeventiende eeuw* (Deventer, 1988), vol. I, pp. 113–14.

[30] P. Hendricksz, *Een ernstige bestraffinge aen de Vlaemsche doops-gesinde gemeinte tot Amsterdam* (Amsterdam, 1670).

[31] The movement of the Collegiants, which recruited its adherents mostly from society's upper classes, was founded around 1620 in the environment of Leiden. About 1680 the Collegiants had 'colleges' in nearly all important towns of the Republic. One hundred years later the movement was extinct. See for the Collegiants: A.C. Fix, 'Mennonites and Collegiants in Holland 1630–1700', *The Mennonite Quarterly Review* 64 (1990), 160–177, and A.C. Fix, *Prophecy and Reason. The Dutch Collegiants in the Early Enlightenment* (Princeton, 1991).

Tolerance and reunion

Tolerance also played a part in the contacts between the different denominations of the deeply divided Mennonite community. Especially after 1600, representatives of these denominations tried to approach each other on the basis of tolerance, which resulted in a number of unions that more or less took root. One of these, the union of the Waterlanders, High Germans, and Young Frisians, which concluded in 1601, proved to be a failure as early as 1613. Mutual tolerance proved to be too weak to hold together groups like Waterlanders and Frisians, who differed strongly in doctrine as well as in organisation. Preserving identity proved to be more important than the longing for unity.

In 1601 the Waterlanders from De Rijp in the north of Holland offered a 'peace proposition' to all other denominations, but especially to the Flemings, again based on mutual tolerance. 'We do not like to be pressed in our conscience and we also dislike to press others', they stated.[32] But the proposal was unacceptable, for the Waterlanders refused to be bound by a confession. The majority of the Flemings still subscribed to the point of view of Hans van Dantzig, who in the same year warned Flemings not to break the covenant with God and introduce novelties. The light could have no conversation with the darkness; there was only one Lord, one baptism, and one faith, so there could also only be one true congregation of God. *Rapprochement* was out of the question.[33]

But within the Flemish denominations, too, several leaders came under the spell of tolerance as a means to restore unity. Claes Claesz, the elder of the Young Flemish congregation of Blokzijl in Overijssel, was the life and soul of this process. He abandoned the concept of his denomination as being the only true congregation of God, and thus removed an important obstacle against an approach to other groups. Claesz stated that antiquity was no argument in favour of the idea that there was only one true congregation: the same argument that was used by the Papists and the Jews. Why, he asked with reference to the clashes between Flemings and Frisians in 1565, should the Flemings accept their view as the only true one?[34] It was contradictory to God's Word to found opinions on

---

[32] *Vrede-presentatie aan de Vriessche en Hoogduitsche Doopsgezinde Gemeentens van de Waterlandsche gemeentens gedaan in den Jaare 1601, den 4 July in de Rijp* (Amsterdam, 1686), p. 3.

[33] Hans van Dantzig, *Een vaderlijcke vermaninghe uyt den grooten schadt er heyliger schrift, daerin dat een vader zijne kinderen vermaent tot een vroom ende volstandich leven* (Haarlem, n.d.), pp. 7, 11, 41.

[34] Claes Claesz, *Eenvuldige vertrouwinge, waer inne naectelijck wt de H. Schrifture aengewesen wort dat Gods gemeente niet op eeniger menschen vroomheyt, oude gewoonten, traditien ofte lange belevingen, dan alleen op den hoecsteen Christum, sijne heylsame leere ende onberispelijck leven ghefondeert staet* (n.p., 1610), pp. 186, 202.

human traditions, for only those commands that are explicitly mentioned in the Bible were binding. There were indeed a number of essential doctrines which a Christian was obliged to believe, such as Christ as the Saviour, the Trinity, and the doctrine of incarnation. These essentials, however, did not include customs like the prohibition on marrying a partner who belonged to another Mennonite denomination. By distinguishing between essentials and non-essentials, Claesz cleared another obstacle to reunion, namely, the different customs to which the various denominations clung. Claes Claesz, however, held on to the concept of the existence of a visible congregation of God, but he no longer thought that it could be found exclusively with the Young Flemings, but with the Old Flemings, the High Germans, and the Frisians as well.[35] In respect of these stipulations he differed from the Waterlander view, according to which the true congregation consisted of Christians scattered over all Christendom.

The negotiations among a number of Mennonite groups did succeed: around 1630 the Flemings, Young Frisians, and High Germans merged and called themselves the United Congregations. Each group had composed a confession and ascertained that there were only minor differences among these confessions which had to be overlooked and tolerated. As for the foundations of faith, Flemings and Frisians had never been in discord; only external matters and organisational issues had caused dissension.[36]

The Waterlanders too were eager to join the United Congregations. Jan Philipsz Schabaelje, one of their leaders, considered the differences between his denomination and the United Congregations as insignificant, but he exaggerated. He pleaded to minimise the differences, but acknowledged that differences could indeed be found in the confessions. The prescription to overcome these differences was tolerance, but the Waterlander interpretation was quite different from that of the United Congregations, which longed for unity, not only regarding certain customs, but especially concerning dogma. In their view the confessions were binding.[37]

The Waterlanders drew up a formal peace proposition in 1647. They sent with it a printed confession of Hans de Ries, but made this gesture worthless by stating that no one was obliged to accept any confession whatsoever and everyone had to be the interpreter of his own words and

[35] Claes Claesz, *Eenvuldige vertrouwinge*, Introduction, pp. 12, 23, 70, 97–101.
[36] *Kort verhael van de vereeniginghe tusschen de doopsgesinde ghemeynten die aen d'eene zijde ghenoemt worden Vlamingen, aen de ander zijde de Vereenigde Vriesen ende Hoogduytschen vreedsaen gheschiet binnen Amsterdam, d. 26 April 1639* (Amsterdam, 1639), pp. 11–12.
[37] I.P. Schabaelje, *Vereenigingh van de principale artijckelen des geloofs eeniger doops-ghesinde gheymenten die men noemt Waterlanderen, Vlaminghen en Duytschen, getrocken uyt hare uytgegevene confessien* (Amsterdam, 1640), fo. A2, p. 52.

positions. The best option was to put away all man-made writings, including the confessions, in a strongbox and to put trust only in the Bible. As for the fundamental issues of faith, both parties were in agreement; as for those issues on which they differed, tolerance should be practised. Differences concerning rites were not important for salvation; for the time being every group should continue to maintain the usual customs. When an elder wanted to serve another denomination, he had to conform to the customs used by the congregation in question.[38]

The Waterlanders, however, were inclined to force their opinions upon the other Mennonite groups and had no understanding for the opinions of the United Congregations. As a pamphleteer rightly put it, the Waterlanders demanded many concessions from the Flemings, but refused to meet them part of the way.[39] As we have already seen, the Waterlanders had a keen aversion to dogmatism. Their strongly pietist bias and dislike of speculation saved them from becoming a conservative, rigid community, but it also prevented them from empathising with the conceptions of the more dogmatic Flemings and Frisians who, precisely on the basis of the confessions, had achieved unification. It would have been too much to ask them to jeopardise this result and to declare the confessions to be null and void, as the Waterlanders proposed. This lack of interest in confessions was exactly why the Waterlanders opined that it was natural for the Flemings to give up their claims and views indiscriminately. They completely misjudged the value of dogma for the preservation of the identity of a group.

The United Congregations reacted to the presentation in 1649. They acknowledged that quarrelling was not suited to the believers, and that they were inclined to reunite, but only with those who wholeheartedly shared their faith. It had yet to be determined whether this was the case with the Waterlander proposal, for not every issue could be solved by proclaiming tolerance. One has to know in the first place what could be tolerated and what could not. The Flemings pleaded for limited tolerance. It is easy to say, they continued, not to impose exact rules, but experience has shown that this approach does not function. The Flemings had their finger on the sore spot, for the Waterlanders refused to make a statement on this issue except for talking generally. The Flemings continued by stating that if the Waterlanders should adjust their doctrines, perception, and ordinances to those of the United Congregations (that is, to subscribe

---

[38] *Vrede-praesentatie (Water-lantsche gemeyntes) aen de vereenighde Vlaemsche gemeynten, etc. midtsgaders vredespoor voor alle doopsgesinde* (n.p., 1648), pp. 4–7.

[39] E. Fredrich, *Discours over de Antwoordt der doopsgesinde Vlaminghen, gegeven op de Presentatie der doops-gesinde Waterlanders, nopende den vreede tusschen hun beyde* (Amsterdam, 1649), p. 39.

to the confessions), a reunion could be possible.[40] The author of this answer was Galenus Abrahamz, the person who a decade later did not want to have anything to do with confessions.

Unlimited tolerance

Within the United Congregations discussion soon flared up about the possibilities and the limitations of tolerance; about 1655 the debates on this issue came to a climax within the United Congregation of Amsterdam. It proved that an overstretched tolerance did not result in an approach, but in a split. Galenus Abrahamsz, who was one of the elders in Amsterdam, had come under the spell of the idea of unlimited tolerance, although he had been sceptical about this issue only six years before. He aimed at the expansion of tolerance, and was even ready to allow persons who were not baptised, like Socinians and Collegiants, to partake in the Lord's Supper with the conditions that they did not use arms and they led devout lives. Galenus showed indifferent towards ideological disputes, but many members of the Amsterdam congregation disagreed with the course he was taking for, according to them, he destroyed the very foundations of redemption. It must be kept in mind that Socinianism had been outlawed by the authorities. For this reason, a number of members of the Amsterdam congregation warned that allowing Socinians to join the congregation would discredit them in the eyes of the government.[41]

From various utterances members of the congregation also concluded that Galenus did not strictly adhere to the confessions. They demanded that he complied with their content and, in addition, they pleaded to maintain the visible congregation which Galenus thought to be superfluous. They also stressed the need for correctly appointed elders, the acceptance of Christ's divine nature, and the maintaining of adult baptism by water. According to them, these issues were essential elements of the Mennonite religion. There was only one solution to this problem: every member of the congregation, especially the elders, had to subscribe to the confessions.[42] The discussion provoked a fierce argument between the adherents of Galenus and his adversaries.

[40] *Antwoort op de Vrede-praesentatie, gedaen door de Waterlanderen aen de Vlaemsch, Duytsche en Vriessche doops-gesinde gemeentens* (Amsterdam, 1664), pp. 4–7.

[41] 'The irritated magistrate will take revenge on us sooner or later' ('Zo zal de magistraat eer langhe door een geterghde wraeck het op ons vergelden'): Radbodus Radbodi, *De ontdekte veinsing der heedendaegsche geest-dryvers en Sociniaenen* (n.p., n.d.), no pages.

[42] *Commonitio ofte waerschouwinge aen de Vlaemsche doops-gesinde gemeynte binnen Amsterdam tegen eenige leeraren onder haer, op welck sy wel hebben te letten aengaende hare leere* (n.p., 1655), fo. A2, p. 16.

These clashes within the Amsterdam congregation were a thorn in the flesh of many members. They tried to find a remedy in order to soften the differences of opinion, and to preserve the jeopardised unity. Their solution was the same as that offered by Galenus, namely mutual tolerance. This argument was put forward, for instance, in a pamphlet written in 1663 and aimed at restoring the peace within the Amsterdam congregation. The author stated that the cause of the clashes lay in the fact that from time immemorial the Mennonites had made an insufficient difference between those issues that were essential to faith, and those that were not. The author, however, failed to respond to the most important question: what were these essentials? According to Galenus there were practically no essentials, while his adversaries stated that the essentials were laid down in the confessions.

The solution provided by the author of the *Zedighe overweginghe* (Moral consideration) was a peculiar one. He exhorted the Amsterdam magistrate to intervene, and to forbid any enforcement of conscience.[43] In other words, freedom of conscience had to be defended by enforcing consciences. Many supporters of tolerance were apparently not aware of the contradiction in this solution. Action from the side of the authorities could misfire for the supporters of tolerance. In the clashes between followers and adversaries of Galenus in 1665 the magistrate of Utrecht had proclaimed that the differences had to be settled on the basis of the confession.[44]

The supporters of tolerance brought forward many arguments. They stated that the confessions were never meant to be exact rules of faith, but were human inventions. Only the main articles of faith had to be subscribed to. One author wrote, with reference to Erasmus' Commentary on Matthew 13, and a quotation from the tolerant Reformed theologian Franciscus Junius who lived in the sixteenth century (*Opera* v, page 723), to distinguish between those issues that were essential to faith and those that were not.[45] As for this author, confessions were merely documents to express the general feeling of a group, and were meant to show that among them there was no glaring heresy. Only Scripture was essential to faith. He further attentively referred to the work of Acontius, 'a treatise

---

[43] *Zedighe overweginghe over den toestandt der jegenwoordighe onlusten en gheschillen in de Vlaemsche doopsgesinde gemeente binnen Amsterdam kortelyck by wijse van Deductie voorgesteldt* (Haarlem, 1663).

[44] *Authentycke copyen der Resolutiën van Utrecht* [broadsheet edn].

[45] The Remonstrants too distinguished between essential issues and non-essentials, a difference that had already been made by Erasmus. Their leader Simon Episcopius had stated this as early as 1627: Israel, 'Toleration in Seventeenth-Century Dutch and English Thought', p. 20.

worthy to be read by all peace-loving Christians'. Acontius' books were often quoted by the defenders of tolerance.[46]

But the supporters of tolerance did not succeed in convincing their opponents. The latter accused them in their turn, and not entirely without reason in view of the appeal of their adversaries to the Amsterdam magistrate, of naked enforcement of conscience, because they demanded that their opponents gave up their views indiscriminately. They clung to the confessions, for only the confession distinguished the Mennonites from other Christian denominations. They also rightly stated that no one was forced to join the congregation but, if anyone did, the confession should be complied with. Moreover, the danger arose that under the cover of tolerance all kinds of dissolute behaviour crept into the Mennonite community. This last comment was a reference to the Socinians.[47]

The confession to which Galenus and his followers paid little attention was of the utmost importance to his adversaries. Even those who were in favour of a limited tolerance of deviant feelings did not go so far as to declare the confessions to be null and void. They quoted the example of the Remonstrants, who indeed accepted almost anyone in their congregation, but did not tolerate their ministers publicly attacking the Remonstrant confession.[48]

The significance of the confessions played a decisive role in the conflict within the United Congregation of Amsterdam that reached a climax in 1664. At stake was the character of the confessions (binding or not?), as well as the scope of tolerance (limited or unlimited?). Galenus, who was deeply influenced by the Collegiants, wished to bar no one from the congregation and was ready to let almost anyone partake in the Lord's Supper. He thought the confessions not binding, and considered any congregational organisation superfluous. His opponents, on the contrary, stressed the importance of confessions. One of them rightly stated that a chaotic situation would emerge when everyone accepted only what he liked, 'for in the Turkish Empire I will say that I accept the Koran as far as it does agree with God's word, in Spain the decisions of the Council of

[46] *Aanmerkingen op de soo-genaamde Vrede-praesentatie door Tobias Goverts van de Wyngaert en sijn mede-stemmers...aen hare mede-dienaren Dr. Galenus Abrahamsz. ende sijne mede-stemmers* (Amsterdam, 1664), pp. 3–4, 14, 24.

[47] [Pieter Apostool], *Verdedigingh der vrede-presentatie door Tobias Govertsz. en medestanders aen Dr. Galenus Abrahamsz en de sijne gedaen* (Amsterdam, 1664), pp. 7, 8, 14, 31.

[48] *Gheleyd-draat voor de Vlaemsche Doopsgesinde gemeente tot Amsterdam om haer te geleyden uyt den doolhof der verwerringen, daer zy door de strijdige gevoelens van haer leeraren zijn ingeraekt* (Amsterdam, 1664), pp. 11, 13–14. Cf. A. van Dale, *Boere-praetje tusschen vijf persoonen, een huysman, een outVlamingh, Remonstrant, Waterlander en Collegiant* (Amsterdam, 1664), pp. 8, 19.

Trent, yes even the Jewish Talmud'.[49] Finally, the opponents of Galenus seceded in June 1664; their group was soon called the *Zonists*, named after a warehouse called *De Zon* (the Sun) where they held their services. A great number of the United Congregations in the Republic agreed with the Zonists and seceded too. Tolerance thus had not brought unity, but only a new rift.

Galenus is usually glorified as the advocate of unlimited tolerance.[50] But his opponents rightly pointed out that without a confession the Mennonite congregations would fall apart from the resulting anarchy. This did indeed happen later to the movement of the Collegiants. They also referred to the tolerant Remonstrants, whose tolerance had its limits: they did not tolerate their confession being under discussion. Galenus' opponents further referred to the fate of the Polish Mennonites, who at first had tolerated the Socinians and were subsequently swallowed by them.[51]

The confession was important to large parts of the United Congregations as well as others. The Waterlanders ascribed no binding authority to their confession, but in practice they did consider it to be binding, or at least their orthodox wing did.[52] After the rift in the Amsterdam United Congregation had taken place, Galenus wished to join the Waterlanders, but they demanded that he had to subscribe to the confession of Hans de Ries.[53] According to them, this was not just a confession composed by a private person, but was endorsed by many Waterlanders and none of their elders or congregations had ever rejected it.[54]

The Waterlanders amended tolerance: it had to be combined with Christian precaution, and a correct course had to be steered between limited and unlimited tolerance; unlimited tolerance would cause quarrelling. The Lord's Supper was accessible for members of the congregation only; the divine nature of Christ, His suffering and satisfaction had

---

[49] W.C. Loopes, *Rechtveerdige Weeghschael voor de christelijcke gemeente die men noemt de Vereen. Vl., Vr. en Hoogd. Doopsgesinde tot Amsterdam* (Amsterdam, 1664), p. 32: 'want in Turckyen komende sal ick seggen, ick neme den Alkoran aen, voor soo veel als de selve met Godts Woordt overeen komt. In Spanje het concilium van Trente, jae selfs den Ioodschen Taelmut.'

[50] See for example the title of his biography by H.W. Meihuizen, *Galenus Abrahamsz 1622–1706. Strijder voor een onbepaalde verdraagzaamheid en verdediger van het Doperse Spiritualisme* (Haarlem, 1954).

[51] *Sedige verantwoordinge, voorgelesen op den 26. Dec. 1669 in de Doopsgesinde kerck (die men tot onderscheyt van andere gemeentens de Waterlantse noemt)* (Alkmaar, 1670), p. 13.

[52] *Demonstrantie of vertoogh dat Coenr. v. Vollenhoven ende sijne medestanders de scheydinghe in de Vl., Vr. en hooghd. Doopsgesinde ghemeente alhier tot Haerlem heeft gemaeckt* (Haarlem, 1667).

[53] *Sedige verantwoordinge*, p. 6. The same is stated by the Waterlander Antonie van Dale in his *Boere-praetje*, p. 8.

[54] *Grondt-steen van vreede en verdraegsaemheyt tot opbouwinge van den tempel Christi onder de doopsgesinde* (Amsterdam, 1674), pp. 13, 20; *Sedige verantwoordinge*, pp. 4–5.

to be acknowledged. This meant the exclusion of the Socinians. They also strongly advised against partaking in the Lord's Supper elsewhere, for instance with the Collegiants. In short, they certainly did not aim at an open congregation, which Galenus favoured.[55] Galenus thus had to renounce the unlimited tolerance he cherished; the congregation remained intact, and was sealed off from other denominations. As for the Waterlanders, they too considered the preservation of their own identity to be of more importance than the wild-goose chase for unlimited tolerance. Galenus and his followers accepted the demands of the Waterlanders, although some of them made angry comments on this 'enforcement of conscience'.[56]

The negotiations of 1671 between the Waterlanders and the Remonstrants in Rotterdam failed for much the same reasons. This fusion had to be made on the base of tolerance but, as we have seen, the Remonstrants opined that tolerance was not unlimited.[57] They could not accept the Mennonite conception of adult baptism and their prohibition to hold public offices. Because neither of the parties was inclined to give up its own view, talks came to a standstill. The urge for preservation of their own identity was once again stronger than the will to unite.[58]

---

[55] *Grondt-steen van vreede*, pp. 9–10, 12–13.
[56] Irenaeus Philalethius, *Aanmerkingen over de sedige verantwoordinge* (Alkmaar, 1670).
[57] L. Bidloo, *Onbepaalde verdraagsaamheyd, de verwoesting der Doopsgezinden* (Leiden, 1742), p. 269.
[58] *Schriftelyke handeling tot christelijke vereeniging voorgevallen tusschen een gedeelte der Waterlandtsche Doopsgesinde en de Remonstrantsche gemeente tot Rotterdam* (Rotterdam, 1671), aenspraeck 5, p. 26.

9   Jews and religious toleration
in the Dutch Republic

Peter van Rooden

The Dutch Republic has been famed as a tolerant haven in an intolerant confessional Europe.[1] The limits and peculiarities of this toleration are equally well known. In the first place, there were stark regional differences. Most representations of Dutch tolerance rest upon the example of the western and maritime province of Holland. The religious order of other provinces, like Overijssel or Groningen, was much closer to the model of the German *Landeskirchen,* while the closest parallel for the religious regime of the Generality Lands is probably to be found in eighteenth-century Ireland. In these areas in the south, conquered by the armies of the Republic in the later stages of the Eighty-Years' War, a mainly rural Catholic population was governed by a small elite of Reformed office-holders on behalf of the States-General. Even within Holland, there were marked differences between the religious policies of the various cities, with Amsterdam and Rotterdam, for instance, being more tolerant than Haarlem and Leiden. In the second place, Dutch tolerance was not founded upon an ideology. Tolerant policies were a mixture of sentiment, tradition, and expediency. There were, of course, ideological debates about toleration within the Dutch Republic, but it is rather difficult to relate them to the actual practices of toleration. It is particularly hard to get a clear picture of what kind of social and religious order the defenders of tolerance actually had in mind. Even more clearly than elsewhere in early modern Europe, ideological debates in the Dutch Republic were overwhelmingly determined by the day-to-day political struggles of which they were but one part.

The predominant interpretation of the struggles about toleration pitches religious zealots against hard-headed practical men, the latter less interested in religious values than in worldly efficiency and secular values. Usually, these two types are exemplified by the *predikanten,* the ministers of the Reformed public Church, as opposed to the regents of

---

[1] See: C. Berkvens-Stevelinck, J. Israel, and G.H.M. Posthumus Meyjes (eds.), *The Emergence of Tolerance in the Dutch Republic* (Leiden / New York / Cologne, 1997).

the cities of Holland. Strangely enough, this interpretation directly challenges the only Dutch defence of toleration which has gained the status of a minor philosophical classic, Spinoza's *Tractatus Theologico-Politicus*. Spinoza does contrast regents and *predikanten*, but he does not represent their conflict as a struggle between persecutors driven by religious zeal and secular defenders of toleration. Instead, he interprets any use of religion for political purposes, for instance using it to mobilise the common people by whipping them up against their social superiors, as a form of irreligion. When the regents suppress such clerical activities they are not only promoting good government and preserving social peace, but are actually defending true and pure religion. Of course, the contradiction between Spinoza's representation of the issues at stake and the dominant interpretation can easily be explained away. We readily perceive the ideological nature of the *Tractatus* as a pamphlet meant to stiffen the resolve of the regents. It has been argued, most famously by Leo Strauss, that Spinoza's definition of true religion and his use of this concept ought not to be taken too seriously, as they are offered 'tongue-in-cheek'.[2] I have argued elsewhere that this interpretation of the *Tractatus* is misleading.[3] Spinoza is serious about the religious duty of the magistrate. He takes for granted the confessional state and its peculiar bond between religion and public order. His arguments in favour of toleration are, like those of almost all enlightened philosophers, based on a distinction between the political and philosophical elite and the common people. Popular religiosity cannot be transformed or eradicated. It presents a problem of control which has to be taken care of by some kind of religious establishment. This widely shared conviction makes the treatment of religious difference in early modern Europe quite different from the modern kinds of toleration that are practised by the nation-state.[4]

I would like to approach this problem in a pointedly round-about way. I propose to examine the most striking example of toleration in the Dutch Republic – the acceptance of the settlement and presence of Jews. More particularly, I want to ask whether the treatment of Jews was a special case, or if they were considered and treated just like other dissenters. The last decades of the sixteenth century witnessed the growth of originally modest Jewish communities in several cities of the Dutch Republic.[5]

---

[2] Leo Strauss, *Die Religionskritik Spinozas als Grundlage seiner Bibelwissenschaft* (Berlin, 1930).

[3] Peter van Rooden, 'Spinoza's bijbeluitleg', *Studia Rosenthaliana* 18 (1984), 120–33.

[4] Peter van Rooden, 'Vroomheid, macht, Verlichting', *De Achttiende Eeuw* 32 (2000), 57–75.

[5] Jozeph Michman, Hartog Beem, and Dan Michman, *Pinkas. Geschiedenis van de joodse gemeenschap in Nederland* (Amsterdam, 1999).

Their origins are wrapped in obscurity. It is clear, however, that the arrival of Marranos, mostly directly from the Iberian peninsula or by way of the Marrano communities in the South of France, formed the most important factor in this immigration. Marranos were, by their own accounts, descendants of baptised Jews who had confessed Catholicism in Spain and Portugal. In the Republic they converted to Judaism, although many of the immigrants had scarcely had any acquaintance with Jewish customs and assumptions in their youth.[6] The religious history of the Dutch Jewish community, which settled mainly at Amsterdam, was fundamentally determined by this descent from converts who had not been imbued with a religious tradition in their youth. In the first half of the seventeenth century, numerous conflicts broke out within the community. After 1603, three different synagogues were set up within fifteen years, dividing among them the small group of Jews, probably only a thousand, who lived in Amsterdam. Even after the synagogues were united after great efforts in 1639, conflicts between more philosophical-rationalistic and mystical-cabbalistic rabbis and between rabbis and prominent laymen continued alongside an undercurrent of radical religious scepticism.[7] Still, the Jews of Amsterdam formed a tightly knit community, based on family ties, a shared immersion in Spanish culture, the use of Spanish and Portuguese as vernacular languages, distinctive economic activities, and their treatment by the Amsterdam city council.[8] Jews could not penetrate the traditional branches of Holland's trade and were excluded from most guilds, but in the trade with Portugal and the Portuguese colonies they retained a virtual monopoly. In the course of the seventeenth century, there emerged a sizable class of Jewish artisans in Amsterdam. They were employed in industries which processed the products of this colonial trade – sugar, diamonds, tobacco, silks, and perfumes. These industries were the basis on which Amsterdam's Jewish community was able to grow into the largest of Western Europe.[9] Since Jews did not usually

---

[6] Y. Kaplan, 'The Portuguese Jews in Amsterdam. From Forced Conversion to a Return to Judaism', *Studia Rosenthaliana* 15 (1981), 37–51; H.R. Salomon, 'The "De Pinto" Manuscript. A 17th Century Marrano Family History', *Studia Rosenthaliana* 9 (1975), 1–62; J.C. Boyayin, 'The New Christians Reconsidered. Evidence from Lisbon's Portuguese Bankers, 1497–1647', *Studia Rosenthaliana* 13 (1979), 129–56.

[7] H.P. Salomon, 'Haham Saul Levi Morteira en de Portugese nieuw-christenen', *Studia Rosenthaliana* 10 (1976), 127–41; H.P. Salomon, *Saul Levi Morteira en zijn 'Traktaat betreffende de waarheid van de Wet van Moses'* (Braga, 1988); A. Altmann, 'Eternality of Punishment. A Theological Controversy within the Amsterdam Rabbinate in the Thirties of the Seventeenth Century', *Proceedings of the American Academy for Jewish Research* 40 (1973), 1–88.

[8] R.G. Fuks-Mansfeld, *De Sefardim in Amsterdam tot 1795. Aspecten van een joodse minderheid in een Hollandse stad* (Hilversum, 1989).

[9] Jonathan Israel, 'The Economic Contribution of Dutch Sephardi Jewry to Holland's Golden Age, 1595–1713', *Tijdschrift voor Geschiedenis* 96 (1983), 505–35.

threaten cross-community economic competition because of the special nature of their commerce, the city patriciate was able to take a very liberal attitude to them. The fact that in 1632–3 the Republic was willing to let peace negotiations with Spain founder on the condition put forward by the Dutch, namely, that their Jewish subjects should enjoy the same rights as their other citizens in trade with Spain and Portugal, so that they should be protected from the Inquisition speaks more eloquently than any declaration of tolerance. This demand, more than any other, roused the Spanish government to fury. Although it is possible that this condition was chiefly defended by those groups in the Republic that were supporters of the continuation of the war, and who therefore tried to put unacceptable demands to Spain, the condition was credible because from 1619 a clearly formulated and consistent policy with regard to Jews had been part of the foreign policy of the Republic.[10] The sizable immigration of Eastern European Jews, from the 1640s onwards, resulted in the emergence of an Ashkenazi community next to the older Sephardic one, but did not change the attitude of the Amsterdam authorities or population towards Jews.

Contemporaries, of course, experienced the toleration extended to Jews as one of the most striking aspects of the religious order of the Republic. A visit to the magnificent Amsterdam synagogues became a staple element in descriptions of journeys through the Dutch Republic. Most Jews were themselves deeply impressed by the treatment accorded to them. At some stage during the first half of the seventeenth century, David Curiel, a prominent member of the Amsterdam Sephardi community, was said to have been attacked by a German robber. Although seriously wounded, Curiel managed to overcome his attacker with the help of his Christian neighbours. The robber was caught, tried, sentenced, and executed. Afterwards, the States of Holland dispatched Curiel a letter expressing their regret at the incident, inviting him to witness the medical lesson on the corpse of the robber in the anatomical theatre of their university at Leiden. This legend has been handed down in at least five different manuscripts preserved in Amsterdam Jewish libraries. It was probably read out at the feast of Purim which, of course, commemorates an earlier attack on the Jews and the spectacular destruction of their enemy.[11] But then, was the treatment accorded to Jews in any way special in its historical context?

[10] Jonathan Israel, 'Spain and the Dutch Sephardim, 1609–1660', *Studia Rosenthaliana* 12 (1978), 15, 26–7.
[11] L. Fuks and R. Fuks-Mansfeld, 'Jewish Historiography in the Netherlands in the Seventeenth and Eighteenth Centuries', in S. Lieberman and A. Hyman (eds.), *Salo Witmayer Baron Jubilee Volume* (Jerusalem, 1974), pp. 436–8.

I want first to turn to the realm of ideology. Were Jews considered to be a special case, different from Christian dissenters? Augustine had justified the presence of Jews in the Christian Empire by enlarging upon Paul's speculations about their special status in God's dispensation. In his eyes, they were unlike Christian heretics or schismatics. Their continuing presence was ordained by God. The expulsion of the Jews from most of Europe during the High Middle Ages was justified by a re-interpretation of this Augustinian argument. The friars distinguished between the ancient Jews of the time before the split between Church and Synagogue and the modern Jews. The former, so the argument went, had actually agreed with the Christians and traces of their views were to be found in rabbinical literature. The thirteenth-century Spanish Dominican Raymundus Martini developed this scheme in the foreword to his *Pugio fidei adversus Mauros et Judaeos*, a huge and extremely learned work in which he ransacked the Talmud, Midrashim, and Targumim to prove his claim. According to this view, modern Jews were actually akin to heretics who had perverted the traditions of their ancestors.[12]

This high medieval interpretative scheme, with its implied research programme, formed the basis of the intellectual reflection on the Jewish presence in the Dutch Republic, both in humanist works and theological treatises. This was not a situation characteristic for the Netherlands alone. All Christian scholars in seventeenth-century Europe – Lutherans, Reformed, Catholics, and dissenters – used this model for their intellectual understanding of Judaism. When the Basle professor Buxtorf the Younger, the most prominent Hebrew scholar of the middle of the seventeenth century, wrote to Cocceius to congratulate him on his appointment as professor for Jewish Controversies at Leiden, he advised him to acquire, 'to use alongside Raymundus: Porchetus, the *Fortalitium Fidei*, *Stella Messiae*, Hieronymus de Sancta Fide, the book that is called *Zelus Christi*, published at Venice, Paulus de St Maria'.[13] These are all Catholic works in the tradition of the *Pugio Fidei*.

The approximation of Judaism to some kind of heresy went even further than this. Judaism was considered to be, like Christianity, a creed-orientated religion. The earliest reaction to the presence of Jews and their religion in the Dutch Republic was written in the vernacular. In 1608 the

---

[12] J. Cohen, *The Friars and the Jews. The Evolution of Medieval Anti-Judaism* (Ithaca, 1982).
[13] Buxtorf to Cocceius, 3 September 1651, in J. Cocceius, *Opera Anekdota theologica et philologica* (Amsterdam, 1706), vol. II, p. 688. Cf. Peter van Rooden, *Theology, Biblical Scholarship and Rabbinical Studies in the Seventeenth Century: Constantijn L'Empereur (1591–1648), Professor of Hebrew and Theology at Leiden* (Leiden, 1989), pp. 158–83.

Reformed minister Abraham Costerus published his *Historie der Joden*, intending to obstruct a request for a synagogue.[14] His work has a simple structure. The first part, making up about half of the book, deals with the faith of the Jews. Starting with Maimonides' thirteen principles of Judaism, it relates the Jewish conceptions concerning God, salvation, and the Messiah. The second and third parts of the book describe the Jewish religious ceremonies, and Jewish customs and rituals when eating, going to bed, marrying, and so on. Costerus' work cannot be considered a great scholarly achievement. It is part excerpt, part translation of Antonius Margarita's *Der gantz Jüdisch Glaub* (Augsburg, 1530) and Johan Buxtorf the Elder's *Synagoga Judaica, das ist teutsche Judenschul* (Basle, 1603). Costerus derived the structure of his argument from this latter work: Buxtorf's *Synagoga*, too, opens with a chapter explicating the Jewish articles of faith on the basis of Maimonides. The following chapters – about 85 per cent of the book – describe Jewish ceremonies and rituals. I suppose that this structure, which derives religious ceremonies, customs, and rituals from articles of faith, ultimately goes back to the first Protestant Confession, the *Confessio Augustana* which uses the same twofold argument.

We find this description of Judaism as a kind of mirror image of Christianity in all works written by Dutch Christians about Jews, whether they are theologians or humanist scholars, orthodox Calvinists, Arminians, or spiritualists. They all consider Judaism to be a creed-orientated religion, attempting to found its principles and practices on revelation.[15] Ethical and legal rules, rituals and ceremonies, the core of normative Judaism, are judged to be secondary. Part of this is probably a reflection of the heavy stress that Sephardic Jews themselves laid upon creed-formulation, overall a rare occurrence in Jewish thought,[16] and the strong educational programme of the Amsterdam Jewish community, by means of which they assimilated newly arrived New Christians from the Iberian peninsula.[17] Most important, though, was the general practice in post-Reformation Europe to discuss religious differences in terms of disagreements about the interpretation of revealed truth.

[14] Abraham Costerus, *Historie der Joden* (Leiden, 1608).
[15] Peter van Rooden, 'Conceptions of Judaism as a Religion in the Seventeenth-Century Dutch Republic', in Diana Woods (ed.), *Christianity and Judaism* (Oxford, 1993), pp. 299–308.
[16] M. Kellner, *Dogma in Jewish Thought. From Maimonides to Abravanel* (Oxford, 1986).
[17] For the internal history of the Jewish communities during the Republic, see J.C.H. Blom, R.G. Fuks-Mansfeld, and I. Schöffer (eds.), *Geschiedenis van de Joden in Nederland* (Amsterdam, 1995), pp. 53–206 and the literature mentioned there in the excellent bibliographical sections.

Judaism was considered to be something akin to a Christian heresy. Not all theologians went as far as Antonius Hulsius, who considered Judaism to be the archetype and origin of all heresies and superstitions: 'Nothing strange to the Christian truth has been introduced into the Church which does not smell of this corrupted Judaism.'[18] But even when such an unpleasant attitude was lacking, the main defect of Judaism was thought to be that it was intellectually wrong, like the doctrines of the Catholics, Arminians, Socinians, and so on. Consequently, the general opinion among theologians was that Judaism ought to be treated like other heresies. Constantijn L'Empereur, one of the most important Dutch Hebraists of the seventeenth century, considered that he:

> should set the truth of Christianity in writing against the errors of the Jews, as the light against the shadow; and with the intention and purpose 'that it may happen that God will grant them a change of heart and show them the truth, and thus they may come to their senses and escape from the devil's snare' [2 Timothy 2:25–26], or, if their obstinacy should prevent this in this age, that the Christians should at least be able to show the fame of the saviour more clearly to them, and better defend their dogmas, and thus establish the faith ever more firmly.[19]

The quote from the Second Epistle to Timothy, which forms the core of this statement, refers to the heterodox in general, not to the Jews. L'Empereur considered a conversion of the Jews very unlikely, and saw his most important duty as the vindication of Christian truth and refutation of Jewish error. This, it seems to me, is the general intellectual attitude towards Judaism in the Dutch Republic. Refutation of error, vindication of the truth, suppression of supposed blasphemies, and attacks on Christianity – these are all much more important than attempts at conversion. Theologically, L'Empereur was not quite representative. Most mainstream Dutch Calvinists would have referred to Romans 11, a text which had been used since Beza to justify the expectation of the conversion of all the Jews.[20] Still, this was a theological difference without practical consequences. Those theologians who maintained that a general conversion of the Jews would occur before the end of the world did not act upon their belief. Characteristically, at the Synod of Dordt in 1618–19, the most important religious meeting during the Dutch Republic, a proposal by the Zeeland delegates to search for means to further the conversion of the Jews was changed into a request to the States-General to stop the Jewish libels of Christ.[21] The public Church

[18] A. Hulsius, *Theologiae judaicae pars prima: de messia* (Breda, 1653), preface.
[19] Constantijn L'Empereur, *Halichoth Olam sive Clavis Talmudica* (Leiden, 1634), ff. *3a–b.
[20] Van Rooden, *Theology, Biblical Scholarship and Rabbinical Studies*, pp. 166–7.
[21] H.H. Kuyper, *De Post-Acta of Nahandelingen van de Nationale Synode van Dordrecht* (Amsterdam, 1899), pp. 268, 291.

repeated the same injunction during the *Grote Vergadering* of 1651, when the States of all the provinces of the Dutch Republic met to discuss the nature of their state after the conclusion of the war with Spain and the death of the Stadholder.[22] In its emphasis on suppression and refutation instead of conversion, this attitude towards Judaism was not different from the stance towards other dissenters. Actual attempts at conversion of individual religious dissenters were extremely rare, as were missionary endeavours in general.[23]

The appointment of two special professors for Jewish Controversies at Leiden University, L'Empereur in 1633 and Cocceius in 1651, cannot be taken as an indication of a special attitude towards the Jews. The appointment of L'Empereur was not connected with Menasseh ben Israel's *Conciliator* (the first theological work by a Jew published in Latin in the Dutch Republic) as has been supposed, but was meant as a consolation prize. L'Empereur had been passed over for a professorship in the faculty of theology.[24] In a similar way, the appointment of Cocceius was part of the negotiations between him and the board of the university about his appointment as Professor of Theology. Cocceius, who drove a hard bargain, insisted upon receiving a higher salary than his colleagues. The Board, which did not want to offend them, had to search for a justification for such a supplement.[25] It actually took them some weeks to come up with the Professorship for Writing Against the Jews. Of course, in both cases such an appointment made sense only against a background in which it was considered a positive good to refute Judaism. But this did not make the Jews special. During many years of the seventeenth century, the Professors of Theology at Leiden University devoted all their teaching to refuting various heresies: polemical theology reigned supreme, and refutations of Judaism were only a small part of the total polemical production.[26]

In the course of the seventeenth century, and even more in the eighteenth, polemics against the Jews waned. Intellectual refutations of Judaism became less popular, as did the study of rabbinical literature. It was replaced by popular prejudice. The stereotype of the *smous* gained wide currency in the eighteenth century. This development, too, finds a parallel in the changing attitudes towards Christian dissenters. High polemics against Catholicism also became more rare and were replaced

[22] J.Th. de Visser, *Kerk en staat* (Leiden, 1926–1927), vol. II, pp. 280–304, especially p. 283; Jonathan Israel, *The Dutch Republic. Its Rise, Greatness, and Fall 1477–1806* (Oxford, 1995), pp. 703–13.

[23] Peter van Rooden, *Religieuze regimes. Over godsdienst en maatschappij in Nederland, 1570–1990* (Amsterdam, 1996), pp. 121–46.

[24] Van Rooden, *Theology, Biblical Scholarship and Rabbinical Studies*, pp. 94–5, 182–3.

[25] *Ibid.*, p. 182 n. 354.   [26] *Ibid.*, p. 215.

by popular prejudice.[27] Popular stereotyping of the Mennonites – *het men-niste zusje* – seems to have become more pronounced in the eighteenth century as well, although this is, admittedly, based on impressionistic evidence. The reasons for this shift from elitist polemics to popular prejudice are to be found in the changes in the actual treatment of religious minorities. This brings us back to the problem of whether or not the treatment of Jews in the Dutch Republic was different from that of other dissenters. To answer this question in a nutshell: initially it was, but over time it ceased to be. However, this was not the result of a change in the way that Jews were treated. On the contrary, the policies towards other dissenting groups became more similar to the way the Jews had been treated all along. The decisive shift seems to have taken place in the second half of the seventeenth century.

It is clear that during the first half of the seventeenth century Jews were treated differently. After the Revolt, all Christian religious groups were reconstituting themselves, building up organisations, defining their identity, gaining support and adherents. The sudden political demise of traditional Catholicism had resulted in a religious situation which was both unprecedented and in flux.[28] It would be wrong to interpret this situation as a free religious market, fought over by different religious suppliers who were trying to maximise their market share. Political support was essential for all groups, and most of them were more interested in building up structures and organisations than in gaining members. The Reformed received by far the most political support and had the clearest ideas about the kind of organisation they wanted to set up. The truth of the thesis that the Dutch were forcefully Protestantised by political means lies in the undeniable outcome of the years up to 1625, which proved that the Reformed were right in their assumption that once the correct structures were in place and political support was assured, the hearts and minds of the population would follow. In all areas where political authority had effectively suppressed dissenting Christian organisation before 1625, the population became homogeneously Reformed. Interestingly, those areas form a continuous belt, running from the south-west to the north-east of the Netherlands along the military front as it had been more or less stabilised at the turn of the sixteenth century.[29]

However, similar mechanisms worked for other religious organisations as well. They, too, had found that power bases and links to existing political and social structures were essential. Consequently, what

---

[27] Results of ongoing graduate research by Edwina Hagen.
[28] Joke Spaans, *Haarlem na de Reformatie. Stedelijke cultuur en kerkelijk leven, 1577–1620* (The Hague, 1989).
[29] Van Rooden, *Religieuze regimes*, pp. 169–99.

is commonly depicted as the struggle about toleration during the first two generations after the Revolt actually involved two different fields of conflict. On the one hand, there were fierce disagreements about the organisation and identity of the public Church; on the other, about the attitudes to be taken towards attempts at religious organisation apart from the public Church and the efforts of dissenting religious organisations to insert themselves within the society of the Dutch Republic. Although this difference is well established in current research, it still needs to be stressed how necessary it is to distinguish sharply between these two contexts, and to locate carefully the various contributions to the debate about toleration within each of them. The outcome of the political crisis during the Truce with Spain and the Synod of Dordt effectively resolved the first conflict, although from time to time we encounter radical (and highly unrealistic) propositions in favour of a public Church with a weak confessional identity to which everybody could belong. The second struggle, about the attitude to be taken towards the attempts at organisation of other religious groups, took much longer to resolve and showed marked local varieties. It was only in the last quarter of the seventeenth century that a recognisable, consistent, and henceforth dominant model was put in place.

In the first half of the seventeenth century, Jews as a group did not fit the two contexts in which the struggle about toleration played itself out in the Dutch Republic. In the first place, they never were contenders in the conflict about the identity of the public Church, as were the Arminians or even the Catholics. In the second place they were, from the beginning, a well-defined group of immigrants which never tried to insert itself within the social body of the Republic. Their organisation and community stood apart. In this context, it is highly significant that in the first half of the seventeenth century, only in the case of the Jews do we find an attempt to formulate a formal constitution for a religious group other than the public Church. One of the drafts for such a decision, Hugo Grotius' *Remonstrantie nopende de ordre dije in de landen van Hollandt ende Westvrieslandt dijent gestelt op de Joden*, has been preserved.[30] Ultimately, no formal arrangement was issued, but all the various local decisions taken, whether in the form of the regulation of an existing Jewish community or else as a list of conditions to allow the settlement of Jews, bear the same character. The presence of Jews, and the exercise of their religious practices, were accepted, but the boundaries of their community were sharply drawn and strictly guarded. Intermarriage and conversion of Dutch subjects

---

[30] Jaap Meijer, *Remonstrantie nopende de ordre dije in de landen van Hollandt ende Westvrieslandt dijent gestelt op de Joden* (Amsterdam, 1949).

were not allowed, the Jews could not become members of most guilds, and they had no claim on common poor relief, being obliged, instead, to take care of their own poor. Because the Jews stood apart from Dutch society, they did not play any role in its debates and struggles about the place of various religious organisations within it. By the same token, solutions similar to the way in which the Jewish presence had been regulated were not applicable to the Lutherans, Mennonites, Arminians, or Catholics. In their case, the question was not the incorporation or exclusion of well-defined groups, but the acceptance or suppression of attempts at religious organisation apart from the public Church: in short, it was not a question of the rights of religious minorities, but of political and social order and concord. The reason that the question was posed in these terms had, in the first place, to do with the widely shared Augustinian conception that individual belief does not spring up by itself, but is the product of social discipline and public order. I return to this point in my conclusion. In the second place, even in the first half of the seventeenth century a confessional division of the inhabitants of the core provinces of the Dutch Republic had not yet fully crystallised across different confessions.[31] The public Reformed Church did not acknowledge all subjects of the Dutch Republic as its members, when all other State Churches in Europe did.[32] It had a core of dedicated members surrounded by a much wider but ill-defined group of sympathisers and people who used some of its services. The situation of the other religious groups was more or less the same. Consequently, the boundaries between the different religious groups were hazy. This was not yet a religiously segmented society. The best image is probably one of an ongoing process in a solution with several crystallisation points.

In the second half of the seventeenth century, this process had worked itself out. All religious minority groups occupied a position which in important aspects resembled that of the Jews, that is, they had become communities with fixed boundaries. All other inhabitants of the Republic were considered to be Reformed. The main mechanism driving this development was, as Joke Spaans has demonstrated, the organisation of poor relief.[33] Like the Jews, the dissenters were forced to take care of their own poor, while all others had either to be members of the public Church to receive poor relief (as in Amsterdam); alternatively, if a public

---

[31] Spaans, *Haarlem na de Reformatie*, p. 104.

[32] A. Duke, 'The Ambivalent Face of Calvinism in the Netherlands', in A. Duke, *Reformation and Revolt in the Low Countries* (London, 1990), pp. 269–94.

[33] Joke Spaans, *Armenzorg in Friesland 1500–1800. Publieke zorg en particuliere liefdadigheid in zes Friese steden: Leeuwarden, Bolsward, Franeker, Sneek, Dokkum en Harlingen* (Hilversum, 1997); see also her chapter in this volume.

poor relief apart from the Reformed *diaconie* still existed, as in Friesland and Groningen, they were considered to be Reformed. In this context, the dissenters and Catholics could actually be treated as the Jews had been treated since the first decades of the century. Their presence was assured, the internal authority of their lay leadership was supported by political authority, they developed their own cultural life, and they were – a hypothesis which needs detailed testing – more and more excluded from public life: not only from the local political elites, as they had been all along, but also from their extensive patronage networks.[34] The religious and social order of the Republic in the eighteenth century was made up of several hierarchically ordered religious groups. Religious dissent was incorporated by giving it a lower position within this order.

Once this had happened, the presence of dissenters could also be recognised formally. Beginning in the last quarter of the seventeenth century, religious dissenters were invited by the municipal authorities to hold religious services on public Days of Prayer, the most important civic ritual of the Republic.[35] The logical implication of this civil religion – that all religious groups in the Republic shared certain basic convictions – was not formulated positively, but was expressed negatively in the form of fierce repression of anti-Trinitarianism and radical dissent.[36]

There were still many differences in the treatment of the various dissenting groups. In contrast to the Catholics, Mennonites, and Arminians, Amsterdam's Lutherans and Jews, both essentially groups of immigrants, were allowed to build highly visible churches and synagogues. No formal ban on marriage between Christians of various confessions was ever suggested, although the rate of intermarriage between Catholics and Protestants seems to have fallen sharply. Only the Jews were ever excluded from the guilds. Eighteenth-century Arminians and Mennonites were quite clearly of higher social standing than Catholics or Lutherans. Nevertheless, all these differences were easily accommodated within the hierarchical religious order which the Republic upheld, and there were remarkably few instances of resistance against this hegemonic order. The Jews seem to have accepted their position more positively than other groups. The Amsterdam Jews were extremely proud of invitations to take part in the public Days of Prayer, or at least, they preserved them much more carefully than any dissenting community. They also bitterly resisted

[34] Van Rooden, *Religieuze regimes*, pp. 17–45.   [35] *Ibid.*, pp. 78–120.
[36] Joris van Eijnatten, *Mutua Christianorum Tolerantia: Irenicism and Toleration in the Netherlands: The Stinstra Affair 1740–1745* (Firenze, 1998); Jonathan Israel, 'The Intellectual Debate about Toleration in the Dutch Republic', in C. Berkvens-Stevelinck, J. Israel, and G.H.M. Posthumus Meyjes (eds.), *The Emergence of Tolerance in the Dutch Republic* (Leiden / New York / Cologne, 1997), pp. 3–36, especially pp. 24–36.

the end of the old religious order, in marked contrast to the Arminians, Mennonites, and Catholics, who welcomed the changes after 1795.[37]

What does all this say about Dutch tolerance or, better, about the nature of the religious order of the Dutch Republic? First, it can help to pose questions about toleration more appropriately. The outcome of the religious development of the Dutch Republic was the establishment of a stable religious and social order, hierarchical in nature, based on exclusions and strong boundaries. The Dutch Republic became a confessional state, based on religious difference and devoted to upholding a religious order by political means. It was a peculiar confessional state, to be sure, but it still fits within a recognisable early modern European continuum, and is thus not exceptional.[38] Across early modern Europe religion occupied a social place which, in important ways, is comparable to the social place of high art today. It is generally accepted that a modern state has a duty to further art, that is to say, has to fund museums and artists, and ought to subsidise forms of art such as opera and poetry which cannot compete on the open market. It is also a generally shared sentiment that people will benefit from enjoying art. Attempts abound to get people to subscribe to this judgement and to interest them in artistic productions. Yet the existence of art and museums is not dependent upon the number of people taking an interest in art, and any defence of the common people's right and ability to define art will meet fierce resistance. In fact, the people who care most passionately about high art usually share the conviction that it is not for everybody. The level of artistic achievement and the state of art is not judged on the basis of its public. Such judgements are not based on demand, but on supply: are the museums any good, are they located in prominent places, do they possess good collections? Are the arts well funded? Are excellent works of art bought or created?

The social location of religion in early modern Europe presents instructive parallels to the position of the arts in the twenty-first century. Churches were funded by public authority, religion had its most important place in the public sphere, and religious organisations were not judged according to the interest in religion they managed to create among the common people; on the contrary, the elites were deeply suspicious of popular tastes in religion and popular forms of religious life. Everybody

---

[37] Blom, Fuks-Mansfeld, and Schöffer (eds.), *Geschiedenis van de Joden*, pp. 191–5.

[38] Cf. Joris van Eijnatten, *Liberty and Concord in the United Provinces: Religious Toleration and the Public in the Eighteenth-Century Netherlands* (forthcoming); Horst Dreitzel, 'Gewissensfreiheit und soziale Ordnung. Religionstoleranz als Problem der politischen Theorie am Ausgang des 17. Jahrhunderts', *Politische Vierteljahresschrift* 36 (1995), 3–34, especially 7.

shared the sentiment that religion was a good thing. Various pietist groups attempted to convince the people of its supreme worth but they, just like modern devotees of high art, tended to be even more limited by strong feelings of social superiority. True religion was thought so marvellous that a common artisan or servant lived a too conscripted life to enjoy it.[39]

The main point on which the comparison breaks down is, of course, the religious intolerance of the early modern state. Modernist architects are not forced to recant their errors in public ceremonies. Conceptual works of art are not burned on the squares in front of museums, although arguably both measures might further the observable presence of beauty. Still, the theoretical justification of intolerance, as developed by Augustine and endlessly recycled by lesser lights (less interesting but more numerous than the defenders of toleration), fits this interpretative parallel very well.[40] Intoleration was mainly justified with the argument that religious consciousness did not instinctively turn to the truth: since people tend to deviate from what is good for them, their errors must be suppressed and they must be led in the right direction. The Christian self can only be created by discipline and force, as there is no other human way to create it. Public order is a necessary precondition for the emergence of a worthwhile inner life.[41] Perhaps the most succinct early modern statement of this view is Luther's answer to the question: where is the true Church to be found? 'Wherever the word is preached correctly and the sacraments are administered in the right way.' Luther was talking about the invisible Church of true believers, who can only be identified by God. The correct preaching and the right administering of the sacraments are not characteristics of a religious organisation, but are a responsibility of public authority. If we want to create Christian selves, public order is the way to go about it.

The voluminous laments and criticisms about the state of religion in the Dutch Republic have to be interpreted against this background. They were not, in any direct way, about the disappointing record of the Dutch state in creating Christian selves, but about its religious order which, they argued, left much to be desired. They were not about a lack of piety, but about a lack of discipline. Visible infringements of the public order were deplored, not secret sins. The jeremiads were about clothes, carriages,

---

[39] An opinion expressed by the Dutch pietist H. Ravensteyn in his anonymously published *Beknopt Onderrigt aan Predikanten* (Amsterdam, 1730), pp. 48–9.

[40] Mark Goldie, 'The Theory of Religious Intolerance in Restoration England', in Ole Peter Grell, Jonathan I. Israel, and Nicholas Tyacke (eds.), *From Persecution to Toleration. The Glorious Revolution and Religion in England* (Oxford, 1991), pp. 331–68.

[41] Peter Brown, *Augustine of Hippo* (London, 1967), pp. 236–8; Talal Asad, 'The Construction of Religion as an Anthropological Category', in his, *Genealogies of Religion. Discipline and Reasons of Power in Christianity and Islam* (Baltimore, 1993), pp. 27–54.

fashion, visible instances of Catholic or Jewish worship, and so on. So it was not the presence of religious dissenters which was decried, but their encroachments upon public space.

This social location of religion in a public order was a general characteristic of early modern European states. Everywhere in Europe, the way to create Christian selves was predominantly found in the strengthening of the public presence of religion.[42] Missionary endeavours or propagandising efforts in a modern sense of the word were far less prominent and always an optional extra. The Dutch practice of incorporating religious minorities by locating them in a hierarchically lower, well-described niche still upheld such a public order. This happened elsewhere as well. The religious settlement of England after the Glorious Revolution was actually quite similar to the religious order of the Republic.[43] In both cases, a hierarchical religious order could be interpreted at the same time as a kind of confessional state, upholding the preeminence of a public Church, and as an example of enlightened toleration accepting the existence of religious dissenters.[44] In both cases, this hierarchical order offered ample scope for political conflicts between dissenters and the public Church, or between clergy and politicians. All these conflicts, however, only served to strengthen the principle that religion was located in some kind of public order.

The Dutch confessional state was destroyed in 1795, yet the separation of Church and State and the emergence of the nation-state did not spell the end of political involvement with religion. What happened was a shift in the social location of religion. Religion was no longer socially produced in a way similar to present-day art, but more like literacy. It was no longer located in a public order, but in the inner selves of the members of the new moral community of the nation. The nineteenth-century state was deeply involved in the production of virtuous and pious

---

[42] This interpretation is based mainly on a reading of W.R. Ward. Cf. W.R. Ward, *The Protestant Evangelical Awakening* (Cambridge 1992); W.R. Ward, 'The Relations of Enlightenment and Religious Revival in Central Europe and in the English-Speaking World', in Derek Baker (ed.), *Reform and Reformation: England and the Continent c. 1500 – c. 1750* (Oxford, 1979), pp. 281–303; and W.R. Ward, 'Power and Piety, the Origins of Religious Revival in the Early Eighteenth Century', *The Bulletin of the John Rylands University Library of Manchester* 63 (1980), 231–52.

[43] J.C.D. Clark, *English Society, 1688–1832. Ideology, Social Structure and Political Practice during the Ancien Regime* (Cambridge, 1985).

[44] There were of course close connections between the Dutch and English religious orders. The international and domestic political exigencies which acted upon the religious policies of William III, the Stadholder-King, are well worked out by Jonathan Israel: see his 'William III and Toleration', in Ole Peter Grell, Jonathan I. Israel, and Nicholas Tyacke (eds.), *From Persecution to Toleration. The Glorious Revolution and Religion in England* (Oxford, 1991), pp. 129–70.

citizens. After 1815, the new Kingdom of the Netherlands undertook massive reorganisations of the various Protestant Churches to enable them to morally inform the Dutch citizens. The Jews had been the religiously dissenting community which the Dutch Republic had found it easiest to incorporate into its religious order, mainly because their community stood so clearly apart. For the same reason, the new Dutch nation-state subjected them to its most ambitious project of social engineering. The Jews were turned into Dutch men and women. Their languages and culture were suppressed, their organisations dismantled.[45] There is no single growth of something called 'tolerance' or 'religious freedom'. There are several ways of managing religious diversity.

[45] Blom, Fuks-Mansfeld, and Schöffer (eds.), *Geschiedenis van de Joden*, pp. 197–239.

10 Religious toleration and radical philosophy in the later Dutch Golden Age (1668–1710)

Jonathan Israel

In the preface to Spinoza's *Tractatus Theologico-Politicus* (1670) there is to be found a famous passage celebrating the toleration and freedom of thought prevailing in Holland during the age of De Witt:

> Now since we have the rare good fortune to live in a commonwealth where freedom of judgement is fully granted to the individual citizen and he may worship God as he pleases, and where nothing is esteemed dearer and more precious than freedom (*ubi unicuique judicandi libertas integra, et Deum exsuo ingenio colere conceditur, et ubi nihil libertate charius, nec dulcius habetur*) I think I am undertaking no ungrateful or unprofitable task in demonstrating that not only can this freedom be granted without endangering piety and the peace of the commonwealth, but also that the peace of the commonwealth and piety depend on this freedom.[1]

The passage is intriguing from several points of view. Sometimes it has been taken at face value, along with Spinoza's positive comments about Amsterdam 'which enjoys the fruits of this freedom',[2] in the final chapter of the *Tractatus*, a grateful eulogy extolling a religious toleration paralleled at the time scarcely anywhere in Europe.[3] A second way of interpreting the passage is to see it as a response to the spate of recent repressive measures on the part of the civic governments to suppress the upsurge of radical ideas which was so striking a feature of the late 1660s in the Dutch Republic. In particular, one might link the passage with the tremendous public outcry against the anonymously published *Philosophia S.Scripturae Interpres* (Amsterdam, 1666) by Spinoza's ally, Lodewijk Meyer (1638–81), and the death in prison, shortly before completion of the *Tractatus*, of Spinoza's friend and 'disciple' Adriaen Koerbagh (1632–69). Convicted of blasphemy, Koerbagh was sentenced by the Amsterdam magistracy to ten years' imprisonment in the *Rasphuis*, a 4,000 guilder fine, and (should

---

[1] Spinoza, *Tractatus Theologico-Politicus*, trans. S. Shirley (Leiden, 1989), p. 51; Spinoza, *Opera*, ed. Carl Gebhardt, 4 vols. (Heidelberg, 1925), pp. iii, 7.

[2] Spinoza, *Tractatus Theologico-Politicus*, p. 298.

[3] See K.W. Swart, *The Miracle of the Dutch Republic as seen in the Seventeenth Century*. Inaugural lecture delivered at University College London, 6 November 1967 (London, 1969), p. 13.

he survive prison) a further ten years' banishment from the city,[4] for writing two books denying the key tenets and 'mysteries' of the Christian faith in violation of the States of Holland's and States-General's anti-Socinian legislation of 1653.[5] At the same time his brother Johan, also a Spinozist, despite the magistrates' failure to prove complicity in the writing of Adriaen's books,[6] only narrowly escaped imprisonment himself. Locked up in the *Rasphuis*, Adriaen Koerbagh's morale and health rapidly broke: he sickened and in 1669, still in prison, he died. Meanwhile Spinoza, for his part, continued to face formidable difficulties in getting his own work published. In this sombre context, it has been argued, his ostensible praise of Dutch toleration may readily be construed as an ironic protest, indeed a piece of carefully wrought sarcasm.[7]

But there is also, I believe, a third way of interpreting his seemingly lavish praise of Dutch toleration. Considering the wider context of the *Tractatus*, and Spinoza's own pressing need to find ways to clear a path for publication of his *Ethics* (his chief work, but one which he felt unable to publish, so forbidding was the atmosphere in which he now found himself during the remainder of his life, despite its being ready for the press and his coming close to attempting publication in Amsterdam, where he spent several weeks during the summer of 1675),[8] it is surely not convincing to argue his eulogy of Dutch toleration in the *Tractatus* was sincere and genuinely felt. On the other hand, given the book is in large part an effort to sway opinion, particularly among the regent elite, in favour of a broader toleration – what he calls *libertas philosophandi* ('liberty to philosophise': a heavily loaded term in Spinoza's work) – by demonstrating that freedom of judgement on all matters does not damage but, on the contrary,

---

[4] K.O. Meinsma, *Spinoza et son cercle. Étude critique historique sur les hétérodoxes hollandais* (1896; revised edition in French, Paris, 1983), p. 368; H.A. Enno van Gelder, *Getemperde vrijheid. Een verhandeling over de verhouding van kerk en staat in de Republiek der Verenigde Nederlanden en de vrijheid van meningsuiting in zake godsdienst, drukpers en onderwijs, gedurende de 17e eeuw* (Groningen, 1972), pp. 180–4.

[5] J.I. Israel, *The Dutch Republic. Its Rise, Greatness and Fall, 1477–1806* (Oxford, 1995), pp. 911–14; J.I. Israel, 'The Banning of Spinoza's Works in the Dutch Republic (1670–1678)', in Wiep van Bunge and Wim Klever (eds.), *Disguised and Overt Spinozism around 1700* (Leiden, 1996), pp. 6–7.

[6] 'Confessie-Boeck', Ms. 5061/318, ff. 115r, 117v, 118r–119v, 122r, Gemeentearchief Amsterdam; Meinsma, *Spinoza et son cercle*, pp. 368–9.

[7] See M. Francès, *Spinoza dans les pays néerlandais de la seconde moitié du XVIIe siècle* (Paris, 1937), p. 61; Meinsma, *Spinoza et son cercle*, pp. 369–75; Etienne Balibar, *Spinoza and Politics*, trans. P. Snowden (1985; reprint London/New York, 1998), p. 23; Gerardine Maréchal, 'Inleiding', in [Aert Wolsgryn, Johannes Duijkerius, *et al.*], *Het Leven van Philopater*, ed. Gerardine Maréchal (Amsterdam, 1991), pp. 23–4; J.I. Israel, *The Dutch Republic*, p. 789.

[8] Piet Steenbakkers, *Spinoza's Ethica from Manuscript to Print. Studies on Text, Form and Related Topics* (Assen, 1994), p. 7.

promotes the well-being of the community and the state, it seems equally improbable that such praise is essentially a sardonic reproach. Rather it seems best to view it as a deliberate piece of exaggeration and subtle propaganda intended as part of a wider strategy to broaden the scope of Dutch toleration.[9] It is surely significant in this context that several hostile critics who denounced the *Tractatus* in the 1670s deemed Spinoza's remarks on toleration an outrageous, even provocative piece of sedition, an attempt fundamentally to alter the status quo and manipulate the intellectual and religious life of the community by falsely insinuating that the authorities approved and condoned a general toleration of a kind which in reality was neither permitted nor generally thought desirable or respectable.[10]

Spinoza might argue that 'in any way to coerce the citizen's free judgement is altogether incompatible with the freedom of the people', and that it ruins the state when the 'law intrudes into the realm of speculative thought and beliefs are put on trial and condemned as crimes'.[11] But this did not change the – for him and his followers – deeply frustrating and unpalatable fact that the Dutch Republic and its laws firmly proscribed his thought and the key concepts of the radical philosophical tradition of which his philosophy formed the backbone. The work of radical Bible exegesis by Lodewijk Meyer, the *Philosophia S. Scripturae Interpres*, was not just widely decried by the public and fiercely condemned by the consistories and synods of the Reformed Church, but actively prohibited and suppressed by city governments in Holland and by the States of Friesland and Utrecht.[12] Adriaen Koerbagh's *Bloemhof van allerley Lieflykheid sonder verdriet*, the first of his two major works denying divine authorship of Scripture, miracles, the divinity of Christ and the Trinity, as well as the immortality of the soul and Heaven and Hell,[13]

---

[9] See J.I. Israel, 'The Intellectual Debate about Toleration in the Dutch Republic', in C. Berkvens-Stevelinck, J.I. Israel, and G.H.M. Posthumus Meyjes (eds.), *The Emergence of Tolerance in the Dutch Republic* (Leiden, 1997), pp. 28–32, 35; J.I. Israel, 'Spinoza, Locke and the Enlightenment Battle for Toleration', in O. Grell and Roy Porter (eds.), *Toleration in Enlightenment Europe* (Cambridge, 2000), pp. 109–11; see also J.I. Israel, 'Locke, Spinoza and the Philosophical Debate concerning Toleration in the Early Enlightenment (c. 1670 – c. 1750)', *Koninklijke Nederlandse Academie van Wetenschappen, Mededelingen van de Afdeling Letterkunde*, New Series 62, 6 (1999), 5–19.

[10] See, for instance, Regnerus van Mansvelt, *Adversus Anonymum Theologico-Politicum* (Amsterdam, 1674), pp. 4, 362.

[11] Spinoza, *Tractatus Theologico-Politicus*, p. 51.

[12] Acta Kerkeraad VIII, res. 14 January 1667, 4 February 1667, and 18 March 1667, Het Utrechts Archief; Israel, 'The Banning of Spinoza's Works', p. 9.

[13] Hubert Vandenbossche, *Spinozisme en kritiek bij Koerbagh* (Brussel, n.d.), pp. 5–6, 9, 22–3, 29, 45; Hubert Vandenbossche, 'Adriaan Koerbagh en Spinoza', *Mededelingen vanwege Het Spinozahuis* 39 (1978), 4–13; H. Jongeneelen, 'La philosophie politique d'Adrien Koerbagh', *Cahiers Spinoza* 6 (1991), 249–50; Wim Klever, *Mannen rond Spinoza (1650–1700). Presentatie van een emanciperende generatie* (Hilversum, 1997), pp. 88–9.

clandestinely published in Amsterdam in 1668, was similarly denounced by the Reformed consistories in Holland and Utrecht and banned by the city governments.[14] Furthermore, despite the conventionally accepted view that it was not until 1674 that the States and *Hof van Holland* banned the *Tractatus*, in reality, as has been shown,[15] there was once again a massive outcry from the moment it appeared, leading to steps being taken in several – or probably most – cities to suppress the book in accordance with the anti-Socinian legislation of 1653. Under the terms of the edict of 1674 banning the *Tractatus*, and still more the States of Holland's edict of 1678 suppressing the *Opera Posthuma*, including the *Ethics* (a measure followed by a decree of the States-General), Spinozism was effectively a banned philosophy in the United Provinces, and publication and distribution of Spinozistic texts was henceforth to incur severe penalties, both fines and terms of imprisonment followed by banishment.[16]

Nevertheless, it was also true that the Dutch Republic afforded a degree of religious toleration and also, up to a point, of intellectual toleration, which went appreciably beyond what could be found in most other European states at the time. Moreover, the regent elite and much of the public had become gradually accustomed to justify, advocate, and even take pride in a toleration which was vigorously championed by De Witt and the anti-Orangist regent faction, and which was at the same time beginning to be admired by a few foreign observers such as the deistically inclined English envoy at The Hague, Sir William Temple. The most zealous republicans, such as the theorists Johan and Pieter de la Court, undoubtedly favoured extending religious toleration still further.[17] This growing support for toleration, and the considerable tension which existed at this time between De Witt's ruling regent faction and the orthodox Calvinist Voetian wing of the public Church, provided a political and cultural framework within which Spinoza and his circle could hope to build on the limited Dutch toleration of the past, using the widespread regent and general public support for it – to be found at any rate in Holland – as an ideological and political lever with which to open the door to a genuinely comprehensive 'freedom to philosophize'. Spinoza's *libertas philosophandi* indeed stretched far beyond what had been conceded to the

[14] Israel, 'The Banning of Spinoza's Works', p. 9.
[15] *Ibid.*, pp. 10–13; J. Freudenthal, *Die Lebensgeschichte Spinozas in Quellenschriften, Urkunden und nichtamtlichen Nachrichten* (Leipzig, 1899), pp. 121–7.
[16] Israel, 'The Banning of Spinoza's Works', pp. 11–14; Israel, 'The Intellectual Debate about Toleration', pp. 30–1.
[17] J.I. Israel, 'Toleration in Seventeenth-Century Dutch and English Thought', in S. Groenveld and M. Wintle (eds.), *Britain and the Netherlands*, vol. XI (Zutphen, 1994), pp. 25–7.

Cartesians under the States of Holland's edict on philosophy of 1656,[18] and ultimately amounted to a demand for freedom to express ideas totally at odds with the theological premises on which contemporary cultural and intellectual life rested. The final objective, presumably, was to undermine the hegemony of theology in society and culture, clearing a path for the progress of radical philosophy.

Spinoza's call for *libertas philosophandi* was echoed both in his own lifetime and subsequently by almost the entire Dutch radical philosophical fraternity. It implied a concept of toleration which not only clashed fundamentally with the Dutch toleration that actually existed, but was intricately entwined with an intellectual and political agenda which was nothing less than revolutionary in scope and implications. Even before Koerbagh, Van den Enden proclaimed the new toleration in the most uncompromising manner in his extremely radical *Vrije Politieke Stellingen* (1665), where, among much else, he saw all ecclesiastical power and priestly ascendancy in society as incompatible with true toleration and individual freedom.[19]

There were similar reverberations in every decade from the 1660s onwards. A notable instance in the 1690s followed publication of the second part of the *Life of Philopater*, a Spinozistic novel written collectively by a radical coterie in Amsterdam among whom the book's publisher, Aert Wolsgryn, seems to have been the central figure.[20] The text appeared anonymously in 1,500 copies at Amsterdam in 1697, provoking an immediate outcry as a 'book tending to the belittling of the divine majesty and mockery and denial of Holy Scripture, as well as many things contained within it necessary for Salvation'.[21] Following Spinoza's strategy, *Philopater* seeks to transform Dutch toleration from an essentially religious freedom within certain strictly defined bounds into an unlimited 'freedom to reason' and to express ideas freely, however different these may be from those accepted by most of society. According to Wolsgryn and his accomplices, 'freedom to reason and to judge' causes all the arts and sciences to flourish, while lack of that freedom causes only decay.[22]

---

[18] On this measure, see Israel, *The Dutch Republic*, pp. 892–4.

[19] Franciscus van den Enden, *Vrije Politieke Stellingen* (Amsterdam, 1992), pp. 196–205; Israel, 'The Intellectual Debate about Toleration', p. 28.

[20] Maréchal accepts the view of the consistory that Johannes Duijkerius was the principal author, but it seems the Amsterdam magistrates took a different view and regarded Wolsgryn as the chief culprit, see Archief Kerkenraad XVII, p. 9, inv. no. 376, Gemeentearchief Amsterdam; Maréchal, 'Inleiding', pp. 11–16.

[21] Archief Kerkenraad XVI, fo. 316r, res. 9 January 1698, inv. no. 376, Gemeentearchief Amsterdam.

[22] [Aert Wolsgryn, Johannes Duijkerius, *et al.*], *Het Leven van Philopater*, ed. Gerardine Maréchal (Amsterdam, 1991), pp. 170–1.

Delegates sent from the consistory to the city hall in January 1698 reported that the burgomasters had been shocked by the 'offensive' extracts read out to them, and promised to take vigorous steps to combat the book, as they duly did.[23] In March Wolsgryn, who we know from other sources was a dedicated Spinozist, was arrested and interrogated. Though he denied being the main author, the magistrates concluded he was the inspirer and person chiefly responsible.[24] Sentenced on 25 April 1698 to a 4,000 guilder fine (3,000 for publishing the book and 1,000 for distributing it) 'in accordance with the edict against printing Spinozistic books' (*volgens 't placcaet aengaende het drukken van Spinosistische boecken*), eight years' imprisonment and, if he survived this, a subsequent twenty-five years' banishment from the city, he too was locked up in the *Rasphuis*, apparently never to be heard of again.[25] Wolsgryn's co-author Johannes Duijkerius, though denounced and condemned by the consistory, escaped punishment by the magistracy.

But the furore over *Philopater* was a minor affair compared with the commotion which erupted in 1703 over a minister of the Reformed Church who, though originally from Zeeland, had preached at Zwolle in Overijssel since the early 1680s by the name of Frederik van Leenhof (died 1711). A key representative of the Dutch radical intellectual movement, though in the past he has often been classified as a religiously inspired 'Christian Spinozist', Van Leenhof had earlier acquired a reputation as a markedly liberal Cocceian theologian. To an even greater extent than the books of Meyer and Koerbagh, however, the chief work of his later years, *Den Hemel op Aarden* (1703), caused a mighty commotion and was denounced throughout the United Provinces – correctly in my judgement – as a Spinozistic work not just completely incompatible with, but actively antagonistic to, Christian doctrine. In this publication, as Van Leenhof's foremost critic in Amsterdam expressed it, 'nothing else but crystal clear Spinozism is taught and propagated' (*niets anders als het klink klaar Spinozismus geleert en voortgeplant wordt*).[26] In Van Leenhof's book, explained another leading critic, everything is reduced to 'obedience towards God', love, peace, and justice towards one's neighbour, and joy, or tranquillity of mind, as regards oneself, with no need for theology – no

---

[23] Archief Kerkenraad XVI, fo. 316r, res. 2 January 1698 and 9 January 1698, inv. no. 376, Gemeentearchief Amsterdam.

[24] Archief Kerkenraad XVII, p. 9, res. 15 May 1698, inv. no. 376, Gemeentearchief Amsterdam.

[25] *Ibid.*; Acta Harderwijk, res. Augustus 1698, art. 'licentieus boekdrukken', Oud Synodaal Archief 85, Synode van Gelderland, Algemeen Rijksarchief Den Haag; Maréchal, 'Inleiding', p. 33; Israel, 'The Intellectual Debate about Toleration', p. 32.

[26] Tacco Hajo van den Honert, *Nodige Aantekeningen Op de Artikelen tot Satisfactie van de Eerw. Kerken-raad tot Zwolle voorgestelt aan D.F.van Leenhof* (Amsterdam, 1705), pp. 2–3.

'Grace', no 'Salvation', no immortality of the soul, no Heaven, no damnation, no Hell, no Christ and in fact 'no belief in God'.[27]

Not the least ruinous of Van Leenhof's ideas, insisted his adversaries, were his efforts to obtain from the civic magistracies the same 'freedom of opinion and speech' which Spinoza calls for in his *Tractatus*, claiming that 'freedom of opinion and speech is such a natural and unalterable right of the individual that it neither should, nor can, be constrained either by religion or the laws passed by government'.[28] Toleration of such 'free minds', complained his antagonists, would mean accepting the right of those who think there is no Hell or damnation, and no Grace, Salvation, or Christ, to air their views freely which, in their view, would simply be altogether 'too scandalous' a state of affairs.[29] According to both the law and practices of the state, there was no freedom to express such opinions in the Dutch Republic, nor, in the view of the vast majority, should there be. In one of his most daring passages, Van Leenhof audaciously asserts that 'the truth' is generally suppressed by persons commonly held to be 'learned because they have a good memory and know how to talk of languages, happenings and antiquities and who thereby strive for authority'.[30] These men, an obvious enough allusion to the Reformed preachers and other clergy, were the reason that the 'noble truth cannot break through and free minds are oppressed' (*dat de edelmoedige waarheid niet en kan doorbreken en dat vrije verstanden onderdrukt worden*).[31] Consequently, held Van Leenhof, false and misleading ideas prevail in society, medicine, philosophy, and theology.

In the future, he urges, one of the chief means whereby society can be improved, peace spread among men, and tranquillity of mind promoted, will be to extend toleration to the sphere of ideas. But in pressing this argument, Van Leenhof carefully guards his flanks by speaking of such intellectual toleration as if it were still religious toleration: 'disdain no-one for his religion, provided he lives peacefully; it is God's work to give faith' (*veragt niemand om zijn Godsdienst, als hy 'er door maar vreedzaam leeft: 't is God's werk het geloove te schenken*).[32] It would be thoroughly helpful, he adds, if men would refrain from entering into theological quarrels.

Van Leenhof's revolutionary concept of 'true religion' which requires no clergy or theology in fact replicates the paradox which lies at the heart

---

[27] Franciscus Burmannus, *'t Hoogste Goed der Spinozisten, vergeleken met den Hemel op aarden van den Heer Fredericus van Leenhof* (Enkhuizen, 1704), pp. 107, 143.

[28] *Ibid.*, p. 143; Frederik van Leenhof, *Den Hemel op Aarden; Of een korte en klaare Beschrijvinge van de waare en stantvastige Blydschap; zoo naar de Reden als de H.Schrift voor alle slag van Menschen en in allerlei voorvallen* (Zwolle, 1704), pp. 77–9, 85, 115; Burmannus, *'t Hoogste Goed der Spinozisten*, pp. 236–40.

[29] *Ibid.*, pp. 143, 236–44.   [30] Van Leenhof, *Den hemel op Aarden*, pp. 74–5.

[31] *Ibid.*   [32] *Ibid.*, p. 115.

of Spinoza's system and the entire tradition of Dutch radical philosophy,[33] the contention that the doctrines of theologians have nothing to do with truth, not only in the sense envisaged by the philosopher or scientist but also in the sense of true 'religion'. As Spinoza famously redefines 'faith' in Chapter Fourteen of the *Tractatus*: 'worship of God and obedience to him consists solely in justice and charity or love towards one's neighbour'.[34] Hence 'it is only by works that we can judge anyone to be a believer or unbeliever, however much he may differ in religious dogma from other believers; whereas if his works are evil, he is an unbeliever, however much he may agree with them verbally'.[35] Spinoza's dictum that 'those who love justice and charity we know by that very fact to be the faithful while he who persecutes the faithful is Antichrist' (*Qui enim justitiam et charitatem amant, eos per hoc solum fideles esse scimus; et qui fideles persequitur, Antichristus est*)[36] means that true religion is something different from Christianity (Catholic or Protestant), Islam, and Judaism and indeed has nothing to do with theology. It implies also that theologians who insist their doctrines are necessary for salvation are enemies of Christ. No doubt it was this Spinozist logic that lay also behind Bernard Mandeville's contention that weakening the clergy as much as possible is the key to a genuine toleration and that 'it is evident . . . that there is no characteristick to distinguish and know a true church from a false one'.[37]

The realisation in Dutch society around 1700 that Spinoza and the Spinozists were claiming there is a true 'universal religion' which has no theological dogmas other than that the true worship of God is the practice of justice and charity, and which requires a comprehensive toleration of thought and freedom of speech and expression, aroused no small anxiety. One of the chief points of the commission of the Zwolle consistory which, with the backing of the town burgomasters, vainly endeavoured to purge Van Leenhof of suspicion of Spinozism by getting him expressly to repudiate a list of proscribed core radical philosophical doctrines was that there is no such thing as a 'universal religion in which all people, including those who are without Christ, can be saved and redeemed and in which

---

[33] Balibar speaks of the 'central paradox' of the *Tractatus Theologico-Politicus* being to 'free faith itself from theology', see Balibar, *Spinoza and Politics*, pp. 7–8; on Van Leenhof's concept of 'true religion', see Hubert Vandenbossche, *Frederik van Leenhof* (Brussels, 1974), p. 38.

[34] Spinoza, *Tractatus Theologico-Politicus*, pp. 222–4.   [35] *Ibid.*, p. 222.

[36] *Ibid.*, p. 223; Spinoza, *Opera*, vol. III, p. 176.

[37] Bernard Mandeville, *Free Thoughts on Religion, The Church and National Happiness* (London, 1720), pp. 234, 246; this Dutchman, settled in London, also maintained that the 'greatest argument for toleration is, that differences of opinion can do no hurt, if all clergymen are kept in awe, and no more independent on the state than the laity': *ibid.*, p. 241; Israel, 'Locke, Spinoza', p. 111.

all opinions are free and must be openly tolerated in the church' (*een Algemeen Godsdienst, waar door alle menschen, selfs ook die buiten Christus zyn, kunnen zalig en behouden worden; en daarom alle gevoelens vry zyn, en openbaar moeten worden geduldet in de kerk*).[38]

Under the Republic's laws Spinozism as well as Spinoza's books were banned and, as one of the pamphlets attacking Van Leenhof pointed out, this had resulted in the suppression of *Philopater*, and imprisonment of Wolsgryn, and ought logically also to entail suppression of Van Leenhof's Spinozistic writings and his being publicly disgraced and punished.[39] Both objectives of the Reformed synods were eventually achieved. But, owing to the political intricacies of the situation, not before a remarkably arduous and protracted battle. According to the usual procedures of the Republic, the other provinces were supposed to wait, before banning illicit books published within the jurisdiction of a given province, for that province to take the initiative. But Van Leenhof's defence that he had ill-advisedly used Spinozist terms and phrases yet was not a Spinozist but a loyal Christian swayed enough of his colleagues in the Zwolle consistory as well as the Zwolle city government – the latter taking the view that the rights and dignity of their city were being impugned by the heavy pressure exerted from outside – to cause a general deadlock over the question in the States of Overijssel. The delay caused a remarkable build-up of anger and pressure in the other provinces. On the initiative of Pensionary Heinsius, the States of Holland eventually banned three of Van Leenhof's publications, including *Den Hemel op Aarden*, in December 1706 'because they contain various gross and blasphemous opinions directly conflicting with God's Word', despite the fact that these writings were still freely circulating in Overijssel.[40] The States of Friesland formally banned Van Leenhof's *Den Hemel op Aarden* on 29 March 1708 as a work 'containing many heterodox, suspicious and Spinozistic propositions'.[41]

The most tragic of the echoes of Spinoza's paean of praise for the toleration afforded by the Dutch Republic was very possibly that of the young

---

[38] Acta Kerkenraad, res. 29 October 1704, art. XVII, point 15, inv. no. 017/6, Gemeentearchief Zwolle; Gottlieb Friedrich Jenichen, *Historia Spinozismi Leenhofiani publica in Belgio avctoritate novissime damnati ex authenticis docvmentis collecta* (Leipzig, 1707), p. 157.

[39] *D. Leenhofs Boek genaamt Den Hemel op Aarde strijdende tegen het Christendom* (Utrecht, 1704) [Knuttel no. 15302], pp. 9, 16–19, 21–3, 42; on the pamphlet war surrounding Van Leenhof, see J.I. Israel, 'Les controverses pamphlétaires dans la vie intellectuelle hollandaise et allemande à l'époque de Bekker et Van Leenhof', *XVIIe Siècle* 49 (1997), 253–64.

[40] Johannes Monnikhoff, 'Aantekeningen', fo. 16v, Ms. 128 G 1 (2), Koninklijke Bibliotheek Den Haag.

[41] Acta Breda, July 1708, art. 17, Oud Synodaal Archief 97, Synode van Zuid-Holland, Algemeen Rijksarchief Den Haag; Acta Vollenhove, June 1708, art. 40, Oud Synodaal Archief 216, Synode van Overijssel, Algemeen Rijksarchief Den Haag.

autodidact of humble background, Hendrik Wyermars (1685–?). Though he read philosophy only in the vernacular and seems to have known no other language than Dutch, Wyermars had a good grasp of the contemporary philosophical scene. An Amsterdam merchant's clerk and a passionate Spinozist, Wyermars held that 'all occurrences happen through the unalterable laws of nature' and that nothing happens against or outside the laws of nature.[42] His only known book, the *Ingebeelde Chaos*, giving his name on the title-page, was published at Amsterdam in 1710, and caused an immediate outcry. In June the Amsterdam consistory denounced the book as 'containing all the gross and blasphemous opinions of Spinoza presented in the clearest and most shameless manner' and sent a delegation of three preachers to reveal its contents to the burgomasters.[43] The argument of his treatise is mainly concerned to show that the world has existed eternally and was not created, and to deny divine providence and revelation.

Wyermars was evidently proud of both the progress of 'philosophy' and the freedom of thought which, he maintained, prevailed in the Dutch Republic. While superstitious belief in demonic power and ghosts still filled the rest of Europe, he notes, 'in our land it is already much diminished'.[44] But especially poignant in view of what was about to happen was his real or professed trust in Dutch toleration. 'Fortunate', he maintains, is the land where toleration and 'freedom of thought' prevails, and 'fortunate the university where such toleration is taught', he adds, referring to the famous address on the subject delivered at Leiden on 8 February 1706 by the eminent jurist, and then rector of the university, Gerardus van Noodt, a plea for religious toleration on grounds of civil freedom which reportedly caught the attention of much of Europe.[45] But as the States of Holland's edicts on Socinianism, Cartesianism, and Spinozism made abundantly clear, Dutch religious toleration was one thing, toleration of radical ideas quite another. On 1 October 1710, Wyermars was arrested by the magistracy and shortly thereafter the remaining unsold copies of his book in the publisher's possession were seized. The publisher too was arrested and tried.

In the interrogations which followed, Wyermars seems to have been more than a little defiant. When accused of denying free will and adhering

---

[42] Hendrik Wyermars, *Den Ingebeelde Chaos* (Amsterdam, 1710), pp. xvii, 132–4, 141–2; Hubert Vandenbossche, 'Hendrik Wyermars' *Ingebeelde Chaos* (1710), een "Tractatus de Emendatione Spinozae"', *Tijdschrift voor de Studie van de Verlichting* 2 (1974), 329–37.

[43] Archief Kerkenraad XVIII, p. 107, res. 26 June 1710, inv. no. 376, Gemeentearchief Amsterdam.

[44] Wyermars, *Den Ingebeelde Chaos*, p. 128.

[45] *Ibid.*, p. xvi; on Van Noodt's peroration, see G.C.J.J. van den Bergh, *The Life and Work of Gerard Noodt (1647–1725)* (Oxford, 1988), pp. 224–8.

to a radical determinism, the absolute necessity of all things, he apparently called his accusers hypocrites who in their hearts believed the same as himself, an outburst which was ill received. On 30 October 1710 he was sentenced, in accordance with the laws against Spinozism, to a 3,000 guilder fine, imprisonment for fifteen years 'without pen, ink or paper' and, in case of survival, subsequent banishment from Holland for twenty-five years.[46] At their gatherings over the following months, the news was reportedly greeted with 'joy' by the Reformed Church classes and synods.[47]

[46] Vandenbossche, 'Hendrik Wyermars' *Ingebeelde Chaos*', 324.
[47] The classis Edam 'verheught zijnde over de geoeffende straffe ontrent den schryver van het Ingebeelde Chaos': Acta Classis Edam VII, 20 July 1711, art. 8 Synodalia, point no. 15 'licientieus boekdrukken', Rijksarchief Noord Holland; Archief Kerkenraad XVIII, res. 9 October 1710, inv. no. 376, Gemeentearchief Amsterdam; and Acta Leiden, 7–17 July 1711, art. 14, Oud Synodaal Archief 97, Synode van Zuid-Holland, Algemeen Rijksarchief Den Haag, where it was merely reported that 'tot Amsterdam uytgekomen was een seer godloos boekje genaamt Het Ingebeeld Chaos door eenen Hendrik Weyermars en hoe dat de kercke-raad aldaar 't selve op de tafel vande burgemeesteren dier stadt hadden geligt, die gunstichlick aangenomen hadden daar op te letten'.

11 The politics of intolerance: citizenship and religion in the Dutch Republic (seventeenth to eighteenth centuries)

Maarten Prak

Over the past two decades, a remarkable shift has taken place in our evaluation of the religious situation in the Dutch Republic. For a long time Calvinism was seen as the dominant force in Dutch society. Textbooks, such as K.H.D. Haley's *The Dutch in the Seventeenth Century* (1972), or J.L. Price's *Culture and Society in the Dutch Republic in the Seventeenth Century* (1974) discussed the position of Catholics, Mennonites, and other so-called minority religions, in terms of toleration. The civic authorities, often liberal in private, had allowed their Churches to practise their rites as long as they did so discreetly, and as long as they were prepared to pay the occasional bribe that persuaded the men in charge to keep looking the other way.[1]

Today, many Dutch historians tend to depict the Calvinist Church as one among the many Churches of the Republic, its membership covering less than half of the population of the Republic. Of course, the Calvinists had their political privileges, but day-to-day practice came closer to a seventeenth-century equivalent of a multi-cultural society. In the fourth volume of A.Th. van Deursen's *Het kopergeld van de Gouden Eeuw* (1981) we see the first signs of this new picture emerging in his discussion of 'popular religion'. By emphasising the magical and non-doctrinal elements in the frame of mind of many Dutch men and women in the seventeenth century, Van Deursen persuaded the reader that many people were indifferent to doctrine as long as the Church managed to alleviate their anxieties. Van Deursen also underlined the self-conscious exclusiveness of the Calvinist Church in Holland.[2] In her *Haarlem na de Reformatie*, Joke Spaans demonstrated how Haarlem's religious divisions sprang the framework of dominance and toleration, not simply in terms of

---

[1] K.H.D. Haley, *The Dutch in the Seventeenth Century* (London, 1972), pp. 84–99; J.L. Price, *Culture and Society in the Dutch Republic in the Seventeenth Century* (London, 1974), chapter 2.

[2] A.Th. van Deursen, *Het kopergeld van de Gouden Eeuw*, vol. IV: *Hel en hemel* (Assen, 1981); translated as *Plain Lives in a Golden Age. Popular Culture, Religion and Society in Seventeenth-Century Holland* (Cambridge, 1991), part 4.

numbers, but also as a consequence of the authorities' attitude towards this situation. Haarlem's regent elite, instead of firmly supporting the public Church, promoted a civic ideal that cut across the doctrinal divides.[3] In a recent article Wiebe Bergsma emphasised, albeit from a somewhat different angle, the civic character of the Reformed Church itself. He describes its role thus:

> The place of the Reformed church in society is epitomised in a seventeenth-century picture of the *Grote Kerk* in Dordrecht. The public character of the building is illustrated by ornaments from guilds and carpenters. Everyday life was thus reflected in the church decorations. The building was open to members and sympathisers, baptised and unbaptised citizens alike. They could go into the church to the sermon or to listen to the news from the pulpit.[4]

All of this must sound most appealing to modern readers, who will have little trouble in recognising in Dutch seventeenth-century religious attitudes a sympathetic, not to say politically correct, answer to a thoroughly modern plight.[5] But was the Dutch Republic really that 'haven in a heartless world'[6] for its non-Calvinist inhabitants? There is some evidence to the contrary that, as I will suggest, provides a less reassuring picture of the popular frame of mind in the Netherlands of the seventeenth century.

This chapter discusses the religious elements of citizenship in a number of Dutch towns in the seventeenth and eighteenth centuries. As I have argued on several other occasions, citizenship was an important element of Dutch social life at the time of the Republic. In the towns under discussion, Arnhem and Nijmegen in the province of Gelderland, Zwolle and Deventer in the province of Overijssel, and finally the city of Utrecht, we will analyse the formal obstacles for non-Calvinists in the acquisition of citizenship rights.[7] This chapter addresses the 'how', 'when', and 'why' of this issue, which has been largely ignored so far in the debate about the religious situation in the Dutch Republic.[8] We begin with a short survey of Dutch citizenship in the seventeenth and eighteenth centuries.

---

[3] Joke Spaans, *Haarlem na de Reformatie. Stedelijke cultuur en kerkelijk leven, 1577–1620* (The Hague, 1989).

[4] Wiebe Bergsma, 'Church, State and People', in Karel Davids and Jan Lucassen (eds.), *A Miracle Mirrored. The Dutch Republic in European Perspective* (Cambridge, 1995), pp. 196–228, here: p. 218.

[5] In one of the latest additions to this literature, Charles de Mooij paints an equally rosy picture: *Geloof kan Bergen verzetten. Reformatie en katholieke herleving te Bergen op Zoom 1577–1795* (Hilversum, 1998).

[6] I have borrowed this evocative phrase from the title of Christopher Lasch's book on the family, *Haven in a Heartless World: The Family Besieged* (New York, 1977).

[7] The five towns discussed in depth in this paper were the largest in the provinces of Overijssel, Gelderland, and Utrecht.

[8] The exception is J.A. Schimmel's study of Nijmegen's citizenship rights: *Burgerrecht te Nijmegen 1592–1810. Geschiedenis van de verlening en burgerlijst* (Tilburg, 1966).

Dutch urban citizenship: a short introduction

The Republic was a federal state with a heavy emphasis on its constitutive parts, the provinces and within those provinces the individual towns. Citizenship rights were dominated by a medieval legacy of local privileges and bylaws that had created the foundation on which early modern rules and practices were built. As a consequence, citizenship in the Dutch Republic was a local, and more specifically, an urban phenomenon. Moreover, citizenship expressed itself variously from town to town, although some general patterns can be observed.[9]

Then, as now, citizenship covered a broad range of issues, many of them explicitly attached to citizenship status.[10] Only citizens were considered full members of the urban community, entitled to the advantages that this entailed. In politics, major offices were exclusively reserved for those who held citizenship status. Given the political make-up of the Republic, this ensured citizens had at least a theoretical possibility of becoming involved in national as well as local politics. Juridically, the citizens were entitled to trial by their peers. All towns insisted that their citizens had to be called to account, in the first instance, before the local bench of aldermen made up, by definition, of citizens. Economically, citizens had exclusive access to the guilds, or 'burgher trades', as they were significantly called. Citizens were also exempt from the payment of tolls in the hinterland of their home towns. Our present evidence strongly suggests that it was particularly the access to the guilds, as provided by citizenship status, that encouraged people to become citizens. Those who lacked the prospect of establishing themselves as independent masters, or who worked outside the guild trades, seem to have been distinctly less keen on citizenship status.

Citizenship could be acquired in several ways. Probably the most common was by birth. Some towns accepted everyone as citizen who was baptised in a local church. But more commonly it was required that one's parents were citizens too. In Amsterdam, moreover, every generation had to reconfirm its citizenship by swearing the citizens' oath before the local

---

[9] Cf. Piet Lourens and Jan Lucassen, ' "Zunftlandschaften" in den Niederlanden und im benachbarten Deutschland', in Wilfried Reininghaus (ed.), *Zunftlandschaften in Deutschland und den Niederlanden im Vergleich* (Münster, 2000), pp. 15–20.

[10] For further references: Maarten Prak, 'Burghers into Citizens. Urban and National Citizenship in the Netherlands during the Revolutionary Era (c. 1800)', *Theory and Society* 26 (1997), 403–20; Maarten Prak, 'Burghers, Citizens, and Popular Politics in the Dutch Republic', *Eighteenth-Century Studies* 30 (1997), 443–8. For comparative purposes, see also the special issue 'Cittadinanze' of *Quaderni Storici* 30 (1995), 281–531, ed. by S. Cerutti, R. Descimon, and M. Prak; M. Boone and M. Prak (eds.), *Statuts individuels, statuts corporatifs et statuts judiciaires dans les villes européennes (moyen âge et temps modernes)* (Louvain/Apeldoorn, 1996); Gail Bossenga, 'Review Article: Rights and Citizens in the Old Regime', *French Historical Studies* 20 (1997), 217–43.

magistrate. Citizenship was not explicitly gendered.[11] By common understanding, the daughters from citizen families were considered members of
the citizenry. The citizens' oath in Zwolle, rephrased in 1767, even made
specific reference to female citizens (*Burgeressen*). They were expected
to help protect the community 'to the best of their abilities', whereas
the men had to promise to do so 'with their body and property'.[12] In
other towns citizenship was not explicitly gendered. But men who married a female citizen, or 'citizen's daughter' as they were usually called,
would become citizens too. A few lucky outsiders were presented with
citizenship status by the local authorities for free. Ministers of the Dutch
Reformed Church could expect this to happen when they accepted a new
appointment. Most outsiders, however, had to buy citizenship status by
paying a fee. They might also be required to demonstrate their legitimate
birth, proper walk of life, and, in some towns, to provide proof of their
religious affiliation.

Citizenship and religion

On 21 August 1654, the *vroedschap* of the city of Utrecht decided that
from then on all applicants for citizenship would have to provide testimony of 'their religion and comportment'.[13] Enquiries into the moral
character of new citizens was not an innovation in Utrecht's civic administration. Fifty years earlier, on 19 March 1604, the council had ruled
that 'quality, comportment, and conduct' should be looked into before
granting admission to the town's citizen community.[14] The insistence on
religious correctness, however, was something entirely new to Utrecht.
Within a year, moreover, it was further specified: 'And no Catholics will
be admitted to this town's citizenship, unless the council, for serious reasons, will unanimously decide to grant dispensation.' At the same time
it was decided that citizens who, after accepting that status, reverted to
Catholicism, were to be deprived of their citizenship.[15]

These rulings of the Utrecht council were not unique. In the Overijssel
town of Deventer similar measures had been introduced in the 1620s.

[11] For the German towns compare: Merry E. Wiesner, 'War, Work and Wealth. The Bases
of Citizenship in Early Modern German Cities', in her *Gender, Church and State in Early
Modern Germany. Essays by Merry E. Wiesner* (London/New York, 1998), pp. 114–25.

[12] Regulations relating to Citizenship and Elections, fo. 169r, 11 March 1767, inv. no. AAZ
01, 258, Gemeentearchief Zwolle [quoted hereafter as: GAZ].

[13] Resolutions of the council, vol. 25, 21 August 1654, inv. no. 121, Stadsarchief [quoted
hereafter as: SA] II, Het Utrechts Archief [quoted hereafter as: UA]. On citizenship in
Utrecht: Ronald Rommes, *Oost, west, Utrecht best? Driehonderd jaar migratie en migranten
in de stad Utrecht (begin 16e – begin 19e eeuw)* (Amsterdam, 1998), pp. 36–43 and *passim*.

[14] Resolutions of the council, vol. 4, 19 March 1604, inv. no. 121, SA II, UA.

[15] *Ibid.*, vol. 25, 12 June 1655.

On 9 January 1623 the Deventer magistrate, together with the Sworn Council, ruled that people who wanted to become citizens had to 'profess of the true Christian Religion', that is, to adhere to the Dutch Reformed Church. They would also be asked to declare quite specifically that they abhorred 'Popish fallacies'. For good measure it was decided at the same meeting that from then on Catholics would be excluded from various municipal offices.[16] In nearby Zwolle the same institutions ruled in 1646 that 'no one, coming from outside into this town and being of the Popish religion, can be admitted as citizen or into any of the guilds'.[17] In the neighbouring province of Gelderland, the Arnhem council decided in 1622 that any Catholic who married a citizen's daughter would be exempt from the rule that only Calvinists could become citizens.[18] In Nijmegen, some twenty kilometres further south, it was decided a year later 'that no person coming into this town from outside and dedicated to the Popish superstitions, will be awarded with this town's citizenship, even if he has married a citizen's daughter'.[19] Thus, within a span of three decades, five of the largest towns in the central and eastern areas of the Republic had deprived their Catholic population of the right to participate in the community on a par with the Calvinists.

Later decisions of the authorities confirmed their determination to stick to these initial policies, although not always in the strictest sense. In May 1674, the Utrecht council decided that Catholics could not become citizens unless they were born within the province of Utrecht.[20] In November it was added that Catholics might also be eligible 'for important, particular reasons'.[21] In 1724 Catholics from all seven provinces of the Dutch Republic were made eligible if they could not merely provide evidence of their comportment, but also a declaration from . . . a Reformed consistory![22] The council of Deventer reiterated its religious policy on several occasions in both the seventeenth and eighteenth centuries. In 1665, for example, it was confirmed that according to the town's

---

[16] Agreements between Magistrate and Sworn Council, lib. C, 9 January 1623, pp. 256–7, 259, inv. no. 125, Republiek [quoted hereafter as: Rep] II, Gemeentearchief Deventer [quoted hereafter as: GAD]. On Deventer's citizenship: B. Woelderink, 'Het Deventer grootburgerrecht', *Gens Nostra* 36 (1981), 114–21; Paul Holthuis, *Frontierstad bij het scheiden van de markt. Deventer militair, demografisch, economisch, 1578–1648* (Houten/Deventer, 1993), pp. 37–9, 110–14, 149.

[17] Resolutions of the Council and Community, vol. 373, 25 June 1646, inv. no. AAZ 01, 21, GAZ. On Zwolle citizenship: J.C. Streng, *'Stemme in staat'. De bestuurlijke elite in de stadsrepubliek Zwolle 1579–1795* (Hilversum, 1997), pp. 91–5.

[18] Resolutions of the Council (Raadsignaat), 24 January 1622, fo. 252v, Oud Archief [quoted hereafter as: OA] 12, Gemeentearchief Arnhem [quoted hereafter as: GAA].

[19] Quoted in Schimmel, *Burgerrecht te Nijmegen*, p. 30.

[20] Resolutions of the council, vol. 29, 4 May 1674, inv. no. 121, SA II, UA.

[21] *Ibid.*, 23 November 1674.   [22] *Ibid.*, vol. 48, 18 April 1724.

constitution, new citizens had to profess the true Christian religion.[23] In 1711, an attempt to clarify the rules repeated that those who wanted to become citizens 'will have to declare that they are favouring (*voorstanders van*) the true Reformed religion, as it is openly practised in this province, and that they detest all Popish superstitions'.[24] In Zwolle it was the same story again. The initial rulings were confirmed in general, but at the same time modified in detail. In 1669 an elaborate decision excluded all foreign Catholics completely and forever from the town's citizenship, but provided certain escape routes for Dutch Catholics.[25] In 1666 the Arnhem council had expressly restated its determination not to admit any Catholics, nor Lutherans for that matter, as citizens into the community.[26]

Nor were these measures allowed to remain a dead letter on the statute books. In all towns under investigation active measures were taken against individuals who did not fit the picture of a proper citizen as perceived by the authorities. In Deventer Herman Berents, blacksmith, lost his citizenship in February 1646. On becoming a citizen in January 1643, Berents was known to have a Catholic background. Two of his colleagues had to vow for his religious opinions. It was explicitly stated in the citizens' register that he would be forced to renounce his citizenship and leave the town if in the future he was found to have misled the authorities.[27] This is exactly what happened when, three years later, it was disclosed that Berents, contrary to his declaration in 1643, continued to participate in Catholic rites. Therefore, he was not merely deprived of his citizen status, but also told to close down his shop and leave Deventer before Easter.[28] In June 1646, Jan Magnus, a tailor and, as it turned out, a Catholic, was stripped of his citizenship and had to close down his shop. He also had to pay a fine of 10 guilders.[29] Half a century later, in June 1700, the authorities in Deventer were still prosecuting Catholic citizens. Jan van Eltrop, Gerrit Egberts and Henrik Berents, all working as tailors, had misled the magistrate by declaring to profess of the Reformed religion, even though they had continued their Popish practices. As a consequence they were deprived of the citizen status they had acquired on false pretext.[30] It was

---

[23] Agreements between Magistrate and Sworn Council, lib. E, 9 January 1665, p. 329, art. 5, inv. no. 125, Rep II, GAD.

[24] Resolutions of Aldermen and Council, lib. 24, 9 June 1711, inv. no. 4, Rep I, GAD.

[25] Regulations relating to Citizenship and Elections, p. 465, 6 April 1669, inv. no. AAZ 01, 22, GAZ.

[26] Resolutions of the Council (Raadsignaat), 28 April 1666, fo. 174v, OA 12, GAA.

[27] According to the Deventer Citizens' Register ('Burgerboek') 1596–1719, fo. 238r, 12 January 1643, GAD.

[28] Resolutions of Aldermen and Council, lib. 14, 9 February 1646, inv. no. 4, Rep I, GAD.

[29] *Ibid.*, 12 June 1646.   [30] *Ibid.*, lib. 22, 27 June 1700.

the same with Adriaen Reinerts, who had been admitted on 9 January
1696 and declared that he 'would diligently frequent the services of the
Reformed Church, and abstain from the Popish religion and Mass'; his
declaration notwithstanding, it was discovered that Reinerts was still a
Catholic.[31]

Other towns followed suit. In Nijmegen Jan van Beugen lost his citizenship in 1637 as a consequence of his religion. The Nijmegen consistory
insisted that Van Beugen had misled them as well as the town's magistrate with promises to change his allegiance from the Roman Catholic to
the Reformed Church. The magistrate, satisfied that this was indeed the
case, decided to deprive him of his citizenship, 'and forbid him all the
burgher trades and freedom'. The shopkeepers' guild, where Van Beugen
was a member, would be notified and told no longer to accept him in their
ranks. Van Beugen, however, had left the authorities little choice. When
asked to account for his conduct, he declared in the consistory's meeting
'that he had been a Catholic as a child, that he still was and planned to
persist with Catholicism for the rest of his life'.[32] In Utrecht Jan Schut-
ter and his wife Johanna van Wijck were deprived of their citizenship in
March 1690 because they had violated the religious rules.[33] It seems that
she had been Reformed and a citizen's daughter, and he had been allowed to become a citizen upon their marriage, provided that Johanna
would stick to the Reformed Church.[34] This, it turned out, she had not
done and now the couple had to face the consequences. In Zwolle, all
applications for citizenship that were turned down before 1750 came from
Catholics. In other words, religion was really the only reason why people
were refused citizenship status in Zwolle.[35]

The clauses against Catholics, and sometimes against other 'minority'
religions,[36] seemed clear-cut at first sight, but contained several infringements of established rights that sometimes called for additional legislation. The first problem was what to do with those Catholics who were
already citizens. This turned out to be easy to deal with. As far as we can

---

[31] *Ibid.*, 1 December 1701.   [32] Schimmel, *Burgerrecht te Nijmegen*, p. 35.

[33] Deprivation of citizenship, 31 March 1690, inv. no. 619, SA II, UA.

[34] This had been laid down in the 'Order on marriages between Reformed and Popists':
Resolutions of the Council, vol. 29, 15 January 1677, inv. no. 121, SA II, UA.

[35] This point is made in a manuscript 'Afwijzen voor het burgerschap', by F.C.
Berkenvelder, the former director of the Zwolle archives, who is investigating local citizenship. I want to express my gratitude to Mr Berkenvelder for sharing his data with me.

[36] In Deventer the clauses against non-Calvinists were also applied to Mennonites: Resolutions of Aldermen and Council, lib. 22, 7 May 1702, inv. no. 4, Rep I, GAD; Minutes of a
Meeting at the Loo Palace, 18 September 1700, inv. no. 99, Rep I, GAD. In Arnhem a ruling relating to the marriages between citizens' daughters and non-Calvinists was directed
explicitly at Catholics and Lutherans alike: Resolutions of the Council (Raadsignaat),
28 April 1666, fo. 174v, OA 23, GAA.

tell, no town tried to take away citizenship rights from these people.[37] As a consequence, all towns must have contained a group of Catholic citizens, and as that status was inherited by one generation after another, even by the end of the eighteenth century Arnhem, Deventer, Nijmegen, Utrecht, and Zwolle must have had Catholic citizens. How many there were is, however, impossible to establish.

A second problem consisted of the position of female citizens.[38] Outsiders who married daughters from citizen families could acquire that status either for free, or at least at reduced rate. It seems that citizenship was considered an asset on the marriage market.[39] In Arnhem it was decided in 1622 that 'Popists, or others who are not of the Reformed religion and have married a citizen's daughter, can be accepted as citizens, provided the Magistrate considers these people's life and qualities to be an asset for the town.'[40] Thus Jan Corneliszn was refused citizenship in 1634 because he was a Catholic but not married to a citizen's daughter.[41] Michiel Remmen, on the other hand, could become a citizen as he had married the widow of one Willem Becker who was presumably a citizen.[42] In 1666, however, for reasons that are not altogether clear, this back door for Catholics aspiring to become citizens in Arnhem was closed.[43] In Zwolle it was decided in 1658 that Catholics from within the province would be allowed to become citizens when they married a citizen's daughter.[44] In Utrecht quite a few Catholics were admitted as citizens as a result of a marriage alliance with a citizen family.[45]

The exclusion of non-Calvinists might deprive individual towns of valuable resources and, perhaps even worse, make these available to other, competing communities. Wary of that prospect, several local governments allowed themselves a certain amount of discretion in the matter. In Utrecht, within a year after the decision to demand a certificate of religious attitudes from prospective citizens, the *vroedschap* decided it

---

[37] This was stated explicitly in a clarification of the initial resolution excluding the Catholics in Zwolle: Resolutions of the Council and Community, p. 376, 14 December 1646, inv. no. AAZ 01, 21, GAZ.

[38] Compare Wiesner, 'War, Work and Wealth'.

[39] Maarten Prak, 'Identité urbaine, identités sociales. Les bourgeois de Bois-le-Duc au xviiie siècle', *Annales ESC* 48 (1993), 927.

[40] Resolutions of the Council (Raadsignaat), 24 January 1622, fo. 252v, OA 12, GAA.

[41] *Ibid.*, 21 January 1634, fo. 65r, OA 15.   [42] *Ibid.*, 22 April 1650, fo. 26r, OA 19.

[43] *Ibid.*, 28 April 1666, ff. 174v–175r, OA 23.

[44] Regulations relating to Citizenship and Elections, p. 465, 24 June 1658, inv. no. AAZ 01, 22, GAZ; see also *ibid.*, 6 April 1669. In 1657, however, it had been decided that this would not be acceptable if the young lady was herself a Catholic: *ibid.*, 29 September 1657.

[45] See e.g. Resolutions of the council, vol. 26, 24 July 1656, 11 August 1656, 1 September 1656, 3 November 1656, inv. no. 121, SA II, UA; or *ibid.*, vol. 29, 10 September 1677.

could wave this condition, albeit only by unanimous decision.[46] In Zwolle, as many as 344 Catholics were awarded citizenship between 1670 and 1784. Another 49 applications from Catholics were initially turned down, but then granted at a second or third attempt.[47]

We cannot even be sure that the stern measures against Catholics were actually put into effect. When in Deventer in June 1700 no less than three tailors were deprived of their citizenship, and at the same time lost their membership of the tailors' guild, we may expect them to have left the town. Unfortunately, from the records no clear picture emerges. During the first half of the seventeenth century, the Deventer magistrate was reputedly 'better in the theory than in the practising' of Reformed orthodoxy. It has been credited with a policy that paid lip-service to the Reformed consistory, but at the same time tried to avoid the execution of firm decisions in this area.[48] Two of the three tailors do not appear at all in the (admittedly incomplete) records of baptisms and burials in Deventer around 1700. The third, Jan van Eltrop, had become a citizen in January 1683 when he arrived from Arnhem. During the next decade five of his children were baptised, in the Reformed Church, but none after 1700.[49] On 7 January 1719 a Jan van Eltrop was buried in the Lebuïnus Church in Deventer, possibly 'our' man, but perhaps his son.

Does all of this mean that the exclusion of Roman Catholics was after all ineffective? It is hard to give a definitive verdict at this point. Nonetheless it seems significant that the Catholic community of Deventer at the end of the eighteenth century, when it comprised 16 per cent of the population, is described as 'an impoverished group', compared to the Reformed majority.[50]

The chronology of religious exclusion

In the five towns under investigation the earliest references to religious preconditions for the acquisition of citizenship status date back to the 1620s. In 1622 Arnhem's constitution already contained exclusive clauses of this type, and in 1623 they were introduced in Nijmegen and Deventer. These examples were followed by Zwolle in 1646 and Utrecht in 1654.

---

[46] *Ibid.*, vol. 25, 12 June 1655.   [47] Berkenvelder, 'Afwijzen voor het burgerschap'.

[48] J.C. van Slee, *De gereformeerde gemeente van Deventer in de eerste veertig jaren na hare wederoprichting in 1591* (The Hague, 1926), pp. 61–2, 83 (quotation).

[49] Baptisms on 9 January 1684, on 11 October 1685, on 21 August 1687, on 4 June 1689, and finally on 27 January 1693.

[50] R.G.A. Brouwer, 'De ontwikkeling van het maatschappelijk en kerkelijk leven van de katholieken te Deventer in de 19e eeuw. Emancipatie en kerkopbouw binnen het katholiek bevolkingsdeel te Deventer, 1795–1890', MA thesis, Katholieke Universiteit Nijmegen (1988), p. 22.

This type of exclusion was not, however, a Calvinist invention. The Nijmegen citizen's oath in the sixteenth century contained a list of commitments, undertaken by the newly sworn citizen. Beside providing a gun or armour for the defence of the town, compliance with the decisions of the authorities, and the maintenance of the Hansa bylaws, citizens of Nijmegen pledged to profess of the Catholic religion.[51] Unfortunately, we do not have the exact date of this oath, and it remains unclear if the religious clause was added during the Revolt, or actually predates it.

There is also no obvious connection between the Revolt and the introduction of anti-Catholic elements into local citizenship rules. There may be some relationship with the start of hostilities after the end of the Twelve Years' Truce, in 1621, but this remains implicit at best. There are no direct references to the resumption of the war in the resolutions. There is, however, more than a hint to suggest that the initiative did not come from the town councils but from other institutions, notably the Common Councils and the consistories of the Reformed Church. In Nijmegen, the town council had defended the rights of Catholic citizens in the early seventeenth century. The consistory, on the other hand, complained time and again about Catholic meetings, and the continuing opportunities for Catholics to marry in their own Church. After the introduction of the anti-Catholic clauses, the consistory was constantly pushing the civic authorities to uphold the decisions. This policy was supported by the *gemeenslieden*, or Common Council.[52] In Utrecht, where there was no Common Council, the commanding officers of the civic militias advised the *vroedschap* on applications for citizenship. Even in 1752, when the measures against Catholics were relaxed in most places, the Utrecht militia officers advised the town council to persist in the exclusion of Catholics from citizenship status.[53] In Zwolle it had been the consistory of the Reformed Church that filed a petition for the exclusion of Catholics. This petition then led to a common resolution of the magistrate and Common Council of Zwolle.[54] In Deventer the records of the meetings of the magistrate with the Common Council make it quite clear that the latter was constantly trying to press the magistrate into firmer action. During the 1630s and 1640s, and again in the 1660s, the

[51] Schimmel, *Burgerrecht te Nijmegen*, p. 5.   [52] *Ibid.*, pp. 30–1, 41, 45–6, 61.

[53] Resolutions of the Colonels and Commanding Officers, 28 February 1752, inv. no. 2064, SA II, UA. Other resolutions on citizenship in the same volume at 13 November 1752; 29 November 1787; 6 February 1789; 4 March 1789; 28 March 1789.

[54] Resolutions of the Council and Community, p. 373, 25 June 1646, inv. no. AAZ 01, 21, GAZ.

magistrate was forced to declare on numerous occasions that the Council was indeed vigilant in this area.[55]

The drive for this type of policy seems to have declined markedly, however, by the start of the eighteenth century. Again it is hard to determine the details, but there are several significant clues. First and foremost, no new rigorous bylaws were introduced in any of the towns under investigation related to the exclusion of Catholics from citizen status. At some occasions the authorities confirmed their position. Most new resolutions were, however, widening the possibilities for Catholics to acquire citizenship. Thus, the Utrecht council decided in 1724 that Roman Catholics from all over the Republic would be eligible, whereas before this had been reserved for Catholics from the province of Utrecht only.[56] In Arnhem it was decided in 1737 that from thereon Catholics would be permitted to become citizens, but on restrictive conditions. Significantly, they were only allowed to exercise wholesale trade, explicitly excluded from the guilds, and had to pay a very high fee of 211 guilders.[57] Although this regulation was withdrawn in 1747 on request of the Arnhem guilds, nevertheless it suggests a different climate.[58] In Zwolle, citizenship was made available to Catholics in 1766, provided they had lived in Zwolle for three years. They could not become overseers of their guilds, however.[59] A second indication is that in the eighteenth century it became very rare indeed to be deprived of one's citizenship for religious reasons. The number of victims had never been large, but now it dwindled to insignificance.

A third indication for the lessening of religious intolerance is, perhaps somewhat paradoxically, that in the eighteenth century Catholics started to take concerted action against their exclusion from the privileges of citizenship. During the seventeenth century such action was notably absent. In the summer of 1749, however, a group of eighteen Arnhem Catholics,

---

[55] Agreements between Magistrate and Sworn Council, lib. D, 21 December 1630, p. 56, art. 8 and 10, inv. no. 125, Rep II, GAD; *ibid.*, 17 December 1639, p. 378, art. 4; *ibid.*, July 1644, p. 518, art. 1; *ibid.*, 14 April 1645, p. 538, art. 1; *ibid.*, 9 April 1646, p. 556, art. 4; *ibid.*, 11 September 1646, p. 562, art. 3; *ibid.*, lib. E, 14 December 1658, pp. 215–16; *ibid.*, 9 February 1665, p. 329, art. 5; *ibid.*, 20 September 1666, p. 364, art. 2.

[56] Resolutions of the council, vol. 48, 18 April 1724, inv. no. 121, SA II, UA; cf. Rommes, *Oost, west, Utrecht best?*, pp. 42–3.

[57] Commissie- en Policieboek, 29 April 1737, pp. 165–6, arts. 17–21, OA 55, GAA. Interestingly, the same regulations permitted Jews to become citizens as well, under the same restrictions. For Jews, citizen status was not inheritable.

[58] *Ibid.*, 16 December 1747, p. 134, OA 58.

[59] Regulations relating to Citizenship and Elections, pp. 164–5, arts. 16–17, Citizenship 1767, inv. no. AAZ 01, 258, GAZ. Again, Jews were permitted to become citizens, but required special permission from the town council (*ibid.*, art. 18).

all respectable middle-class men, filed a petition for the restoration of the bylaw of 1737 that had granted their fellow Catholics the right to become citizens. They stated that there were 'no obvious reasons why they would not be allowed to enjoy citizen status in Arnhem and become members of the guilds', as Catholics could 'in Nijmegen and hence in this province, as well as in Holland and other provinces of the United Netherlands'.[60] Their argument was dismissed by the magistrate, as the claims were incompatible with Arnhem's ancient constitution. References to other towns were irrelevant 'as each town has its own particular constitution'. Moreover, the economy of Arnhem was in such a bad shape that even the Reformed found it hard to make a living.[61] The Arnhem Catholics failed to win their case, but in the eighteenth century they at least made a point of fighting for their rights.

In the 1780s, during the so-called Patriot era, the struggle re-emerged. In Deventer radical Patriots, not necessarily Catholics themselves, proposed to drop the religious clauses from the town's citizenship regulations. This caused an uproar among the guilds that so far had supported the Patriot cause. The guilds even switched their allegiance to the conservative Orangist wing on the council in protest. However, many hundreds of Deventer citizens continued to support a new draft constitution that would give citizenship status to the Deventer Catholics.[62]

Citizenship and religious discrimination

According to Deventer's town secretary, Gerard Dumbar, the exclusion of Roman Catholics in particular had its roots in the struggle for national independence. It had, he said, 'without doubt taken its first origin in the times of the severe persecution of the Reformed in the Netherlands by these heretics and idolators'.[63] Dutch history, in other words, had perceived Roman Catholics as the main opponents of the Reformed Church. Therefore they had been singled out in the bylaws over the Lutherans, Mennonites, and Arminians. This explanation, convincing as it may seem at first sight, is deficient in at least two respects. First of all, its chronology is wrong. Had Dumbar been right, we should have expected these measures to be already in place in the early seventeenth century. This,

---

[60] Petition by Catholics, 1749, OA 1231, GAA.
[61] *Ibid.*, reply by Aldermen and Council, 13 October 1749.
[62] Wayne Ph. te Brake, *Regents and Rebels: The Revolutionary World of an Eighteenth-Century Dutch City* (Oxford, 1989).
[63] Notes by Dumbar Sr on the town's constitution, L.1, titul 3, art. 8, Collectie Dumbar, 3, GAD.

however, was not the case.[64] Secondly, Dumbar's geography was wrong. His explanation should have applied throughout the Republic. The fact is, however, that on the contrary the exclusion of Catholics from urban citizenship was far from general.

Even though this topic warrants further investigation in other towns beyond those discussed in this chapter, our present data strongly suggest that in the western territories of the Dutch Republic no equivalent discrimination of non-Calvinists existed in relation with local citizenship. In Amsterdam there was only one clause concerning religion, and this related to the Jews. They were admissible as citizens, but on restricted conditions. Jews were only allowed to participate in wholesale trade, and could not enter the guilds. Jewish citizens could not transfer their status to their children.[65] It is very likely that in many towns Jews were simply turned away when they requested citizenship. Catholics, on the other hand, had no problems becoming citizens of Amsterdam, or Haarlem, where the civic community could no longer claim to coincide with the religious community.[66]

Not so, obviously, in Arnhem, Deventer, Nijmegen, Utrecht, or Zwolle; so why the difference? Two possible explanations seem to suggest themselves. Economically, the towns of the central and eastern regions of the Republic were past their prime. Their heyday had been the late Middle Ages, when Utrecht was the largest city in what would later become the Dutch Republic.[67] As members of the Hansa-league, the towns along the river IJssel had profited from the dynamics of this northern commercial network.[68] In the fourteenth century, however, Holland's economy began a transformation that would eventually enable it to overtake competitors in the east. The policies towards Roman Catholics in the towns as discussed here might be interpreted as a 'natural' reaction of exclusion during a phase of economic stagnation. This sort of reflex was felt

[64] I am referring specifically, of course, to the limitation of citizenship rights. Measures against Catholics and the practising of their rites were introduced during the 1580s in obvious connection with the progression of the Revolt.

[65] See p. 337 of the special issue 'Cittadinanze' of *Quaderni Storici* 30 (1995), 281–531, ed. by S. Cerutti, R. Descimon, and M. Prak; also R.G. Fuks-Mansfeld, *De Sefardim van Amsterdam tot 1795. Aspecten van een joodse minderheid in een Hollandse stad* (Hilversum, 1989), pp. 39–40, 58.

[66] Gabriëlle Dorren, 'De eerzamen. Zeventiende-eeuws burgerschap in Haarlem', in Remieg Aerts and Henk te Velde (eds.), *De stijl van de burger. Over Nederlandse burgerlijke cultuur vanaf de Middeleeuwen* (Kampen, 1998), pp. 76–7.

[67] Figures in Jonathan I. Israel, *The Dutch Republic. Its Rise, Greatness, and Fall, 1477–1806* (Oxford, 1995), pp. 114, 332. More detailed figures are supplied by Piet Lourens and Jan Lucassen, *Inwoneraantallen van Nederlandse steden ca. 1300–1800* (Amsterdam, 1997).

[68] Hubert Nusteling, *Welvaart en werkgelegenheid in Amsterdam 1540–1860. Een relaas over demografie, economie en sociale politiek van een wereldstad* (Amsterdam/Dieren, 1985), pp. 73–80.

in Holland itself during the later seventeenth century, when economic growth slowed down perceptibly.[69] The timing of the anti-Catholic legislation seems to fit this explanation. Apart from Zwolle, which managed to continue its growth into the second half of the century, the towns mentioned here all changed gear, from a trajectory of slow growth to one of outright population decline, somewhere during the middle decades of the seventeenth century.[70] A general feeling of crisis may have been further aggravated by the reductions in garrison sizes that hit the economies of towns such as Arnhem and Nijmegen, and the east generally, after the conclusion of peace at the Westphalia settlement in 1648.[71] On the other hand, such economic arguments were hardly ever mentioned in relation to restrictions of citizenship for religious minorities. Perhaps the second possible explanation can help us to shed light on this issue.

Arnhem, Deventer, Nijmegen, Utrecht, and Zwolle were not just different from the western towns in their economic development, they also had a special constitutional history. In Utrecht, until 1528, the guilds had dominated the town government. When Charles V became the new lord of Utrecht, he had immediately abolished the guilds' role in government, and installed a permanent council – *vroedschap* – of the Holland type. Nonetheless, the people of Utrecht remained involved in several areas of administration. The guilds were superseded by the civic militias as representatives of the citizens of Utrecht. Significantly, the officers of the militia were asked for advice on individual applications for citizenship status. The guilds, at the same time, remained involved in community affairs. The Utrecht guilds maintained strong links with the Church. Several guilds had their own vaults, where 'brothers and sisters' of the guild were laid to rest. Some guilds sponsored chandeliers for local parish churches.[72] The fishmongers, for instance, had one in the Buur Church that could

---

[69] Jan de Vries, 'The Labour Market', in Karel Davids and Leo Noordegraaf (eds.), *The Dutch Economy in the Golden Age. Nine Studies. Economic and Social History in the Netherlands* (Amsterdam, 1993), vol. IV, pp. 66–9; Jan de Vries and Ad van der Woude, *The First Modern Economy: Success, Failure, and Perseverance of the Dutch Economy, 1500–1815* (Cambridge, 1997), pp. 632–54.

[70] Holthuis, *Frontierstad bij het scheiden van de markt*, p. 109; Lourens and Lucassen, *Inwoneraantallen*, pp. 17, 25, 83–4. Rommes, *Oost, west, Utrecht best?*, p. 25, states that Utrecht's growth stagnated during the second quarter of the century, but picked up again during the 1650s and 1660s, only to be broken off again in 1672.

[71] Israel, *The Dutch Republic*, pp. 612–16.

[72] According to a survey in 1799, 15 guilds out of a total of 36 listed owned graves: Algemeen rapport van den Staat der (gesubsisteerd hebbende) gilden, Historisch werkmateriaal (arch. 354), 644, UA. For more details, see Maarten Prak, 'Politik, Kultur und politische Kultur: die Zünfte in den nördlichen Niederlanden', in Wilfried Reininghaus (ed.), *Zunftlandschaften in Deutschland und den Niederlanden im Vergleich* (Münster, 2000), pp. 76–80; and Benjamin J. Kaplan, *Calvinists and Libertines: Confession and Community in Utrecht, 1578–1620* (Oxford, 1995), especially chapter 3.

easily be recognised because it sported three tiny fish. The linen-weavers' sick box had its annual accounts read to the members in the St Jacob Church (in even years) or the St Nicholas Church (in odd years), even though the guild had only been established in 1596 after the introduction of the Reformation in Utrecht.[73]

Similar observations can be made for other towns. In both Deventer and Zwolle the Common Council (*Gezworen gemeente*) represented the inhabitants of the towns' districts in a permanent representative assembly. The local constitutions allowed the Common Councils to have a say in major policy decisions. The annual election of the magistrate, that is, the local government, was also in the hands of the Common Councillors.[74] It was the Deventer Common Council that repeatedly argued in favour of a restrictive policy towards the Catholic community. In Arnhem, whenever there was a vacancy on the magistrate's bench, the guilds proposed one candidate as a replacement, the Common Council another.[75] The guilds' involvement was underlined in 1707 when, after years of public unrest in Arnhem, the guilds were co-signatories to the new local constitution.[76] During the early eighteenth century a strong republican current had dominated public political debate in Arnhem, as well as in Nijmegen. In both towns, the guilds claimed an important political role.[77]

All of this suggests that the level of popular influence on the shaping of local policies was a major factor in deciding the contents of citizenship. In the west, town councils were dominated by merchant interests and favoured liberal access to their communities. They faced no institutionalised popular opposition.[78] In Utrecht and the eastern towns, local

---

[73] Account book of the linen-weavers' sick box, Bewaarde archieven I, 42, UA.

[74] For the constitution of Zwolle: Streng, '*Stemme in staat*', pp. 95–119; on Deventer: Te Brake, *Regents and Rebels*, pp. 24–32.

[75] J.F. Pols, 'Arnhemse regenten in de achttiende eeuw', *Bijdragen en Mededelingen Gelre* 87 (1996), 85–9.

[76] Regulation on the Government of the Town of Arnhem, 22 December 1707, OA, 1152, GAA.

[77] On Arnhem, see *Deductie van de regten ende privilegien der vrye Stadt Arnhem, het Collegie van de Geswoore Gemeente, Gildens, Borgerye ende Ingesetenen van dien competerende; ofte apologie van de wettige Regeringe, na de oude gronden van de vrye Stadt Arnhem* (Arnhem 1703) [Knuttel no. 15033]. Also Arjan van Dixhoorn, ' "Voorstanden van de vrije wetten". Burgerbewegingen in Arnhem en de Republiek tussen 1702 en 1707', *Tijdschrift voor Sociale Geschiedenis* 25 (1999), 25–54. On Nijmegen: *Justificatie van het Recht, dat de Magistraat, neffens de Gildens, en de Gemeensluyden der Stadt Nymegen als een vrye Ryks-stadt van ouds heeft gehad ende als nog competeert, om hare Magistraat, ende vrye keure van dien by haar selfs te doen, volgens hare Privilegien, Rechten, Plebisciten ende Usantien, ende waartoe deselve al nu tot meesten dienst, ende welstand van de stad ende Burgerye berechtigt ende bevoegt sijn* (n.p., n.d.) [Knuttel no. 14844].

[78] A similar constellation protected the Jewish community in Amsterdam in the seventeenth century: Miriam Bodian, *Hebrews of the Portuguese Nation: Conversos and Community in Early Modern Amsterdam* (Bloomington, IN, 1997), chapter 3.

economies relied to a much greater extent on artisanal manufacturing, and they did not profit from the Golden Age to the same extent as the Holland towns. Moreover, local politicians were confronted with well-organised, often institutionalised, popular opponents who saw it as their interest to restrict access to declining markets. Depriving non-Calvinists of citizenship rights was one of the means to this end.

This argument is further reinforced if we take a brief look across the Republic's eastern border.[79] In complexity, from both a religious and a constitutional point of view, the Holy Roman Empire far outstripped the Dutch Republic. Whereas Dutch authorities had one official religion, and were confronted with several subversive other Churches, the Holy Roman Empire had three dominant Churches. A first understanding – really a territorial division of the Empire – had been established at Augsburg in 1555. These arrangements were, after a lot of bloodshed, notably during the Thirty Years' War, further refined at the Treaty of Osnabrück, in 1648, as part of the Westphalian peace settlement. The Treaty made Catholicism, Lutheranism, and Calvinism into the established Churches. It allowed sovereign princes to determine which of the three would prevail in their territories. It was more or less assumed that the members of the other Churches would then move to a place where they could worship in freedom, but the Treaty of Osnabrück did not allow the sovereign to force religious minorities to move, nor could he seize their property.[80] Thus, some sort of accommodation had to be reached. According to a survey by Etienne François, this resulted in three patterns.[81] In a very limited number of cases, in southern Germany – with Augsburg as the most notable example – a system of power-sharing was developed. In Augsburg this implied that all political positions in the city were scrupulously divided between Lutherans and Catholics, even though the two communities were not of equal size.[82] In small towns dominated by middle-class guildsmen there was no question of accommodation. Here, religion was seen as one of the foundations of the community and the community's preservation as depending on religious unity. In newly established towns and capital cities, on the other hand, religious minorities were protected by absolutist princes and enjoyed a reasonable degree of toleration. The situation in Prussia is a case in point. This was not so much because the

---

[79] Cf. Lourens and Lucassen, ' "Zunftlandschaften" in den Niederlanden'.
[80] Joachim Whaley, *Religious Toleration and Social Change in Hamburg 1529–1819* (Cambridge, 1985), pp. 5–6.
[81] Etienne François, 'De l'uniformité à la tolérance: confession et société urbaine en Allemagne, 1650–1800', *Annales ESC* 37 (1982), 783–800. I am grateful to Benjamin Kaplan for referring me to this article.
[82] More details on this arrangement: Etienne François, *Protestants et catholiques en Allemagne: identités et pluralisme, Augsbourg 1648–1806* (Paris, 1993).

rulers of Prussia, or any of the other German princes, were firm upholders of individual rights, but because they believed it was in the interest of their states, and therefore of themselves, to be moderately tolerant. In the new towns and capital cities, these sovereigns were able to overrule the objections against minority religions there may well have been among the population.

So it seems that in the Dutch Republic as much as in the Holy Roman Empire socio-political relations were an important determinant of religious toleration. In the eastern Netherlands political representation of the middle classes provided opportunities for the sort of religious bigotry that may or may not have existed as an undercurrent in Holland. In the west, however, the dominance of the elites effectively precluded the systematic harassment of non-Calvinists outside the domain of religion itself.

Select bibliography

Augustijn, C. and E. Honée (eds.), *Vervreemding en verzoening. De relatie tussen katholieken en protestanten in Nederland 1550–2000* (Nijmegen, 1998).

Bergsma, W., *Tussen Gideonsbende en publieke kerk. Een studie over het gereformeerd protestantisme in Friesland, 1580–1650* (Hilversum, 1999).

Berkvens-Stevelinck, C., J.I. Israel, and G.H.M. Posthumus Meyjes (eds.), *The Emergence of Tolerance in the Dutch Republic* (Leiden/New York/Cologne, 1997).

Bodian, M., *Hebrews of the Portuguese Nation: Conversos and Community in Early Modern Amsterdam* (Bloomington, IN, 1997).

Bots, H., 'Tolerantie of gecultiveerde tweedracht. Het beeld van de Nederlandse tolerantie bij buitenlanders in de zeventiende en achttiende eeuw', *Bijdragen en Mededelingen betreffende de Geschiedenis der Nederlanden* 107 (1992), 657–69.

Davids, K. and J. Lucassen (eds.), *A Miracle Mirrored: The Dutch Republic in European Perspective* (Cambridge, 1995).

Deursen, A.T. van, *Bavianen en slijkgeuzen. Kerk en kerkvolk ten tijde van Maurits en Oldenbarnevelt* (Assen, 1974).

Plain Lives in a Golden Age: Popular Culture, Religion and Society in Seventeenth-Century Holland (Cambridge, 1991).

Duke, A., *Reformation and Revolt in the Low Countries* (London, 1990).

Frijhoff, W.T.M., 'La coexistence confessionnelle: complicités, méfiances et ruptures aux Provinces-Unies', in J. Delumeau (ed.), *Histoire vécue du peuple chrétien*, 2 vols. (Toulouse, 1979), vol. II, pp. 229–57.

'Le seuil de tolérance en Hollande au XVIIe siècle', in *Homo religiosus. Autour de Jean Delumeau [Avant-propos d'Alain Cabantous]* (Paris, 1997), pp. 650–7.

'La tolerance sans édit: la situation dans les Provinces-Unies', in J. Delumeau (ed.), *L'acceptation de l'autre de l'Edit de Nantes à nos jours* (Paris, 2000), pp. 86–107.

Fuks-Mansfeld, R.G., *De Sefardim in Amsterdam tot 1795. Aspecten van een joodse minderheid in een Hollandse stad* (Hilversum, 1989).

Gelder, H.A. Enno van, *Revolutionnaire Reformatie. De vestiging van de Gereformeerde Kerk in de Nederlandse gewesten, gedurende de eerste jaren van de Opstand tegen Filips II, 1575–1585* (Amsterdam, 1943), pp. 9–10.

Vrijheid en onvrijheid in de Republiek. Geschiedenis der vrijheid van drukpers en godsdienst van 1572 tot 1619 (Haarlem, 1947).

The Two Reformations in the Sixteenth Century: A Study of the Religious Aspects and Consequences of Renaissance and Humanism (The Hague, 1961).

'Nederland geprotestantiseerd?', *Tijdschrift voor Geschiedenis* 81 (1968), 445–64.

Getemperde vrijheid. Een verhandeling over de verhouding van kerk en staat in de Republiek der Verenigde Nederlanden en de vrijheid van meningsuiting in zake godsdienst, drukpers en onderwijs, gedurende de 17e eeuw (Groningen, 1972).

Gijswijt-Hofstra, M., *Een schijn van verdraagzaamheid. Afwijking en tolerantie in Nederland van de zestiende eeuw tot heden* (Hilversum, 1989).

Grell, O.P. and B. Scribner (eds.), *Tolerance and Intolerance in the European Reformation* (Cambridge, 1996).

Groenveld, S., *Huisgenoten des geloofs. Was de samenleving in de Republiek der Verenigde Nederlanden verzuild?* (Hilversum, 1995).

Guggisberg, H.R., 'Veranderingen in de argumenten voor religieuze tolerantie en godsdienstvrijheid in de zestiende en zeventiende eeuw', *Bijdragen en Mededelingen betreffende de Geschiedenis der Nederlanden* 91 (1976), 177–95.

Güldner, G., *Das Toleranzproblem in den Niederlanden im Ausgang des 16. Jahrhunderts* (Lübeck, 1968).

Hamilton, A., S. Voolstra, and P. Visser (eds.), *From Martyr to Muppy. A Historical Introduction to Cultural Assimilation Processes of a Religious Minority in the Netherlands: The Mennonites* (Amsterdam, 1994).

Hsia, R.P., *Social Discipline in the Reformation. Central Europe 1550–1750* (London, 1989).

Israel, J.I., 'Toleration in Seventeenth-Century Dutch and English Thought', in S. Groenveld and M. Wintle (eds.), *Britain and the Netherlands*, vol. XI (Zutphen, 1994), pp. 25–7.

Kaplan, B.J., 'Dutch Particularism and the Calvinist Quest for "Holy Uniformity"', *Archiv für Reformationsgeschichte* 82 (1991), 239–56.

'Hubert Duifhuis and the Nature of Dutch Libertinism', *Tijdschrift voor Geschiedenis* 105 (1992), 1–29.

Calvinists and Libertines: Confession and Community in Utrecht, 1578–1620 (Oxford, 1995).

Mooij, C. de, *Geloof kan Bergen verzetten. Reformatie en katholieke herleving te Bergen op Zoom, 1577–1795* (Hilversum, 1998).

Mout, M.E.H.N., 'Spiritualisten in de Nederlandse Reformatie van de zestiende eeuw', *Bijdragen en Mededelingen betreffende de Geschiedenis der Nederlanden* 111 (1996), 297–313.

Pollmann, J., *Religious Choice in the Dutch Republic: The Reformation of Arnoldus Buchelius (1565–1641)* (Manchester, 1999).

Posthumus Meyjes, G.H.M., 'Protestants irenisme in de 16e en eerste helft van de 17e eeuw', *Nederlands Theologisch Tijdschrift* 36 (1982), 205–22.

Price, J.L., *Holland and the Dutch Republic in the Seventeenth Century: The Politics of Particularism* (Oxford, 1994).

Rooden, P. van, *Religieuze regimes: over godsdienst en maatschappij in Nederland, 1570–1990* (Amsterdam, 1996).

Schilling, H., 'Der libertär-radikale Republikanismus der holländischen Regenten', *Geschichte und Gesellschaft* 10 (1984), 498–533.

Spaans, J., *Haarlem na de Reformatie: stedelijke cultuur en kerkelijk leven, 1577–1620* (The Hague, 1989).

'Unity and Diversity as a Theme in Early Modern Dutch Religious History: An Interpretation", in R.N. Swanson (ed.), *Unity and Diversity in the Church* (Oxford, 1996), pp. 221–34.

Tracy, J.D., 'Public Church, Gemeente Christi, or Volkskerk: Holland's Reformed Church in Civil and Ecclesiastical Perspective, 1572–1592', in H.R. Guggisberg and G.G. Krodel (eds.), *Die Reformation in Deutschland und Europa: Interpretationen und Debatten* (Gütersloh, 1993), pp. 487–510.

Woltjer, J.J., 'De plaats van de calvinisten in de Nederlandse samenleving', *De Zeventiende Eeuw* 10 (1994), 3–23.

Tussen vrijheidsstrijd en burgeroorlog. Over de Nederlandse Opstand 1555–1580 (Amsterdam, 1994).

'Political Moderates and Religious Moderates in the Revolt of the Netherlands', in Ph. Benedict, G. Marnef, H. van Nierop, and M. Venard (eds.), *Reformation, Revolt and Civil War in France and the Netherlands 1555–1585* (Amsterdam, 1999), pp. 185–200.

Wouters, A.P.F. and P.H.A.M. Abels, *Nieuw en ongezien. Kerk en samenleving in de classis Delft en Delfland, 1572–1621*, 2 vols. (Delft, 1994)

Index